CAMBRIDGE COMMENTARIES ON
WRITINGS OF THE JEWISH AND CHRISTIAN WORLD
200 BC TO AD 200
VOLUME I PART I

Jews in the Hellenistic World

CAMBRIDGE COMMENTARIES ON
WRITINGS OF THE JEWISH AND CHRISTIAN WORLD
200 BC TO AD 200

General Editors:

P. R. ACKROYD

A. R. C. LEANEY

J. W. PACKER

JEWS IN THE
HELLENISTIC WORLD

JOSEPHUS, ARISTEAS,
THE SIBYLLINE ORACLES, EUPOLEMUS

JOHN R. BARTLETT

Lecturer in Divinity and
Fellow of Trinity College Dublin

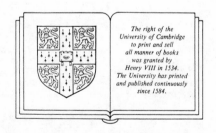

The right of the
University of Cambridge
to print and sell
all manner of books
was granted by
Henry VIII in 1534.
The University has printed
and published continuously
since 1584.

CAMBRIDGE UNIVERSITY PRESS

Cambridge

London   New York   New Rochelle

Melbourne   Sydney

Published by the Press Syndicate of the University of Cambridge
The Pitt Building, Trumpington Street, Cambridge CB2 1RP
32 East 57th Street, New York, NY 10022, USA
10 Stamford Road, Oakleigh, Melbourne 3166, Australia

First published 1985

Printed in Great Britain by the
University Press, Cambridge

Library of Congress catalogue card number: 85-3840

British Library cataloguing in publication data
Jews in the Hellenistic world. – (Cambridge
commentaries on writings of the Jewish and
Christian world 200 BC to AD 200; v. 1, pt. 1)
Josephus, Aristeas, the Sibylline oracles,
Eupolemus.
1. Church history – Primitive and early church,
ca. 30-600 2. Judaism – History – Pre-exilic
period, 586 B.C.–210 A.D.
I. Bartlett, John R.
270 BR163

ISBN 0 521 24246 0 hard covers
ISBN 0 521 28551 8 paperback

Contents

v

Maps and Plans

General Editors' Preface

The three general editors of the Cambridge Bible Commentary series have all, in their teaching, experienced a lack of readily usable texts of the literature which is often called pseudepigrapha but which is more accurately defined as extra-biblical or para-biblical literature. The aim of this new series is to help fill this gap.

The welcome accorded to the Cambridge Bible Commentary has encouraged the editors to follow the same pattern here, except that carefully chosen extracts from the texts, rather than complete books, have normally been provided for comment. The introductory material leads naturally into the text, which itself leads into alternating sections of commentary.

Within the severe limits imposed by the size and scope of the series, each contributor will attempt to provide for the student and general reader the results of modern scholarship, but has been asked to assume no specialised theological or linguistic knowledge.

The volumes already planned cover the writings of the Jewish and Christian World from about 200 BC to AD 200 and are being edited as follows:

1 i *Jews in the Hellenistic World: Josephus, Aristeas, the Sibylline Oracles, Eupolemus* – John R. Bartlett, Trinity College, Dublin

1 ii *Jews in the Hellenistic World: Philo* – R. Williamson, University of Leeds

2 *The Qumran Community* – M. A. Knibb, King's College, London

3 *Early Rabbinic Writings* – H. Maccoby, Leo Baeck College, London

4 *Outside the Old Testament* – M. de Jonge, University of Leiden

5 *Outside the New Testament* – G. N. Stanton, King's College, London

6 *Jews and Christians: Graeco-Roman Views* – Molly Whittaker, University of Nottingham

A seventh volume by one of the general editors, A. R. C. Leaney, *The Jewish and Christian World 200 BC to AD 200*, examines the wider historical and literary background to the period and includes tables of dates, relevant lists and maps. Although this companion volume will preface and augment the series, it may also be read as complete in itself and be used as a work of general reference.

P.R.A.   A.R.C.L.   J.W.P.

Jews in the hellenistic world

In recent years, an increasing amount of scholarly time and attention has been devoted to the literature written in Greek by the Jews of the hellenistic age. Interest in this literature is hardly surprising in an intellectual tradition founded on the Graeco-Roman classics and the Judaeo-Christian scriptures. Most scholars, however, have been content to focus on the more classical writings or on the Hebrew scriptures; the hellenistic literature, whether from the Greek or the Jewish world, has been of more limited interest. But in the last century there has been new emphasis on the importance of the links in the hellenistic period between the Greek world and the Jewish world.

The history of Greek contact with the Levant is a long one. As early as the fifteenth century BC Mycenaean pottery was beginning to reach Late Bronze-Age sites on both sides of the Jordan. In the tenth century BC King David apparently employed mercenaries from Crete (Kerethites: 2 Sam. 8: 18) in his army; in the late seventh century BC Greek mercenaries fought in Palestine in the pay of the Egyptian Pharaohs. In the fifth and fourth centuries Persian rule reached west from Susa to the shores of the Aegean and Mediterranean seas, where it clashed with the maritime interests of the Athenians and other Greeks. In 490 and 481 BC the Persians invaded Greece and were driven back; in 401–400 the Persian Cyrus marched eastwards through what is now Turkey with Greek mercenaries in rebellion against his brother, the Persian king Artaxerxes II; and in 331 Alexander the Great marched his Macedonian troops through Samaria and the borders of Judah to Egypt, before turning east to Mesopotamia and India. All these movements and many others brought the Greeks into contact with the Jews and other peoples of the Levant, but it is generally agreed that it was in the aftermath of Alexander's conquests that the Jewish people began to be closely involved with the hellenistic world and to look west rather than east.

The process of hellenisation was not a simple one. The Persian province of Yehud or Judah became hellenised by degrees as it became subject to the administration and bureaucracy of the Ptolemies, the Greek dynasty that seized power in Egypt after the death of Alexander.

The book of Ecclesiastes (5: 8f; 10: 20) may hint at the political situation in Judah in this period:

> 'If you witness in some province the oppression of the poor and the denial of right and justice, do not be surprised at what goes on, for every official has a higher one set over him, and the highest keeps watch over them all. The best thing for a country is a king whose own lands are well tilled. Do not speak ill of the king in your ease, or of a rich man in your bedroom; for a bird may carry your voice, and a winged messenger may repeat what you say.'

The correspondence of Zenon, who toured Palestine and Transjordan in 259 BC as the administrator of the Egyptian finance minister Apollonius, shows that Greek was used officially for purposes of provincial administration. Particularly interesting is the record of Zenon's purchase in Transjordan of a slave-girl, which reveals the presence there of soldiers and others with Greek names from various parts of the Mediterranean world: 'In the reign of Ptolemy [II Philadelphus]...at Birta of Ammanitis, Nicanor son of Xenocles, Cnidian, in the service of Toubias, sold to Zenon son of Agreophon, Caunian, in the service of Apollonius the chief minister, a Sidonian girl named Sphragis, aged about seven, for fifty drachmas.' The guarantors and witnesses included a Persian and a Macedonian from Toubias' personal troops, and four government officials, one from Athens and three from hellenistic cities of the Turkish coast (Miletus and Colophon in Ionia, and Aspendus in Pamphylia; see Map 1). The seller and buyer respectively came from Cnidus and Caunus in south-west Turkey. One should note also that the land of the Old Testament Ammonites is now named in Greek fashion Ammanitis; similarly Moab had become Moabitis and Gilead Galaaditis.

The growing importance of the Greek language, culture and institutions in Judah through the third, second, and first centuries BC is well documented. Even Judas Maccabaeus' diplomat had a Greek name, Eupolemus (see below, pp. 56–9). The Hasmonaean kings used both Greek and Hebrew titles on their coins, and the Nabataean king Aretas III (c. 85–62 BC) could style himself 'Phil-hellene' on the coins he issued from Damascus. Greek manuscripts of the scriptures have been found at Qumran; Herod the Great employed a hellenised Syrian, Nicolaus of Damascus, as his secretary and court historian. The city of Samaria was called Sebaste, the Greek equivalent of the Latin Augusta, after the Emperor Augustus. Greek was one of the three languages used on the title affixed to the cross of Jesus, and it is not impossible that Jesus like other Galilaeans understood at least some Greek. Places like Samaria, Caesarea, Marisa, Tiberias, Paneas, and Philadelphia (see Map 5) were hellenised towns; Jesus visited the Decapolis (Mark 7: 31), the group of ten cities in northern Transjordan, and one of these, Gadara south-east of the Sea of Galilee, was the home of such well-known Greek writers as Menippus the Cynic (third century BC) and Meleager the epigrammatist and anthologist (*c.* 60 BC), whose couplet saying 'Greetings!' in three languages illustrates the present point:

> If you are a Syrian, '*Salaam!*'; if a Phoenician, '*Naidios!*';
> If you are a Greek, '*Chairē!*'; and say the same in return.
> (*Anthologia Graeca* VII.419)

However, while Judah was under the administration of Egyptian officials who spoke and wrote Greek, Jews from Judah were settling elsewhere. There had been Jews in Egypt already for several hundred years; Jer. 41: 16 – 44: 30 tells of Jewish emigration to Egypt after Nebuchadnezzar's destruction of Jerusalem in 587 BC, and papyri found on the island of Elephantinē near Assuan at the end of the last century revealed the presence there from the early sixth century BC to the end of the fifth century of a Jewish garrison settlement. In 312 BC Ptolemy I settled captive Jews in Egypt (Letter of Aristeas 10–12; see p. 19). 2 Maccabees is an abbreviated version of a work written in Greek by Jason, a Jew from Cyrene in North Africa, and 2 Maccabees was prefaced at an early stage of its history by two letters written in the second century BC to Jews in Egypt by the Jerusalem authorities, urging them to keep the feast of the reconsecration of the Temple. By the time of Philo in the first century AD it is said that there were a million Jews in Alexandria (*In Flaccum* VI.43), and their claims to Alexandrian citizenship led to riots and the sending of delegations from both sides to the emperor himself in AD 38 (see pp. 182–8). But there were also large numbers of Jews settled elsewhere; Josephus refers to Jews transported by Antiochus III to Phrygia from Babylonia (*Ant.* XII.3.4 (147–53)). 1 Macc. 15: 22ff suggests that Jews might have been found in the mid second century BC at Delos, Myndos, Sicyon, Caria, Samos, Pamphylia, Lycia, Halicarnassus, Rhodes, Phaselis, Cos, Sidē, Aradus, Gortyna, Cnidus, Cyprus, and Cyrene (see Maps 1 and 4), as well perhaps as Sparta and Rome, to which the Maccabaeans sent embassies (1 Macc. 8: 17–32; 12: 1–23). By 59 BC the Roman lawyer Cicero was complaining that the jury was being unduly influenced by the large numbers of Jews in court. In AD 44 the Emperor Claudius had a number of Jews expelled from Rome (Acts 18: 2). The writings and travels of Paul of Tarsus witness to the presence of Jewish communities throughout the Mediterranean world in the mid first century AD.

It is thus not surprising that from the third century BC onwards there were Jews who found it natural to write in Greek. There were many reasons why a Jew might write in Greek. The author might be a hellenised member of the Jerusalem aristocracy parading his learning, or a diplomat engaged in his profession, a travelling business-man, an Alexandrian scholar using his native or adopted Greek, a tradesman in a Greek city presenting his accounts, and so on. A writer might be addressing fellow diaspora Jews, or Greek Gentiles who knew no Hebrew or Aramaic. It is not always clear whether a piece of Jewish apologetic written in Greek was primarily intended to persuade gentile unbelievers of the merits of Judaism or to boost the morale of Jews living in a gentile society. Educated Jews, anxious to be accepted as members of the aristocracy of the hellenistic world, might become acquainted with the Greek classics, but there is little or no evidence that the educated Greek had very much concern to read the Jewish scriptures. Jewish apologetic works in Greek were probably read primarily and largely by Jewish readers, just as today works of Christian apologetic are read more by the believer than by the unbeliever.

The Jewish hellenistic literature that remains to us is mostly of this nature. It owes its preservation, however, mainly to Christian writers. The writings of Philo of Alexandria became of greater interest to Christian theologians than to Jewish; the first known important writer to make use of Josephus was Eusebius, the early fourth-century Bishop of Caesarea, closely followed by the fourth-century biblical scholar Jerome. The Sibylline Oracles of Jewish origin were preserved by being taken over and developed by the Christian Church from the second century onwards. The writings and even the names of most minor Jewish hellenistic writers are known to us chiefly and sometimes solely from references in Josephus' works and from a series of fragments collected by Alexander Polyhistor in the first century BC and preserved by Eusebius in his *Praeparatio evangelica* in the fourth century AD. Perhaps the most important monument of Jewish hellenistic literature is the Septuagint, the Greek translation of the Old Testament begun at Alexandria in the third century BC. This too owed its continued existence after the first century AD to the Christian Church, which adopted this Greek version of the scriptures as its own. In addition to translations of earlier Hebrew writings, the Septuagint includes a number of writings from the second or first century BC, such as the

Wisdom of Solomon and the Greek translations of Ecclesiasticus, Daniel, and Esther, all of which qualify as Jewish hellenistic literature.

The main part of this book is devoted to passages selected from the Letter of Aristeas to Philocrates, the Sibylline Oracles, and from the writings of Eupolemus and Josephus. The first two works derive from Alexandria; Eupolemus and Josephus, however, were both of Jewish priestly families connected with Jerusalem. Eupolemus visited Rome in 161 BC as a diplomat, and Josephus lived in Rome and wrote his books there from the end of the Jewish War until the end of the first century AD. Alexandria, Jerusalem, and Rome were important centres of Jewish life and activity, though not, as we have seen, the only ones. Alexandria was particularly important as a place of learning and literature, and it is hardly accidental that more hellenistic Jewish literature can be located here than anywhere else. In addition to the translation of the Septuagint, the Sibylline Oracles and the Letter of Aristeas, we can perhaps credit to Alexandria the writings of the chronographer Demetrius (late third century BC), Aristobulus the philosopher (perhaps mentioned in 2 Macc. 1: 10), the historian Artapanus (late third to mid second century BC), the playwright Ezekiel (mid second century BC), and possibly Pseudo-Hecataeus and Aristeas (second century BC). The grandson of Jesus son of Sirach settled in Egypt – probably in Alexandria – and translated his grandfather's work there in the reign of Ptolemy VIII, Euergetes II (145–116 BC). The Greek translation of the book of Esther was brought to Egypt – again, probably to Alexandria – in 78–77 BC by Dositheus (Rest of Esth. 11: 1). The Wisdom of Solomon was almost certainly written at Alexandria in the second half of the first century BC or the early first century AD. The romance of Joseph and Aseneth and the book 3 Maccabees both derive from Egypt in the late first century BC, when relationships between Jews and Greek citizens of Alexandria had deteriorated. The hostility shown in 3 Maccabees towards hellenism, the king, and those Jews ready to acknowledge the cult of Greek gods for the sake of Alexandrian citizenship has suggested to some that this work comes from the less hellenised lower-class Jews from the countryside (the *chōra*) rather than from the city of Alexandria itself.

Other Jewish hellenistic writings are harder to locate with certainty. Pseudo-Eupolemus (mid second century BC), Cleodemus Malchus (second to first century BC), Theophilus (before mid first century BC), and Thallus (first century AD), together with the late second-century BC epic poet Theodotus have all been connected with Samaria and taken to be Samaritan authors. The most likely of these to be Samaritan is Pseudo-Eupolemus, who appears to emphasise the importance of the

Samaritan holy place on Mount Gerizim near Shechem (destroyed later in the second century BC by John Hyrcanus) at the expense of Jerusalem. It is hardly surprising to find material from this century reflecting the relationships between the Jews and the people of Samaria and Shechem (cp. Ecclus. 50: 26; 'the senseless folk that live at Shechem'), but there is nothing in Cleodemus Malchus, Theophilus, and Thallus that compels us to identify them as Samaritans, and the case for Theodotus as a Samaritan writer has recently been overturned. Theodotus reflects rather an anti-Samaritan view that justifies Hyrcanus' attack on Shechem.

It is likely that some of this literature comes from Jerusalem itself. We know from 2 Macc. 4: 14f that the priests there were not slow to adopt hellenistic ways, and we have extant five fragments of the work of Eupolemus, who came from a priestly family and wrote in Greek. Two Greek letters from Jerusalem to the Jews in Egypt are preserved at the beginning of 2 Maccabees. A certain Philo the Elder wrote a poem in Greek hexameters entitled 'On Jerusalem' (if the title given by Polyhistor is to be trusted; the poem itself includes much else), and Philo himself may have been a native of Jerusalem or Judaea. We are on firmer ground with the colophon of the Greek book of Esther (Rest of Esth. 11: 1), which tells us clearly that the original authentic book had been translated 'by Lysimachus son of Ptolemaeus, a resident in Jerusalem' and had been brought – presumably to Alexandria – in the fourth year of the reign of Ptolemy and Cleopatra (i.e., probably 78–77 BC). In view of all this, it is not impossible that there were at least some Jerusalem priests involved in the translation of the Septuagint at Alexandria (the Letter of Aristeas says that the whole team of translators came from Jerusalem); but on the other hand, the Jerusalem priesthood was probably less hellenised in the third century BC (to judge from 2 Maccabees) than in the later-second and first centuries. Even in the second century they may have preferred to write in Hebrew or Aramaic rather than Greek; Jesus son of Sirach (*c.* 180 BC) wrote his book in Hebrew, and the Book of Daniel is written (for whatever reason) in a combination of Hebrew and Aramaic. 1 Maccabees was originally written in Hebrew, and later translated into Greek – probably before Josephus used the book. The annals of the high-priesthood of John Hyrcanus (1 Macc. 16: 24) were probably written in Hebrew or Aramaic. Josephus himself says that he wrote the first version of his *Jewish War* in Aramaic for readers in the east, later turning it into Greek for readers in the west (see p. 96).

Little is known of Jewish hellenistic writings from other places.

2 Maccabees describes itself (2 Macc. 2: 19ff) as the abridged version of a five-volume work by Jason of Cyrene, though whether Jason wrote in Cyrene or Alexandria or Jerusalem is hard to say; we know from Mark 15: 21 of another Cyrenean who found his way to Jerusalem. Perhaps Alexandria is the most likely place, both for the original work and for the abridgement; it was presumably at Alexandria that it acquired the two letters addressed to Egypt that now preface the work. Doubtless hellenistic Jews in other cities wrote letters and other works in Greek; Paul of Tarsus, for example, wrote to and from places like Ephesus, Corinth, Rome, Galatia, Philippi, Colossae, and Laodicea (see Map 1). But it seems to have been Christian rather than Jewish writings that have survived from these places, and, as we have seen, even the Alexandrian Jewish literature was preserved by Christian rather than by Jewish agency.

The main interests of these hellenistic Jewish writers are clear. Inevitably their work revolves round the interpretation of Jewish history, for which their major source was usually the Septuagint. Jews were not the only people concerned to present their history in Greek. In the third century BC an Egyptian priest called Manetho wrote in Greek his *Aegyptiaca* chronicling Egyptian history down to the time of Alexander the Great. In Babylon, Manetho's contemporary Berosus, a priest of Bel, used the priestly chronicles to write a Greek history of Babylon. One of the earliest hellenistic Jewish writers was Demetrius (late third century BC), whose main concern was to present a chronology of Jewish history from patriarchal to monarchic times. A similar concern for chronology can be seen in Eupolemus and Thallus. A fragment of Eupolemus notes that there were 5149 years between Adam and his own day (which he gives as the fifth year of Demetrius I Sōtēr and the twelfth year of Ptolemy VIII of Egypt, i.e., probably 158–157 BC), and 2580 years between the Exodus and the same date. If the Jews were compelled to admit that the Egyptian civilisation was older than their own, they could counter by tracing their physical descent back beyond the beginnings of Egyptian history. A related interest lies in showing that Israel's ancestors were men of learning; Pseudo-Eupolemus asserts that Abraham discovered both astrology and Chaldaean science, and taught the motions of the sun and moon to the Phoenicians and astrology to the Egyptians. Pseudo-Eupolemus adds that this knowledge was first acquired by Enoch, whom he identifies with the Greek Atlas. Artapanus also notes that Abraham taught astrology to the Egyptians; he portrays Joseph as the founder of the Egyptian system of land allotment, and presents Moses as a successful general, crediting him with the invention of ships, cranes, Egyptian weapons, machines for drawing water, and philosophy. Moses is thus shown to be the perfect hellenistic man. Eupolemus similarly portrays Moses as the first wise man, the originator of the alphabet, and the first lawgiver. Josephus in his *Antiquities* follows the same tradition (see pp. 149–50). The theme can be traced back to the Old Testament itself, which presents Joseph (Gen. 41: 39) and Moses (Exod. 7: 11f) as superior to the wise men and magicians of Egypt.

Naturally the Law was important. The Letter of Aristeas is especially concerned to defend the authority of the Greek translation of the Law of Moses. According to Josephus, Pseudo-Hecataeus 'demonstrates our respect for the laws, and how we choose to suffer to the end rather than transgress them, and think this a fine thing' (*Apion* 1.22 (190)). 3 Maccabees illustrates this theme with a vivid story of how Ptolemy IV incited intoxicated elephants to trample on Jews who had refused to apostatise (the Jews were saved when the elephants turned on Ptolemy). According to the Letter of Aristeas (see p. 15), the Law is a fence to preserve the Jews from having too much contact with the impurities and vanities of the Gentiles. The priesthood is given less emphasis than the Law in this literature – probably because the priesthood was less well known outside Jerusalem – though Pseudo-Hecataeus and the Letter of Aristeas speak highly of the intellectual, business, and administrative capacities of the high priest. More attention is given to the Jerusalem Temple, an important focal symbol of Judaism. Pseudo-Hecataeus and the Letter of Aristeas describe it, and Eupolemus devotes much space to his account of David's preparation and Solomon's building of the Temple, underlining the friendly assistance given by the rulers of Syria and Egypt.

The importance of the Temple and the fame of David and Solomon naturally led to an interest in the city of Jerusalem itself; hence Philo the Elder's poem (see above, p. 6), of which Eusebius has preserved twenty-four rather obscure lines. Pseudo-Hecataeus and the Letter of Aristeas (see pp. 24f) both describe Jerusalem, though their descriptions may owe more to convention than to first-hand knowledge. Josephus' description is more likely to be accurate, and has been verified in many particulars by recent archaeological work in Jerusalem.

Whether these writings were mainly intended for Jewish or gentile reading, there is no doubt that the authors were at all times conscious of the position of the Jews in a gentile world. It was important to demonstrate to fellow Jews and perhaps to outsiders that the Jews were an ancient people, with wisdom, learning, literature, history, achievements, and godliness of their own. It was important to show that Jews could play a responsible part in the political and military affairs of whatever country they had made their home, while making their own distinctive contribution to it. Thus a Jewish soldier campaigning for his hellenistic ruler demonstrated the futility of taking auspices from a bird by shooting the bird, with the remark that if the bird had possessed divinatory powers it would not have allowed itself to be shot (*Apion* 1.22 (200–4)). And it was sometimes important to underline that there were occasions when a Jew had to face persecution or persuade the authorities that the Jews were loyal citizens in spite of false accusations to the contrary. It was particularly important to a man like Josephus to demonstrate to the Romans that the Jews were not all such awkward trouble-makers as the rebellion suggested, and to his fellow Jews that the Romans were not such brutal tyrants as their destruction of Jerusalem seemed to demonstrate. On another level, it was important to deal with the difficulties that arose when a Jewish boy fell in love with a gentile girl; in the romance of Joseph and Aseneth (late first century BC), Aseneth willingly embraces the Jewish faith, and, once the gentile villain has died of injuries received trying to abduct the heroine, all is well.

On the level of theology, there were a number of issues important to the Jewish hellenistic writers. In their polytheistic world they needed to underline for their Jewish readers the first two commandments, 'You shall have no other gods to set against me', and, 'You shall not make a carved image for yourself.' Stress on the second commandment was perhaps made necessary by the ever-present temptation to accommodate one's Jewish beliefs to the religion of the hellenistic city-state, with its temple and cult-statue of the presiding deity. Egyptian religion, with its animal-headed deities and native priesthood, was probably less subtly tempting, and it drew Jewish scorn rather than argument. Scathing attacks on idolatry are prominent in Jewish hellenistic works from Egypt such as the Sibylline Oracles or the Wisdom of Solomon. Stress on the first commandment, with its corollary that 'God, the creator of all, is one' (Jos. *Ant.* 1.7.1 (155); see p. 145), was a reaction to the general acceptance throughout the Graeco-Roman world of the Olympian gods. It is hardly surprising to find that Greek gods or heroes were subordinated to the Jewish God by being linked with the antediluvian or patriarchal ancestors of Israel; thus Heracles joins with Abraham's sons in a campaign against the Libyans and marries one of Abraham's grand-daughters (Cleodemus Malchus in Eusebius, *Praeparatio evangelica* IX.20.4), and Atlas is identified with Enoch (Pseudo-

Eupolemus in Eusebius, *P.E.* ix.17.9). According to Artapanus, Orpheus, the founder of the Greek religious movement known to us as Orphism, was taught by Moses, and it was Moses also who assigned to the Egyptians their native gods (Eusebius, *P.E.* ix.27.4). The gods many and lords many of the hellenistic and Egyptian worlds are thus firmly put in their place. The Greeks responded with the charge that the Jews were *atheoi* and *asebeis* – godless and impious – to which the Jewish hellenistic writers replied by presenting the Jewish patriarch Abraham both as the first theologian to teach monotheism and as a model of piety (see p. 145). The Letter of Aristeas takes a different line; in the Letter, Aristeas makes the point to Ptolemy that

> '...the same God who gave the Jews their Law is the one who
> directs your kingdom...for the God who watches over and
> creates all things is the God whom they worship, the God whom
> all men worship, the God whom we ourselves worship, your
> Royal Highness, except that we address him by other names such
> as Zeus and Dis.'

(Cp. p. 14, and Josephus, *Apion* ii.19 (179–81), p. 87.) It was important to show that Judaism could match the rationalism of the Greek philosophers. Josephus shows Abraham as a rational theologian and apologist; Philo actually calls him a philosopher. Josephus himself attacked the doctrines of the Epicurean philosophers (see p. 170) and supported those of the Stoics (see p. 81), and apparently intended to write a treatise 'About God and his being, and about the laws' (see pp. 88f). Of course, he judges Greek philosophy in the light of the philosophy of Abraham and Moses, and so he sees Plato, the greatest of the Greek philosophers, as in certain matters following Moses (*Apion* ii.36 (257)). He tells a story from Clearchus to make the point that Plato's famous pupil Aristotle respected the Jews as philosophers (see pp. 179f). Not all Josephus' apologetic was on this high philosophical plane, however, and in the *Apion* he gives much space to rebutting less intellectual views of Judaism (see below, pp. 86f).

These and other concerns of the Jewish hellenistic writers will be illustrated through the following selections from the Letter of Aristeas, the Sibylline Oracles, Eupolemus, and the writings of Josephus.

The Letter of Aristeas

The Letter of Aristeas is not a letter, in spite of its usual superscription, 'Aristeas to Philocrates'. Josephus, who paraphrased much of the work, called it 'the book of Aristaios', and Eusebius entitled it 'On the translation of the law of the Jews'. The author himself called his work a discourse; the Greek word *diēgēsis* is the word used by Luke at the beginning of his gospel to describe the narrative accounts of his predecessors (Luke 1: 1). The author of the Letter uses a number of regular forms and conventions – for example, in his setting the story at a cultured court, in his reference to well-known literary and philosophical people and their ideas, in his description of works of art (51–82), the city of Jerusalem and its surrounding country (100–20), and the banquet at which Ptolemy sought his guests' views on kingship and government (187–299). He ends his work expressing the hope that it will give Ptolemy greater pleasure than the works of the romancers. Whatever his purpose, the author belonged to the hellenistic literary world. He gave himself a Greek name, Aristeas, and, though it is probably a pseudonym, I will use it for convenience when speaking of him.

The purpose of the Letter

The purpose of his discourse is not immediately clear. Aristeas apparently sets out to tell how the Jewish Law was translated into Greek at Alexandria in the reign of Ptolemy Philadelphus (283–246 BC). The king's librarian, Demetrius of Phalerum, brought to the king's notice the library's need of a translated copy of the Jewish Law (9–11) and submitted a memorandum (28–33). The king wrote to the Jewish high priest Eleazar, asking for translators and sending an embassy, on which Aristeas served, with gifts for the Temple (34–41). Eleazar replied favourably (41–6), and a list of the translators' names is appended to his letter (47–51). The author digresses to explain how he persuaded the king to release large numbers of Jewish captives from service in Egypt (12–27), to describe Ptolemy's gifts in detail (51–82), and to describe the Temple, the priesthood, the city of Jerusalem and the country of the Jews (here making some comparison with the city of

11

Alexandria and the country of Egypt) (83–120). He returns to the story of the translation with a few paragraphs on the selection of the translators (121–7) before digressing again to give Eleazar's apologia for the Jewish Law (128–71). In paragraph 172 the translators arrive at Alexandria, but the sequel is delayed by a lengthy account of a seven-day banquet in which the king questions each of his seventy-two guests in turn about the problems of good government (187–294), at the end of which Aristeas apologises for the length of the section (295–300). The book closes with a brief account of the work of translation and its acceptance by the Jewish community in Alexandria and by the king (301–21), and with a final paragraph to Philocrates.

Though the translation of the Law into Greek provides the story-line of the discourse, clearly the author's purpose was not limited to satisfying Philocrates' scholarly curiosity about Septuagintal origins. The purpose is apologetic rather than simply historical. Some scholars argue that the author is defending Judaism, its antiquity and philosophical respectability, to the gentile world. Certainly the address to Philocrates, the description of the Temple, the priesthood, Jerusalem and Judaea compared with Alexandria and Egypt, and the high priest's defence of the Jewish Law and the elders' demonstration of their wisdom before the King of Egypt all appear at first sight to support that view. But Jewish apologetic deliberately aimed at the Gentiles is not well attested before the first century AD (one thinks of Philo, Josephus, and Paul of Tarsus), and Aristeas may have a Jewish audience in mind. He goes out of his way to underline the friendliness and reasonableness and even respect shown by Ptolemy and his counsellors for Judaism; Ptolemy is even presented as bowing down seven times before the Law. Eleazar's explanation of the significance of the clean and unclean beasts is aimed at hellenised Jews for whom the Law is no longer comprehensible rather than at non-Jews, who would first require some explanation of such obviously distinctive practices as circumcision and sabbath observance. But perhaps the most cogent reason 'for supposing that the addressees were in the first place Jews is the book's obvious aim of justifying the translation into Greek of the Jewish Law, hitherto restricted to Hebrew. This is shown as being supported by the Jerusalem high priest, who supplied a basic text and translators, and as being accepted first of all by the Jewish community in Alexandria, whose leaders declare that it was accurate in every detail and that no revision of any sort should take place.

Much scholarship has been devoted to this point. The author is apparently supporting the authority of the Greek translation of the

Jewish Law made in Alexandria. He may be defending it, together with the whole approach of diaspora Judaism, against the attitude of Palestinian Jews, ever ready to accuse Jews living abroad of a tendency to syncretism or laxity in matters of Jewish Law. To such charges the answer was that the translated Law was the equal of the original Hebrew version, and that the high priest, Eleazar, had the interests of diaspora Jews at heart and respected Ptolemy, who was no persecutor but himself welcomed Jews and respected their wisdom. An influential suggestion has been that the translation referred to in the Letter of Aristeas was not the original third-century BC translation but a revision made *c.* 140 BC to meet the needs of the Jewish community; more recently it has been argued that Aristeas is defending the original third-century BC translation against a revision made *c.* 140 BC – a revision recently identified with the version used by the Jewish community established some twenty years earlier at Leontopolis in the Delta region of Egypt (Map 3) under the refugee high priest Onias IV. In this case, the Letter of Aristeas is Jewish propaganda directed against the Leontopolis temple, priesthood, and scriptures. The difficulty with these views is that they lose sight of the undoubted pro-hellenistic attitude of Aristeas. The author seems concerned to defend a form of Judaism that was thoroughly at home in hellenistic Alexandria. He is demonstrating to his Jewish contemporaries in Alexandria (surely the most obvious addressees) that their scriptures are fully legitimate and need no revision, that their own position in the state is respected, and that they can hold up their heads as Jews among the educated hellenistic society of Alexandria. Indeed, a Greek-speaking Alexandrian Jew could be proud of the fact that his own scriptures could bear their witness to the one God of heaven and earth in the language common to all educated people in the Mediterranean world. If the book came into the hands of interested non-Jewish Alexandrians, they might be reassured, by an apparently gentile author, about the acceptability – political, cultural, and intellectual – of the Jewish community in their midst. The author quite deliberately seems to reduce the cultural gap between the Jew and the non-Jew. Thus he describes the translators chosen by Eleazar as

'...the finest of men, whose academic distinction matched their distinguished parentage. They had not only acquired a sound grasp of Jewish literature but had made it their serious business to study Greek literature as well. They were therefore well trained for diplomatic work, which they undertook whenever necessary.

They had great natural ability for conferences and discussions about the Law. They assiduously cultivated a balanced approach (for this is the best course), firmly rejecting crude and uncivilised notions and similarly avoiding conceited and superior attitudes towards others. In conversation they were prepared to listen carefully and to give a proper answer to each questioner.'

(121–2)

The author's purpose is seen clearly in the theological ideas he presents. His view is that Jewish monotheism is not inconsistent with the best in Greek philosophy. Thus, in the person of Aristeas urging Ptolemy to release Jewish captives, he pleads

'As a man of mature and generous mind, release the men confined under such hardships. The same God who gave the Jews their Law is the one who directs your kingdom... for the God who watches over and creates all things is the God whom they worship, the God whom all men worship, the God whom we ourselves worship, your Royal Highness, except that we address him by other names such as Zeus and Dis.'   (15f)

The Jewish high priest, expounding Moses' teaching to the king's ambassadors, says, 'First of all he demonstrated that God is one; that his power is revealed universally, every place being filled with his sovereignty; that no secret, human, earthly activity escapes his notice but all human deeds and all future events are revealed to him' (132). The replies of the translators to Ptolemy reveal much of the author's theology; the third reply (190) tells Ptolemy to observe how 'God is a benefactor of the human race, providing them with health and food and everything else in due season', a phrase reminiscent both of the psalms (104: 27; 145: 15) and of the speeches of Paul to Gentiles at Lystra and Athens (Acts 14: 15–17; 17: 25), where Luke shows Paul presenting Jewish–Christian belief as compatible with Athenian wisdom. God does not smite people according to their sins but is forbearing (192), guides people's actions (195), grants power and beauty of speech (201), loves the truth (206), mercy (207) and righteousness (209), grants kings their glory and wealth (224), or takes away prosperity and leads others to glory (263; cp. the Magnificat, Luke 1: 52f). The gentile king is told on every possible occasion that he rules by the help and grace of God. The translators frequently deliver sentiments that would be commonplace in the Greek world; thus when the king asks: 'What is the highest form of government?', they reply:

'To be in control of oneself, and not to be carried away by one's desires... in all things moderation is a fine thing' (222–3), and in answer to the question: 'What is the teaching of wisdom?', they reply with a form of the Golden Rule of 'do as you would be done by' (207). Much in this section of Aristeas reflects the concerns of popular hellenistic philosophy – for example, how to avoid being carried away by passion, and have pleasure and enjoyment in life (221, 223, 277), how to have untroubled sleep (213), how to avoid envy or grief (224, 232), and in particular with such things as the need for *philanthrōpia* (humanity) (208) and *euergesia* (practical generosity) (205) and justice (189) in a king. But though Aristeas may owe something to hellenistic treatises on kingship and to popular hellenistic philosophy, he may also owe much to the Wisdom tradition of the ancient Near East, well represented in Judaism by such works as the book of Proverbs and, nearer Aristeas' own time, Ecclesiasticus, the wisdom of Jesus son of Sirach. This book, though written by a scholar in Jerusalem in the early second century BC, has in common with Aristeas that it was published in Greek in Egypt, probably in Alexandria, 'for the use of those who have made their home in a foreign land, and wish to become scholars by training themselves to live according to the law' (Preface to Ecclesiasticus). The translator of Ecclesiasticus, the grandson of the author, differs from Aristeas in that he mistrusts the Greek translation of the Law, the prophets, and the rest of the writings: 'It is impossible for a translator to find precise equivalents for the original Hebrew in another language. Not only with this book, but with the law, the prophets, and the rest of the writings, it makes no small difference to read them in the original' (Preface to Ecclesiasticus).

Aristeas, however, for all his hellenistic language and culture, is distinctively Jewish in his theological teaching. His concern is primarily with the Law: it is 'most philosophical and faultless, seeing that it is divine' (31), 'solemnly drawn up for the sake of righteousness, to promote holy contemplation and the perfecting of character' (144). Eleazar says of it that Moses

> '... fenced us round with impenetrable barriers and iron walls, his purpose being that we should have no familiar contact at all with other nations but should remain pure in body and soul, free of worthless opinions, honouring the one almighty God above the entire creation. For this reason, the priests who guide the Egyptians... call us men of God, a title that does not apply to the rest of mankind but only to those who worship the true God.'
>
> (139–40)

Israel's separatism remains important, even to Aristeas, though it is significant that his main criticism falls on the Egyptians (138), with their worship of animals, rather than upon the Greeks, and this is natural enough at Alexandria where, in Ptolemaic times, there was a great social gulf fixed between the hellenistic governing classes and the native peasantry of the country.

All this reveals the author as a cultivated, educated, upper-class Jew of Alexandria, and this assessment is underlined by Aristeas' attitude towards the monarchy. Ptolemy is shown as a benevolent philosopher king who studies the needs of his people (219, 283), checks abuses (271, 283), sees that fair wages are paid (258), and discourages informers (166) – here one is reminded of the advice of Eccles. 10: 20 (see above, p. 2). Above all, Ptolemy will accept the advice of the Jewish wise men on how to rule. Aristeas finds gentile rule agreeable and accommodating; his book would encourage Alexandrian Jews to be loyal citizens and Alexandrian Gentiles (if they met the book) to recognise the Jewish contribution. If it reached Jerusalem, the book might also reassure the Jewish leaders that under a friendly hellenistic regime in Alexandria Jews could live in conformity with the Law.

The date of the Letter

This book is harder to date than to place. References to past and present administrative practice under the Ptolemies (128, 182) show that the writer is looking back over a fairly lengthy period of time. Historical inaccuracies appear: Demetrius of Phalerum was not librarian at Alexandria, and died, out of favour, soon after the beginning of Ptolemy II's reign. The philosopher Menedemus of Eretria (201) was dead by 277 BC and is not known or believed to have visited Philadelphus' court. The description of Philadelphus' naval victory over Antigonus (180) does not exactly fit the circumstances either of his victory at Cos (260 BC) or of his defeat at Andros (245 BC). Certain Greek expressions used by Aristeas have been thought to demonstrate a date in the second half of the second century BC (e.g., the formula 'greeting and health' in Ptolemy's letter (35), the phrase 'if it seems [good to you]' (32), and the plural use of the Greek word for 'keepers of the bodyguard' (40), but more recent examination has shown that these phrases can be traced back to the third century BC. Arguments based on the geographical references to an apparently independent Idumaea (which was first subjugated by Judaea in 127 BC), and on other minor details of political geography, are useful only if the author was not picturing an idealised, biblical Palestine rather than the real, contemporary one. A more reliable guide to the dating may be the relationship of the Letter of Aristeas to other literature. The author probably knew and was influenced by the Books of Ezra and Nehemiah. He clearly depends upon the Greek translation of the Law for the descriptions of the shewbread table (51–72), for the high priest's vestments (96–9), and for the occasional quotation (155). He quotes Hecataeus of Abdera, who lived and wrote in the days of Alexander the Great and Ptolemy I of Egypt. He cites a decree of Philadelphus about the liberation of Jewish slaves (12–27), which probably has its origin in an authentic decree of 262–261 BC. Aristeas certainly shows (with some pride) knowledge of the protocol of the Ptolemaic court (295–300) and of the economic pressures of the late third or early second century BC in Egypt (109). Possibly the first writer to use Aristeas is the Alexandrian Jew Aristobulus who, in an apologetic work addressed to Ptolemy Philometor (180–145 BC), appears to follow important details of Aristeas' account. It may be, however, that Aristeas is dependent upon Aristobulus; but in that case one has to explain why all subsequent writers see Aristeas, not Aristobulus, as the prime source of the story. Also ambiguous for dating purposes is a minor similarity in phraseology between paragraph 37 and 1 Macc. 10: 37. Later in the first century BC, 3 Maccabees may have used the Letter of Aristeas, though presenting a totally different view of Jew–Gentile relationships in the Alexandrian community. Matters become clearer in the first century AD, when Philo probably and Josephus certainly base themselves on Aristeas. The probable conclusion is that the Letter of Aristeas should be dated in the middle of the second century BC – a little earlier if the work is used by Aristobulus, a little later if the dependence is the other way round.

THE AUTHOR'S PREFACE

1 Since the narrative of our meeting with Eleazar, the high priest of the Jews, is worth recording, Philocrates, and since you yourself are particularly concerned (as you keep reminding me) to hear the whys and wherefores of our embassy, I have tried to set out the

2 matter clearly for you. I know your scholarly frame of mind; it is indeed a most important human function, as the poet says,

always to learn, and add to one's mind's store,

whether by historical research or through experience of events. For in this way, by seizing on what is finest, the mind is developed to a pure state; and as it aims at the crown of all virtues, piety, it works with the help of an unerring guide.

3 It was because I had this interest in the careful study of theological matters that I offered myself for the embassy to the man I have just mentioned, a man highly honoured for his excellence and fame both by his fellow citizens and by others. He has brought the greatest possible advantage to his fellow Jews, whether living as his neighbours or elsewhere, in the matter of the translation of the divine Law (for they have it in their possession written on

4 parchments in the Hebrew script). I undertook this assignment, then, with enthusiasm, and I began by seizing the opportunity of an audience with the king about those who had been exiled to Egypt from Judaea by the king's father when he first gained possession of the city and took charge of affairs in Egypt. (This event is also worth

5 explaining to you.) For I am confident that you, with your exceptional inclination to holiness and your sympathy with those who live according to the holy Law, will be happy to listen to what we purpose to reveal, since you have only recently arrived among us from the island and are willing to hear whatever conduces to

6 the good of the soul. Indeed, on a former occasion I sent you an account of matters I thought worthy of record, an account of the Jewish people that I had from the most learned high priests throughout the most learned land of Egypt.

The author introduces his work in a manner reminiscent of Luke's gospel and many other literary works of the hellenistic world. He addresses Philocrates, apparently his patron, as a man of learning and holiness, and a worthy recipient of the story, and he presents himself as a conscientious historian. He explains that he relies on excellent sources, and that he himself played an important part in the events described, acting as ambassador between Ptolemy and the Jewish high priest. All this, however, is a literary affectation if the author is writing a century after the events he describes.

1. He calls his *narrative* a *diēgēsis* (cp. Luke 1: 1), a technical term for a literary genre described by Cicero as 'an exposition of events as they took place or as they might have taken place'. This *Philocrates* is otherwise unknown, but the Greek name ('lover of strength') is common enough in Ptolemaic Egypt and may have been chosen to suggest to the reader that there need be no difficulty in intellectual

intercourse between Jew and Greek in Alexandria. Aristeas himself appears as a hellenised Jew, equally at home with the king in Alexandria or the high priest *Eleazar* in Jerusalem. This high priest is otherwise unknown apart from Josephus, who makes him the successor of Simon the Just (= Simon I) and dates him (clearly depending on the Letter of Aristeas) to the time of Philadelphus. But Josephus' high-priestly succession list is suspect on several counts, one being that Simon the Just should more probably be identified with Simon II (*c.* 200 BC). One notes also that, according to 2 Macc. 6, a priestly Eleazar of great saintliness was martyred by Antiochus IV. It seems likely that Aristeas chose the name Eleazar for its associations rather than from reasons of historical accuracy.

2. The quotation, in Greek a line of iambic verse perhaps taken from the classical playwright Sophocles (496–406 BC), reveals the author's literary pretensions.

3. The author underlines his motives and the quality of his sources. The Greek, slightly ambiguous, might mean either that Eleazar was himself of some usefulness to translators, or that Eleazar had documents of importance for the translation of the Law (though the word 'documents' is not in the Greek). *the divine Law* refers to the Pentateuch alone (cp. the Preface to Ecclesiasticus). *on parchments in the Hebrew script*: according to the Mishnah (Meg. 2: 1f), a man does not properly fulfil his obligation of reading the Law unless 'it was written in Assyrian writing [i.e., in the square Hebrew script], on parchment and with ink'.

4. Aristeas underlines his own Jewish patriotism by giving a full account (12–27) of his part in the emancipation of Jewish captives *exiled to Egypt from Judaea by the king's father* (Ptolemy I) *when he first gained possession of the city* (Alexandria) *and took charge of affairs in Egypt*. Ptolemy became Satrap of Egypt after Alexander's death in 323 BC. In what year he took Jewish captives to Egypt is less clear. He invaded Palestine in 320, 312, 302, and 301 BC. Aristeas quotes a decree of emancipation (21–6) that may be based on an authentic decree of Ptolemy Philadelphus (preserved in Papyrus Rainer 24512), dating from 261 BC, which is a demand for the legal registration of captured Syrians and Palestinians with a view to freeing those whose slavery was in fact illegal. Not all Jews in Egypt, however, were slaves; Jews had been employed in Egypt as mercenary soldiers from the sixth century BC at least, as we know from the Elephantinē papyri, and the practice continued down to the first century BC.

5. The *island* may be Pharos, then offshore but not part of Alexandria, or it may be, as some have guessed, Cyprus.

6. The *former occasion* is unknown; possibly the author is identifying

himself with the historian Aristeas and referring to his book *About the Jews* (known to us from the *Praeparatio evangelica* of Eusebius; see above, p. 4).

In the following paragraphs, Aristeas narrates how Philadelphus, hearing from his librarian, Demetrius of Phalerum, of the existence of Jewish books of Law and of the library's need of a translation of them, ordered a letter to be written to the Jerusalem high priest. Aristeas then describes how he initiated the process leading to the emancipation of Jewish captives in Egypt. That completed, Ptolemy Philadelphus orders Demetrius to draft a memorandum about the transcription of the Jewish books.

THE MEMORANDUM OF DEMETRIUS

28 When this business had been dealt with, he ordered Demetrius to submit a memorandum about the copying of the Jewish books. For at the court of these kings, everything was managed by means of decrees, and with maximum security, and nothing was done in an offhand or casual manner. I have therefore recorded the copy of the memorandum and the copies of the letters, and the list of gifts sent and the description of each, because each of them was of extraordinary quality and craftmanship. This is a copy of the memorandum:

29 To the Great King, from Demetrius.

In accordance with your Majesty's order concerning the library, that books needed to complete the collection should be acquired and added, and that those accidentally damaged should receive suitable attention, I submit the following report, having attended to my responsibility in the matter in no casual

30 manner. Books of the Law of the Jews, with some few others, are wanting. For it happens that these books are written in the Hebrew script and language, but, according to the evidence of the experts, have been somewhat carelessly committed to writing and are not in their original form; for they have never

31 had the benefit of royal attention. It is important that these books, duly corrected, should find a place in your library, because this legislation, in as much as it is divine, is of

philosophical importance and of innate integrity. For this reason writers and poets and the great majority of historians have avoided reference to the above mentioned books and to the people who have lived and are living in accordance with them, because, as Hecataeus of Abdera says, the view of life

32 presented in them has a certain sanctity and holiness. If, then, your Majesty approves, a letter shall be written to the high priest in Jerusalem, asking him to send elders of exemplary lives, expert in their country's Law, six from each tribe, so that, having established the agreement of the majority and obtained an accurate translation, we may give the book a distinguished place in our library, in keeping both with the importance of the affair and of your own purpose. May you ever prosper!

33 In view of this memorandum, the king ordered a letter on the subject to be written to Eleazar, informing him also of the accomplished emancipation of the prisoners. In addition, he gave for the crafting of the bowls and flagons, table, and libation cups fifty talents weight of gold and seventy talents of silver and a fully adequate quantity of precious stones (ordering the treasurers to leave the choice of materials to the craftsmen), and up to a hundred talents of coined money for sacrifices and other details.

This memorandum appears to describe the circumstances that made the translation of the Jewish Law into Greek necessary; Demetrius complains that these Jewish books are not part of the library's collection because they are foreign books and no accurate texts are available, and proposes that an accurate translation should be commissioned from Jerusalem.

28. *this business*: the emancipation of the Jewish slaves. *at the court of these kings*: this sentence suggests that the author is familiar with administrative practices at the Ptolemaic court, and also that he is looking back over several reigns. *gifts*: see on paragraph 33 below, p. 23.

29. The king's *order* as given in paragraph 11 made no reference to repairs.

30. If the books of the Jewish law are *wanting* (i.e., not in the library), what does the following sentence mean? Demetrius knows that the Jewish Law was written in Hebrew (and not, as some think, in Aramaic, as he explained earlier to the king), but the precise meaning of his

complaint is less clear. The Greek verb *sesēmantai* (here translated 'committed to writing') used to be translated 'have been interpreted', and it was supposed that Demetrius was referring to a previous, inferior translation into Greek. In this case, the Letter of Aristeas may have been written to support a Greek revision of the original Greek translation. It has been suggested that such a revision was made *c.* 140 BC (see above, p. 13); but why would the author support such a revision with the obvious pretence that it was made in the reign of Philadelphus? The whole thrust of Demetrius' argument seems to be that the Law was wanting because of lack of care in the transmission of the text, and therefore it seems better to follow the majority of recent scholars and take *sesēmantai* to mean simply 'committed to writing'. Another suggestion is that the Greek sentence, slightly repunctuated, means 'They happen to be written in the Hebrew script and language, but somewhat carelessly, and they have no meaning (*sesēmantai*) as they now exist.' In either case, Demetrius is saying that there are no accurate Hebrew copies to be had in Alexandria, for Hebrew manuscripts have never had the skilled attention that the king's scholars had given to Greek texts. He goes on to argue that an accurate text of these books should be included in the library (31), and that an accurate translation should be made (32). In the sequel, Aristeas tells us that a copy of the Law was sent from Jerusalem (46) and that a translation was made in Alexandria (301–7).

However, it must be admitted that the precise translation of this paragraph, so crucial for our understanding of the history of the Septuagint, remains uncertain.

31. Demetrius justifies the inclusion of *these books* on the ground that the Jewish Law, being divine, is *of philosophical importance and of innate integrity*, a description that might appeal to both Greek and Jewish minds, and certainly to a hellenised Jew. The explanation of the lack of reference to these writings in pagan authors is elaborated at the end of the Letter, when the translation is read to the king, where it is explained that certain Greek writers who had tried to publicise the Law were physically prevented by God; thus Theopompus was shown in a dream that 'he was taking too much upon himself in wishing to reveal divine truths to ordinary men' (315). Aristeas apparently approves of the translation of the Law into Greek for the benefit of Alexandrian Jews and for their patron, the king, but has reservations about allowing it into the hands of the pagan public at large. So at the end of the story the king 'ordered that great care should be taken of the books,

and that they should be preserved in holy manner'. *Hecataeus of Abdera*: see below, p. 148.

32. *If...your Majesty approves*: for the possible implications of the underlying Greek phrase for dating the Letter of Aristeas, see p. 16. *elders...six from each tribe*: as by the third century BC the twelve-tribe system was no longer a political reality, this provision seems idealistic. A total of seventy-two translators seems to conflict with the tradition that the Greek translation was made by 'the seventy' (cp. the name 'Septuagint'), behind which may lie the biblical account of the seventy elders who accompanied Moses at Mount Sinai (Exod. 24: 1, 9). It has been noted that in the story of the banquet preceding the actual translation (182–294) seven rounds of questions are put to the translators. In each of the first five rounds, ten men are questioned, but in the last two rounds eleven men are questioned (i.e., seventy-two men in all), and it has been suggested that the author has adapted the account in this way to meet the needs of his own original scheme of six translators from each tribe.

The emphasis is on the obtaining of an *accurate translation*, based on the majority verdict of the elders. The committee technique of translation is historically much more credible than the later accounts, which describe the miraculous total verbal agreement of translators working separately. Aristeas is concerned to demonstrate that this Greek translation is fully authoritative, accurately based on a text sent from the Jerusalem high priest (paragraph 46) and agreed upon by *elders of exemplary lives, expert in their country's Law*.

May you ever prosper! is the usual closing formula of a letter from a subordinate.

33. The gifts here mentioned are described in detail later in the book (51–82). The major piece was the table (52–72) designed to carry the shewbread. It is pictured as being of complex craftsmanship, bearing designs in relief and inlays of precious stones, 'completed in wonderful and memorable manner, with inimitable craft and superb beauty' (72). The description owes something to the Septuagint description in Exod. 25: 23ff and 37: 10ff. The *bowls* (*kratēres*), again elaborately wrought (73–8), were large, holding about 80 litres (17½ gallons) each. Their purpose is not clear. In the Septuagint bowls of this sort are used by Moses as receptacles for the blood of calves when he sacrifices on Mount Sinai (Exod. 24: 6). The *flagons* (*phialai*) (Josephus says there were thirty of them), engraved with vines, ivy-wreaths, myrtle, and olive (79), were part of the equipment of the altar of burnt-offering

(Exod. 27: 3). The *libation cups (spondeioi)* are not described later; in the Septuagint, such cups belonged with the shewbread table and were for drink-offerings (Exod. 25: 29). It seems clear that the author has in mind the account in Exodus of the furnishings of the Tabernacle and the craftsmanship of Bezalel and his colleagues (Exod. 31: 1ff).

It seems unlikely that in fact sacred furniture and vessels for the Temple would have been accepted as gifts from Ptolemaic Egypt. The author is again stressing that the Egyptian court was benevolent towards Judaism, and that Jews could maintain close and friendly relations with it without incurring pollution.

The author goes on to describe the Temple, the priesthood, and the citadel of Jerusalem.

JERUSALEM AND ALEXANDRIA — A COMPARISON

105 The city is of moderate size, being so far as one can tell about forty stades in circumference. In the arrangement of the towers and the exits through them, the city has the appearance of a theatre, with cross streets appearing some at a higher and some 106 at a lower level. For as the city is built on a mountain, the place is on a slope, and there are stairways to the cross streets. Some people make their way at a higher level, others below them; and as they go, individuals keep their distance from one another to prevent those in a state of purity touching anything unfitting. 107 The fine proportions used by the founders in the building of the city were not unplanned, but the result of wisdom and forethought. For as the country is large and fine, some parts (the region called Samaritis and the region abutting Idumaean territory) being flat, others [those parts abutting Judaean territory] being mountainous, continual attention to farming and agriculture is vital in order that the latter regions also may produce a good harvest. Since such careful attention is given, 108 the whole country is farmed with great profit. The larger (and consequently more prosperous) cities have a high population, but their surrounding country is neglected, for everyone is inclined to seek his own personal enjoyment, all men by nature being

109 prone to pleasure. This was the case at Alexandria, a city
surpassing all others in size and prosperity. For when country
people visited the city, they stayed some time and so reduced
110 the level of farming-activity. The result was that the king, to
prevent countrymen remaining in the city, ordered that they
should not reside in the city for more than twenty days, and gave
written instructions to the officials that if individuals had to be
summonsed, decisions were to be made within five days.
Emphasising the importance of the matter, he appointed special
judges, with assistants, in every district, so that the farmers and
their agents in the cities might not take their own profits to the
disadvantage of the city's stocks (I mean, of agricultural
production).

The author, having described the Temple, the priesthood, and the
citadel of Jerusalem, continues with a brief description of the city. His
main purpose, however, is to compare the ways in which the cities of
Jerusalem and Alexandria respectively relate, economically and socially,
to their surrounding countries. Such comparisons were a regular feature
of hellenistic literature, as were also geographical descriptions, whether
serious and factual (like the work of Herodotus in the fifth century BC
or Pausanias in the second century AD) or more romantic (like Antonius
Diogenes' *Wonders beyond Thule*, c. AD 100). Josephus (*Apion* 1.22
(197–9)) preserves a description of Jerusalem from Hecataeus that has
some similarities with Aristeas' account.

105. *forty stades*: 7.2 kilometres or $4\frac{1}{2}$ miles, the stade being about
180 metres or 200 yards. Hecataeus gives 50 stades, and Josephus 33
(at the beginning of the war with Rome). As Josephus' figure seems
to tally approximately with what is known of the first-century AD city
boundaries from archaeological evidence, and as the Jerusalem of Herod
the Great and his successors was somewhat larger than that of his
predecessors, the figures of Hecataeus and Aristeas are exaggerated.
Alexandria was certainly much larger. Strabo (late first century BC)
describes it as the shape of a spread-out cloak (roughly rectangular),
30 stades east–west by 7 to 10 stades north–south. By comparison with
this, Jerusalem was certainly *of moderate size*. The author explains the
advantage of this below (107ff). *the arrangement of the towers* . . . : the text,
construction, and translation of this sentence are all disputed. Aristeas
seems to think of a walled city, with gate-towers guarding the main

exits, with *cross streets* and stepped streets leading to them. Similar features can be seen in the Old City (i.e., late medieval city) of Jerusalem today. The comparison with a theatre becomes clearer if one remembers the design of the ancient theatre: viewed from the stage, the stone seats, divided by stepped gangways and transverse gangways, rise in wedge-shaped blocks towards the encircling wall or hillside. Aristeas is perhaps picturing Jerusalem as seen from its south-east corner or the Temple area, from which the streets and houses rise towards the north-west.

106. What Aristeas means by this description of people moving apparently on two levels is not entirely clear; possibly Aristeas himself misunderstood what he had been told about the topography of Jerusalem. His description is not inconsistent with the real Jerusalem, but it does not seem to be the description of an eye-witness. In the hellenistic world, however, it would be instantly recognisable, with its towers, gateways, and cross streets, as a very standard *polis* or city. The author conceals the absence of a theatre as best he can by describing the city itself as theatre-shaped. If the Greek word *summetrōs* in paragraph 105 means 'symmetrical' rather than 'moderate' (as here translated), the author perhaps had in mind the grid-pattern arrangement of streets common in Greek cities since Hippodamus of Miletus in the fifth century BC. Whatever the extent of his knowledge, Aristeas certainly presents Jerusalem as a hellenistic city.

Aristeas is right to note that pedestrians would be careful to avoid accidental physical contact with those who might be in a state of ritual uncleanness (cp. Lev. 15, especially verse 31), but wrong if he is suggesting that the clean and the unclean travel at different levels.

107. The author turns to the surrounding country and its relationship to the city. The countryside round the comparatively small Jerusalem is cultivated, both hill and plain, to best advantage (being thickly populated; cp. paragraph 113), so that the city is fully supplied with food, while the huge city of Alexandria suffers from rural depopulation and an unproductive agricultural industry. *Samaritis* is the name of the Ptolemaic administrative region of the Old Testament Samaria, to the north of Judaea. The *Idumaean territory* lay south of Judaea. The *flat* region *abutting* it is probably the coastal plain north of Idumaea and west of Judaea. Aristeas apparently sees Idumaea and Samaria as independent of Judaea, which suggests that he is writing before the reign of John Hyrcanus (134–104 BC), who annexed them to his kingdom. *those parts abutting Judaean territory* (or *city*?): these words have been supplied to restore a lacuna in the text. Their omission may have been caused by haplography after *abutting Idumaean territory*. Alternatively we might read simply 'in the centre'.

110. According to Aristotle, similar measures were taken by Peisistratus, Tyrant of Athens, *c.* 520 BC. It has been argued that this passage is full of terms taken from current administrative vocabulary, and that it reflects the time of Philometor (180–145 BC) rather than Philadelphus, in whose reign agriculture was still flourishing. The temptation was clearly for farmers to make more money by dealing in the city. The precise function of the *prostatai* (here translated *agents*) is not known.

THE LAND OF JUDAEA

112　We owe this digression to Eleazar's excellent exposition to us of the matters just discussed. The devotion of the farmers to their work is great. Their country is planted with numbers of olive trees, with cereal crops and leguminous plants; it has also vines and plenty of honey. There is no numbering their other fruit

113　trees and date palms. They have many cattle of all kinds, and rich pasturage for them. Thus they saw clearly that their districts needed sufficient manpower, and they arranged the city and the

114　villages accordingly in due proportion. A great quantity of spices and precious stones and gold is imported into the region by the Arabs, for the country is organised for trade as well as for farming; the city is full of technical skills and has no shortage

115　of anything that can be imported by sea. For it has harbours well placed to serve trade – Ascalon, Joppa, Gaza, and similarly the royal foundation of Ptolemais. It is centrally placed compared with the others just mentioned, and is not far from them. The country has plenty of everything, since it is generally well

116　watered and enjoys great security. The perennial river called the Jordan flows round it. Originally the country was of not less than six million *arourai* (though later it suffered the encroachment of neighbouring peoples), six hundred thousand men becoming holders of lots of one hundred *arourai* each. The river, like the Nile, becomes full in the period just before harvest and irrigates

117　much of the land. The Jordan's stream discharges into another river in the region of Ptolemais, and this flows out into the sea. Other wadis, as they are called, run off the hills; their catchment

118　area is Gaza and the land belonging to Azotus. The land is ringed

with natural defences, and is difficult of access and impossible
for large numbers of men on account of its narrow passes with
deep cliffs and ravines on either side; the entire mountain range
surrounding the whole country is rough terrain.

The author now turns to the country apart from Jerusalem, presenting
it in idealistic and biblical terms. Among its virtues are the careful
balance between city and country, its self-sufficiency in food, its
technical ability, trade, harbours, the central position of the capital city,
the water supply, and the natural defences.

112. Here as elsewhere the author makes a rhetorical apology for the
length of his discourse. The reference to *Eleazar's excellent exposition*
is not clear; Eleazar's speech to the embassy follows in paragraphs 128ff.
For the description of the country's produce, compare Num. 13: 27;
Deut. 8: 7–10, and the much earlier description in the Egyptian story
of Sinuhe (twentieth century BC): 'It was a wonderful land called Yaa.
There were cultivated figs in it and grapes, and more wine than water.
Its honey was abundant, and its olive trees numerous. On its trees were
all varieties of fruit. There were emmer corn and barley, and there was
no end to all varieties of cattle.'

113. See the comment on paragraph 107 above.

114. *Arabs*: compare the vivid description of the trade of Tyre in
Ezek. 27: 12–24, especially verses 21f, where 'the choicest spices, every
kind of precious stone and gold' are brought by the Arabian dealers
from Sheba and Raamah. The picture of Jerusalem as a commercial
centre, *full of technical skills* and with *no shortage of anything*, is probably
exaggerated, in order that Jerusalem should not appear too provincial
beside Alexandria.

115. *Ascalon* was an ancient trading-city on the coast, long associated
with Egypt and Tyre but never owned by Judah. *Joppa*, another ancient
city (modern Jaffa), became an important port under the Ptolemies;
Judas Maccabaeus burnt the harbour (2 Macc. 12: 6), Jonathan captured
the town (1 Macc. 10: 75f) in 147 BC, and Simon garrisoned it in 143 BC
(1 Macc. 12: 34). *Gaza*, further down the coast towards Egypt, had
a similarly turbulent history, firmly opposing such invaders as Alexander
the Great and the Seleucid Antiochus III, and also the Maccabaean
Jonathan (1 Macc. 11: 61f). In 96 BC Gaza was destroyed after a year's
siege by Alexander Jannaeus. *Ptolemais*, modern Akko, re-founded by,
and re-named after, Ptolemy II Philadelphus (261 BC), was another city
with a history of enmity towards the Jews (cp. 1 Macc. 5: 15; 2 Macc.

6: 8). (See Map 5.) At no time in the last three centuries BC were all these cities simultaneously under Judaean rule; at best this reference to them suggests that the Letter of Aristeas' was written some time between 261 and 96 BC. But in spite of their generally unfriendly attitude to Judah, these ports probably were gateways through which much foreign produce reached Jerusalem. *centrally placed*: Jerusalem was about 55 kilometres (34 miles) from Joppa, 65 kilometres (40½ miles) from Ascalon, 75 kilometres (46½ miles) from Gaza, and 130 kilometres (81 miles) from Ptolemais. The author may also, however, have an ideal in mind. The central position of a capital would be desirable for practical reasons; the book of Ezekiel four centuries previously had set Jerusalem and the Temple at the centre of its idealised reconstruction of the tribal territories of Israel (Ezek. 48).

116. *round it*: again, the author has the ideal rather than the real country in view. His picture of the River Jordan, encircling the country, may owe something to the mythical river that flowed out of Eden to water the garden (Gen. 2: 10–14); it divided into four rivers, two of which are said to flow round the whole land of Havilah and the land of Cush. Similarly, Aristeas' calculation of *six million arourai* is based on the biblical number of the Israelite males who came out of Egypt at the Exodus (Exod. 12: 37) and the Ptolemaic practice of rewarding army veterans (in some cases) with 40½ hectares (100 acres) of land. (The *aroura*, according to Herodotus, *Histories* II.168, was a square of 100 Egyptian cubits, and so the equivalent of 2700 square metres, or about two thirds of an English acre.) *like the Nile*: this comparison with the annual inundation of the Nile is a little forced, but is probably part of the author's wider comparison of Jerusalem and Alexandria, Judaea and Egypt. *becomes full...just before harvest*: the author is clearly using Josh. 3: 15 (cp. Ecclus. 24: 26). The Jordan in fact floods in April, when the snows on Mount Hermon melt, but it does not irrigate the land.

117. The Jordan empties into the Dead Sea, not via any other river into the Mediterranean (whether *in the region of Ptolemais* or 'of the Ptolemaeans', i.e., Egyptians, in accordance with the manuscript evidence). This idea is a consequence of the idea that the Jordan encircles the land. *Other wadis*: Nahal Lakhish flows into the Mediterranean just north of Azotus (Ashdod), and Nahal Besor a few miles south of Gaza. Aristeas is comparatively well informed about the parts of Palestine nearest to Egypt.

118. There is some ground for this description of a defensible, mountainous country; *the entire mountain range surrounding the whole*

country is perhaps to be taken as referring to the mountains of Sinai, Transjordan, Hermon and Upper Galilee. Yet the land of Israel has suffered many invasions in the course of its history.

Aristeas follows his description of Jerusalem and the land by resuming his narrative thread and explaining how Eleazar selected for Ptolemy men who 'had not only acquired a sound grasp of Jewish literature but had made it their serious business to study Greek literature as well' (121), and sent them off with an accompanying letter to Ptolemy requesting their safe return. Aristeas then mentions that he and his fellow ambassador, Andreas, had inquired of the Jewish high priest 'why, given that creation is one, some things are held to be unclean for food, and some even to touch'.

THE HIGH PRIEST'S APOLOGIA FOR THE LAW

134 With this as his basic premise, he demonstrated that, apart from us, all other men believe in the existence of many gods – though men themselves are much more powerful than the gods they

135 vainly worship. They make images of stone and wood, describing them as the images of those whose discoveries were of advantage to human life. They reveal all too clearly their lack of perception

136 by worshipping these images. For that a person should become divine on account of some discovery that he has made is utterly senseless. Such people indeed took certain parts of creation and put them together and went on to demonstrate their usefulness, but they did not actually create them. It is thus idle and foolish

137 for men to deify their fellows. For in our own time also there are many who are more inventive and learned than their predecessors, but men would be in no hurry to worship them. Those who concoct and put out such tales actually believe that

138 they are the wisest of the Greeks! Why should we even mention the other particularly foolish peoples – the Egyptians and those like them – who have put their faith in wild animals and the majority of creeping things and brute beasts, worshipping them

139 and sacrificing to them, both dead and alive? Our lawgiver, therefore, divinely endowed with omniscience, having con-

sidered each detail, fenced us round with impenetrable barriers
and iron walls, his purpose being that we should have no
familiar contact at all with other nations but should remain pure
in body and soul, free of worthless opinions, honouring the one
almighty God above the entire creation.

Aristeas' and Andreas' question introduces a long speech from Eleazar
giving a rationalistic explanation designed for the hellenistic mind
(whether Jewish or gentile) of the Jewish laws of cleanliness. Eleazar
speaks of the 'way of allegory', an approach much used by Philo,
a later Jewish apologist from Alexandria (see the accompanying volume
in this series by R. Williamson). Eleazar's address is in the homiletic
form regularly used by Stoic and Cynic preachers familiar in a city like
Alexandria.

134. *With this as his basic premise*: Eleazar began his apologia by
emphasising the influence on men for good or evil of the company they
keep (compare the proverb quoted by Paul, 1 Cor. 15: 33: 'Bad
company is the ruin of a good character'), and by outlining the teaching
of Moses that a man's actions are manifest to the one God whose
sovereignty is universal. Misdeeds bring retribution. This emphasis on
the unity, power, and omniscience of God is the standard Jewish
counter to the *bête noire* of idolatry. Compare the commandments:
'You shall have no other god to set against me. You shall not make
a carved image for yourself' (Exod. 20: 3f).

135. Trenchant satires on the senselessness of idolatry may be read
in Isa. 44: 9–20 and in Wisd. of Sol. (another Jewish writing from
Alexandria, a century or so later than Aristeas) 13: 10–19. If the Letter
of Aristeas comes from the Maccabaean period, when 'the abomination
of desolation' was set up on the altar of burnt-offering (cp. 1 Macc.
1: 54; Dan. 11: 31), this attack may be all the more relevant, but
Aristeas does not seem to have that particular act of desecration in mind,
and may be thinking of the danger of idolatry ever present to the Jew
in a city like Alexandria.

136f. Aristeas refers to the belief propounded by the philosopher
Euhemerus, who wrote a novel at the end of the third century BC
describing life on an imaginary island in the Indian Ocean. A
monument on the island revealed that the senior Greek gods, Uranus,
Kronos, and Zeus, had originally been kings and benefactors and had
been given divine honours by their grateful subjects. The theory may
have been particularly welcome at the court of a king like Philadelphus,

yet Aristeas has no hesitation in firmly rejecting the deification of men as *idle and foolish*, even though the theory may come from people who regard themselves as *the wisest of the Greeks*.

138. Aristeas' scorn for the Egyptians reflects the cultural chasm between the sophisticated Alexandrian Greek and the native Egyptian. The caricature ignores the Egyptian perception of animals as super-human symbols of the unchanging, static life of the universe. For the Jew, animals were part of God's creation, some clean, some unclean, but all subordinate to man.

139. The idolatry and theriolatry of the Greeks and Egyptians just described explains why the *lawgiver* (Moses) provided laws fencing the Jews off from other peoples. The apologist reverts to his starting-point: the Jews are to be *pure*, avoiding association with evil, and they are to hold strictly to monotheism. This passage has often been contrasted with an earlier passage (paragraph 16), where the author accepts that 'the God who watches over and creates all things is the God whom they [the Jews] worship, the God whom all men worship, the God whom we ourselves worship...except that we address him by other names such as Zeus and Dis'. But this passage is completely consistent with Aristeas' stress on monotheism.

INTERPRETATION OF CERTAIN PROVISIONS OF THE LAW

144   Do not accept the outmoded view that Moses drew up these laws
       with such care solely for the sake of mice or weasels or other
       similar creatures. On the contrary, all these laws have been drawn
       up with solemn purpose to develop righteousness, pious
145   contemplation and perfection of character. For all the winged
       creatures used by us – pigeons, doves, grouse, partridges, and
       also geese and their like – are tame; they are distinguished by
       their cleanliness and they feed on wheat and leguminous plants.
146   The winged creatures forbidden to us, however, you will find
       to be wild, and carnivorous; they use their strength to oppress
       the other birds and employ unfair means to get their food at the
       expense of the tame birds just mentioned – and not just tame
       birds, but they also take as their prey lambs and kids, and inflict
147   indignities upon the dead as well as the living. Moses, therefore,
       by calling these animals unclean, used them as an illustration that
       those for whom the Law was drawn up must practise spiritual

righteousness, oppressing and robbing nobody by reliance upon
their own strength, but ruling their lives by principles of
justice – just as the tame creatures among the birds mentioned
above eat the leguminous plants growing on earth but do not
148   practise oppression to the destruction of their fellow birds. By
such lessons, then, the lawgiver handed down an indication to
those capable of understanding it that they should act justly,
neither gaining their ends by use of force nor oppressing others
149   by reliance on their own strength. For if it is improper even to
touch the above-mentioned animals on account of their individual natures, surely we must use every means possible to prevent
150   our own characters from being degraded to the same level? All
these provisions, therefore, about the legal use of these or other
creatures have been put before us by way of allegory.

The apologist explains that 'there is a profound reason why we abstain
from the use of some things and join in the use of others' (143), and
offers the examples of the mouse and weasel, and carnivorous birds,
which the Law judges unclean. Why such animals were originally
designated unclean is not certain; possibly man's innate fear of them
played a part. The apologist rejects any such rationalism, arguing that
such observances exist to aid the pursuit of righteousness and
philosophical belief. But he interprets the biblical provisions 'by way
of allegory' (150), and by this means makes them more acceptable to
the hellenistically educated Jews (and perhaps others) in Alexandria.

144. *the outmoded view*: compare 1 Cor. 9: 9, where Paul similarly
argues that the Law's command, 'you shall not muzzle a threshing ox',
was not given out of God's concern for oxen, but should be interpreted
to refer to the rewards due to the human worker. Josephus, however,
writes, 'he has taught us the lessons of gentleness and humanity to the
extent that we are not to undervalue dumb animals; on the contrary,
he enjoins that they are to be used only in accordance with the Law,
and he forbids all other use of them' (*Apion* II.29 (213)). *mice or weasels*:
Aristeas reverses the order of Lev. 11: 29. The mouse is probably a
jerboa, and the weasel a mole or mole-rat. The unclean animals of Lev.
11: 29 are carnivores, and may have been forbidden on the grounds
that they eat the blood of the animal they kill (cp. Gen. 9: 4f).

145. The apologist develops his case by reference to birds, distin-
guishing the graminivorous and carnivorous species. *partridges* (Greek

attagai) is a conjecture, based on Eusebius' reading of the text, for
'locusts' (*attakoi*); though locusts are allowed as edible by Lev. 11: 20–2,
they seem out of place in the present list.

146. For *winged creatures forbidden to us* see Lev. 11: 13–19; Deut.
14: 11–18. The list includes vultures, kites, owls, and hawks.

147. The 'unclean' creatures are thus taken as *an illustration* or
'allegory' (150) of the unrighteous oppressors. Aristeas may conceivably
be warning Alexandrian Jews obliquely against injustice, violence, and
arrogance towards their neighbours. According to Diodorus Siculus
(*World History* XXXIV.1), Antiochus' advisers said of the Jews that they
were the only nation that refused to mix with other nations, and that
they regarded all men as their enemies. For a sharp criticism of Jewish
clannishness, see Tacitus, *Histories* v.5: 'among themselves the Jews
have a fierce loyalty and ready sympathy, but to everyone else they
show inimical hatred. They eat apart, they sleep apart; they are a race
greatly inclined to lust, but they abstain from sleeping with foreign
women; between themselves anything is lawful. They introduced
circumcision so that they might be recognised by this difference.'

149. *even to touch*: cp. Lev. 11: 8, 31.

150. *by way of allegory*: allegorical interpretation of Greek poets such
as Homer had long been known and practised, first by philosophers
(including the Stoics) and then by the grammarians. Some, including
many Alexandrian scholars, rejected the use of allegory; others used
it to defend Homer from charges of being morally offensive in certain
passages. Aristeas is using allegory as a way of defending the Jewish
scriptures from a charge of irrelevance or obscurantism, and making
them more acceptable to the community.

The Sibylline Oracles

Origins

The collection of Jewish and Christian writings known as the 'Sibylline
Oracles' came into being between the second century BC and the fourth
century AD. There are allusions and references to this material in
Josephus (*Ant.* 1.4.3 (118)), the Shepherd of Hermas, Clement of Rome,
Justin Martyr, Clement of Alexandria (who says that Paul used the
Sibyl), Lactantius (who quoted many lines from the Sibylline Oracles),
and Augustine. The oracles seem to have been popular; the second-
century anti-Christian intellectual Celsus complained that the Church
invented false oracles, and the third-century satirist Lucian parodied
them. The collection was eventually numbered in fifteen books,
perhaps by the fourth century AD, though there are no surviving
manuscripts earlier than the fourteenth century, from which period
comes also the famous hymn used in the Mass for the Dead, the 'Dies
Irae', the opening verse of which quotes the Sibyl alongside scripture
as an authority for the coming doom:

> Day of wrath and doom impending,
> David's word with Sibyl's blending,
> Heaven and earth in ashes ending.
> (trans. by T. W. Irons, *English Hymnal*, no. 351)

'Sibyls', or inspired prophetesses, were well known in the Graeco-
Roman world and had a long history. The first-century BC Roman poet
Virgil announced in his Fourth Eclogue (40 BC) that the last age
prophesied by the Sibyl at Cumae on the Italian coast near Naples had
arrived. (See Map 6.) Virgil was perhaps using an early Jewish oracle
here in order to proclaim the new golden age of Augustus. In his epic
poem, the *Aeneid*, Virgil makes his hero Aeneas take the Sibyl as his
guide through the underworld. She utters her prophecies possessed by
the god Apollo:

> '"Look, the God! The God is here!" As she spoke the words,...
> suddenly her countenance and her colour changed and her hair
> fell in disarray. Her breast heaved and her bursting heart was wild
> and mad; she appeared taller and spoke in no mortal tones, for
> the God was nearer and the breath of his power was upon her.'
> (*Aeneid* VI.45ff, trans. by W. F. Jackson Knight)

35

According to Plutarch (*On the Pythian Oracles* 6.397A), Heraclitus (*c.* 500 BC) said that the Sibyl, uttering in ecstasy awful things, with the help of the god made her voice reach a thousand years. The Sibyl is always portrayed as an old woman. She was credited with having given oracles at the time of the Trojan Wars, at the dawn of Greek history. In origin she was probably from the East; the towns of Marpessus and Erythrae on the west coast of modern Turkey (see Map 1) each claimed to be her original home. She later became connected with the famous Greek shrine of Delphi, and from then on her oracles were presented (like those of the Delphic oracle) in Greek hexameter verse. She soon became connected with Cumae in Italy, and according to legend offered nine books of her verses to Tarquinius Superbus, the last king of Rome. He said that her price was too high; she destroyed the last three books and offered the remaining six at the same price, and Tarquinius finally bought three books for the price originally sought for the nine. These formed the basis of the oracles officially preserved at Rome, which were consulted by command of the Senate at serious political crises. They were all destroyed when the Capitol was burnt in 83 BC, but a new collection was formed in AD 12 and deposited by Augustus (after some weeding out of suspect oracles) in the temple of Apollo on the Palatine hill, where they lasted until the fifth century AD. Not surprisingly, the Sibyl became known to Jews living in the Graeco-Roman world, and in their apologetic they adopted her as 'a prophetess of the high God' (Sib. Or. III.818f), the more readily as prophetesses were known to the biblical tradition (cp. Deborah, Judg. 4: 4; Huldah, 2 Kings 22: 14–20). The Jewish tradition knows the eastern origins and the Greek adoption of the Sibyl:

> 'I tell you these things, after leaving the long Babylonian walls of Assyria, stung to frenzy, a fire sent to Greece, prophesying God's anger [*or*, revelations] to all mortal men...so that I prophesy to humans the divine riddles. Throughout Greece men shall speak of me as from another country, the shameless one of Erythrae. But others shall say that I am the demented, lying Sibyl whose mother was Circe and whose father was Gnostos. But when everything comes to pass as predicted, then you will remember me, and none shall any longer call me, a prophetess of the great God, demented.'
>
> (Sib. Or. III.809–18)

But the passage goes on to claim that the Sibyl was the daughter-in-law of Noah (III.824–7), thus incorporating her into the biblical history.

The message of the Oracles

The Roman Oracles are almost entirely lost to us, a few quotations apart. Plutarch (*On the Pythian Oracles* 9.398D) says that they spoke of 'many upheavals and migrations of Greek cities, many appearances of barbarian armies and destructions of empires', which is consistent with the fact that the Romans consulted them in time of crisis. Similar interests appear in a section of Sib. Or. III, usually ascribed in origin to the oracle of Erythrae: for example, lines 449ff:

'A Lydian earthquake shall strip the Persian lands, bringing the most horrible sufferings upon Europe and Asia. The murderous king of the Sidonians, and the battle-cry of others will bring deadly destruction across the sea to the Samians. The ground will flow to the sea with the blood of murdered men, and wives with elegant daughters will lament the shameful outrage done them...

On you, Italy, no foreign warmonger shall come, but civil carnage, deeply lamented, totally destructive, and infamous, shall ravage you in your shamelessness.'

The similarity of such hellenistic oracles to Old Testament prophecies against foreign nations may have encouraged the Jewish–hellenistic author to borrow the form and language of the Sibylline Oracles in order to present his own similar message. The Jewish Sibylline books also share the disorder that characterised the hellenistic and Roman collections. (Virgil's Aeneas warns the Cumaean Sibyl not to entrust oracles to writing on leaves 'lest they disperse in air our empty fate' (*Aeneid* VI.74f).) The third book of the Sibylline Oracles in particular is an assembly of independent oracles with several insertions and additions of later date, 'composed in a traditionally wild, chaotic and obscure style in which the sequence of thought and subject must be followed across intervening sections, and the events referred to are rarely identifiable beyond dispute' (P. M. Fraser, *Ptolemaic Alexandria* (Clarendon Press: Oxford, 1972), vol. I, p. 711). The first Jewish Sibylline Oracles probably derive from Alexandria, or possibly from a Jewish military colony in Leontopolis (Tell el-Yahudiya: see Map 2), in the reign of Ptolemy VI Philometor (181–146 BC), in whose reign 'the seventh king of Egypt, a Greek by birth' is expected to usher in a new age for God's people (III.193f).

Book Three

The earliest Jewish strata of the Sibylline Oracles are found in Book
III, lines 97–349 and 489–829. The author or compiler begins by
combining Jewish and Greek legends about primeval times (97–154),
and goes on to review a somewhat tangled sequence of worldly empires
(156–210) and sketch the nature, history, and future prospects of the
Jewish people (211–94). In particular he underlines the Jewish
aversion to magic and idolatry. There follows a series of oracles and
woes against the foreign nations (295–349, 489–529), into which a
varied assortment of oracles of different dates has been inserted,
probably in the first century BC. The lengthy final section of the book
appears to contrast the coming misery of Greece, conquered by Rome
in 146 BC (520–72), with the enviable position of 'a holy race of
god-fearing men' (573) who 'have their portion in the righteousness
of the Law of the Most High' (580). This section contrasts Jewish and
Greek religion and morality, and warns the Greeks to repent before
the end, of which 'unerring signs' are given (797ff). (Similar signs are
described by Josephus, *War* VI.5.3 (288–98) and Luke 21: 10ff in
connection with the siege of Jerusalem, and by 2 Macc. 5: 2–4 with
reference to Antiochus' invasion of Egypt.) Much in this lengthy
passage can be paralleled from the Old Testament and the New
Testament, including the idea that the Gentiles will attack Jerusalem
and the Temple (664ff; cp. Ps. 2; Zech. 14), and the picture of the
fertility and peace of the earth in the age to come (741ff, cp. Isa. 11:
6–9; 35: 1–10; 65: 17–25). Particularly interesting is the statement that
'From the sun, God shall send a king, who shall make the whole earth
cease from evil war' (652f). Behind this expectation lies the Egyptian
mythology, which saw the Pharaohs, and later the Ptolemies, as the
incarnation of the sun god. The Alexandrian Jewish author is drawing
on Egyptian royal language to describe a messianic figure whom he
seems to identify with a Ptolemaic ruler. Men will hide their idols for
shame, he says, 'when a young king, the seventh in succession from
the rule of the Greeks, reigns in Egypt' (608f). This expectation
probably reflected, and was intended to contribute to, the good
relations that existed between the people of Alexandria and the Jews
in the reign of Ptolemy VI Philometor.

This brief résumé, which is no substitute for reading the book as
a whole, shows that a major concern of the second-century BC Jewish
community in Alexandria was to convince itself that not only did the
Jewish people play an important part in the history of the world (which

could not be limited to that of the Greek-speaking peoples) but also that the hellenistic world was ultimately subject to the Jewish God. The Jews are 'the guides of life to all humankind' (195); without the Jews, the heathen peoples are doomed. The oracles threaten woe upon Egypt (315ff), Ethiopia (320ff), Libya (324ff), Phoenicia (492ff), Crete (505ff), Thrace (507ff), and others, and promise suffering to Greece (520ff); but there is an unmistakable sympathy in the appeal to Greece to repent: 'but you, wretched Greece, cease from proud thoughts; pray to the immortal, great-hearted God, and beware' (733f). With this may be contrasted the Sibyl's attitude to the native Egyptians and their religion, seen in a fragment preserved by Theophilus: 'You foolish people, who worship snakes, dogs, cats, and honour birds and animals that crawl on the ground, stone images, statues made by human hand, roadside cairns – these are your gods, these and many other foolish and unmentionable things' (Fragment III.27–31).

These oracles derive from hellenised Jews, happy to write in the hexameter verse made famous by Homer and studied throughout the Greek-speaking world. (Lines 420ff claim that Homer himself used the Sibylline prophecies.) These men were familiar with the world of Greek myth, perhaps as interpreted by the Macedonian philosopher Euhemerus (*c.* 316 BC), who argued that the Greek gods were in origin distinguished mortals, deified after death, and they accommodated the Greek story of the Titans to the Genesis account of the tower of Babel (97ff; cp. Gen. 11). The view of world history as a succession of empires (see the commentary on III.162–96 below) is perhaps also basically hellenistic; a similar presentation appears in the almost contemporary Book of Daniel. The oracles show a wide knowledge of the second-century BC Mediterranean political world, including the growing power of Rome. The themes of the expected destruction of the world and of the arrival of a saviour figure would have been intelligible in both Greek and Jewish contexts. In due course, the early Christian Church found it easy to accept these oracles as pointing to their own Saviour and their own eschatological hopes.

Book Five

It is possible to trace the development of the collection of the Sibylline Oracles by observing their increasing preoccupation with the power of Rome and her relationship with Egypt. Book III.46–62, 75–92, 350–80 may refer to the politics of Cleopatra's day if the 'three men' of line 52 refers to the Second Triumvirate (Antony, Lepidus, and

Octavian) and the 'mistress' of line 360 to Cleopatra as the incarnation of the goddess Isis. Certainly Rome is now seen as the enemy ruler of Egypt, whose depredations upon Asia must in due course be revenged (350–5). The oracles of Book v, however, must be dated about a century and a half later in the early second century AD, first because an historical prologue in cryptic fashion lists the Roman emperors from Julius Caesar to Hadrian (and in an additional note updates the list to the reign of Marcus Aurelius, line 51), and secondly because the book uses the established legend of the return of the Emperor Nero to conquer Rome, presenting him as a demonic, destructive figure of the last days before the final transformation of the world (cp. Rev. 17: 9–18). Apart from an approving description of Hadrian in line 50, Book v is firmly anti-Roman, understandably so after Rome's destruction of Jerusalem in AD 70, and it is equally critical of Egypt and Ethiopia (179–214, 484–511), probably largely as a result of the development of anti-Jewish feeling in Alexandria through the first century AD. Conflict in Caligula's reign led to an edict of his successor Claudius that allowed the Jews religious liberty but denied them full citizen rights in Alexandria (see below, p. 184). Further trouble arose in Alexandria in AD 66 (Josephus, *War* II.18.7 (487ff)), and again in 115–18, when the Jews destroyed Egyptian temples. This may be reflected in the expectation (Book v.484ff) of the destruction of the shrines of Isis and Sarapis.

Book v consists largely of oracles threatening destruction upon Egypt and Rome in particular, but also upon Gaul, Ethiopia, Asia, Thrace, Macedonia, and Babylon. Destruction is not limited to the nations of the earth; the book ends with a dramatic picture of the war of the stars and their final destruction, which leaves the heaven empty: 'the sky stood starless'. The last days will be marked by the return of the Emperor Nero as the final adversary (93ff, 137ff, 214ff, 361ff). But the increased feeling of hostility to the world in general and to Rome and Egypt in particular found in Book v is balanced to some extent by the theme of a coming king who will save his people. After Nero's reappearance to destroy Jerusalem, 'a king sent from God against him shall destroy all mighty kings and all the finest men' (108f); in 155f, after Nero's return, 'a great star shall shine and by itself destroy the whole earth', including the sea, Babylon, and Italy. (In AD 134 a rebellion in Judah against Rome was led by a man who took the name Bar Kokhba, meaning 'son of a star', probably a direct allusion to Balaam's oracle in Num. 24: 17: 'a star shall come forth out of Jacob'.) Similarly, after the appearance of 'an obscure and unholy king to throw down this place [i.e., the Temple] and leave it a ruin' (408f), 'there came from the heavenly regions a blessed one, a man holding a sceptre that God had put into his hand, and he gained noble dominion over all, and to all the good he returned the riches that earlier generations had taken from them' (415ff). In all this there is a combination of Jewish traditional language and mythology and not-dissimilar hellenistic conceptions, according to which stars or similar portents could mark the appearance or birth of illustrious figures, and the collision of the stars would be one feature of the final *ekpurōsis*, a Stoic term describing the fiery extinction of the universe in preparation for its re-creation.

Book v does not hold out much hope for the world. Some sympathy for Greece is apparent, as in Book III, from the references to 'thrice-wretched' Greece and to the 'sad overthrow' of Corinth at Nero's hands (137ff, 215ff), but there is no sympathy for the native peoples of Egypt, Asia, and Rome. The book's Jewish–Egyptian origin is revealed by the hope that at the end 'there shall be in Egypt a great, holy temple, and into it God's own created people shall bring sacrifices; and the immortal God shall grant them to dwell there' (501–3); but this temple is destroyed by the Ethiopians, who in turn suffer the wrath of God (504–11). There is one passage picturing a paradisal future for the Jews (247–85): interestingly, among other blessings it promises that 'the unclean foot of the Greek shall no longer walk freely through your land, for he shall have in his heart the intention to keep your laws' (264f).

These oracle collections were taken over and expanded by the early Church. A Christian addition, or perhaps a substitute for an original Jewish messianic oracle, appears in v.256–9: 'and there shall return from heaven a certain most eminent man, who spread out his hands upon the fruitful tree, the best of the Hebrews, who shall stop the sun in its course, calling upon it with fair speech and holy lips'. This appears to portray the cross as the tree of life, a piece of symbolism that was made explicit in the second century AD by Justin Martyr and later became very popular.

Later Sibylline books

The later books of the Sibylline Oracles are both Christian and Jewish. Books VI–VIII are Christian, from the second to third centuries, comprising a hymn to Christ, a collection of prophecies and moral teaching, and a discourse on the nature of Christ. Books XI–XIV are of third- to fourth-century Jewish origin, and present a history of the world from the flood to the time of writing. The separate origin of

Books XI–XIV is shown also by the fact that Books I–VIII and XI–XIV were preserved in independent manuscript traditions. Books I–VIII were first printed in 1545; further manuscript material was discovered in the early nineteenth century and printed as Books IX–XIV. Book IX, however, repeated Books VI–VII.1 and VIII.218–428, and Book X repeated Book IV. No Book XV exists, though in some manuscripts Book VIII.1–9 is given as a fragment of it.

A SEQUENCE OF KINGDOMS

III.162   Then there arose inside me the voice of the great God, (163) ordering me to prophesy through every (164) land, and to kings, and to bring to their minds future events. (165) And the first thing he brought to my knowledge was (166) the number of human kingdoms that will arise.

167   The house of Solomon shall rule first of all, (168) and the Phoenicians, invaders of Asia and of other (169) islands; also the Pamphylian race, the Persians, the Phrygians, (170) the Carians, the Mysians, and the race of wealthy Lydians.

171   And then the Greeks, proud and impious; (172) another people, from Macedonia, great and diverse, shall rule, (173) coming upon men as a fearsome cloud of war. (174) But the heavenly God will utterly destroy them.

175   But then shall arise another kingdom, (176) white and many-headed, from the western sea. (177) It will rule much land, overthrow many people, (178) and bring fear in its wake to all rulers. (179) It will also plunder much gold and silver (180) from many cities – but there will be gold again in the God-given earth, (181) and then too both silver and finery, (182) and they will bring trouble upon men. But those men will meet great (183) disaster when they begin their proud and unjust ways. (184) Immoral behaviour will be forced on them at once; (185) male will lust with male, they will place boys (186) in dens of vice, and in those days (187) men will be afflicted with great distress confusing all, (188) confounding all, and filling all with evil (189) through sordid greed and ill-gained wealth, (190) in many lands and especially in Macedonia. (191) Among them shall arise hatred

and every form of trickery, (192) until the seventh reign, the reign (193) of an Egyptian king of Greek birth. (194) And then the people of the great God shall once again be strong; (195) they will be the guides of life to all humankind.

In this section, which follows the account of the tower of Babel and the story of the Titans, the author or compiler presents a 'prophecy' of the sequence of empires and kingdoms, culminating in the restoration to its rightful role of the Jewish nation. The major interest seems to be in the Roman destruction of the Macedonian people and in the coming reign of the seventh Greek (i.e., Ptolemaic) ruler of Egypt, which is expected to introduce the rule of the people of God. This passage, then, in origin probably reflects the political interests of the mid second century BC after 168 BC, when the Romans defeated the Macedonians at the battle of Pydna and ejected Antiochus IV of Syria from Egypt. It also reflects the hopes of the Jewish community in Egypt in the reign of Ptolemy VI Philometor.

162. *the voice of the great God, ordering me to prophesy*: divine compulsion is a regular feature of such accounts of prophetic commissioning, whether Jewish or Graeco-Roman. Virgil, for example, shows the Cumaean Sibyl acting under the compulsion of the 'great god' Apollo (*Aeneid* VI.77f, 100f).

164. *to kings*: prophets and seers of the Old Testament regularly addressed themselves to the court, and the author represents himself as influential in the highest quarters; perhaps he has in mind the Ptolemaic court. But in fact his verses are addressed more to the king's Jewish subjects than to the king.

166. *kingdoms*: a similar preoccupation with the sequence of coming kingdoms is found in the second-century BC book of Daniel; cp. Dan. 2: 31ff; 7: 23f; 11: 2ff.

167. *first of all*: the author begins his historical sequence of kingdoms with the famous Jewish kingdom of Solomon and his successors. It seems odd that he should ignore David, but the reason may be that Solomon, as builder of the Temple and personification of human wisdom, seemed much the greater figure in hellenistic Egypt. This preference for Solomon is perhaps also witnessed by the Alexandrian origin of the first-century BC Wisdom of Solomon.

168. The author's history here has a Mediterranean rather than a Mesopotamian outlook. The *Phoenicians* (whose contact with Solomon is documented several times in 1 Kings 3–12) were at the height of their powers between the tenth and the sixth centuries BC. A vivid

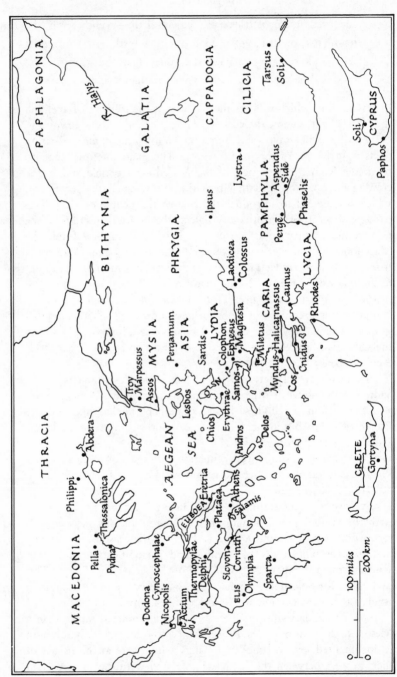

Map 1 The hellenistic Mediterranean world

picture of the range of their trading-contacts is given in Ezek. 27, and
it is trade, rather than war, that is meant by the phrase *invaders of Asia*.
Later in Book III the burning of the Phoenician cities is prophesied;
perhaps the destruction of Sidon by Artaxerxes III and of Tyre by
Alexander the Great are in mind.

169. For the next historical period, the author turns to the western
half of what is now Turkey. From a Mediterranean viewpoint, this is
not an inaccurate picture. The Persians controlled this region for most
of the fifth and fourth centuries BC. The other peoples mentioned
became more or less important in the subsequent hellenistic world
inaugurated by Alexander, until they were incorporated one by one
into the Roman Empire. Pamphylia, a fertile plain on the central
southern coast of Turkey, owed its name to its original colonisation
by a group of minor Greek tribes. In the fifth to fourth centuries
BC it was subject to Persia; in the third century, after a brief occupation
by the Ptolemies, it became part of the Seleucid Empire; in 189 BC
Antiochus III was compelled to yield it to Rome. It was an important
area, but it was not an independent kingdom. The *Persians* controlled
an enormous empire reaching from the borders of India in the east to
the Mediterranean seaboard on the west, divided into administrative
regions called satrapies. Their empire began when Cyrus the Great
overthrew Babylon in 539 BC, and ended when Alexander the Great
defeated Darius III in 331 BC. From a Mediterranean viewpoint the
Persians could certainly be seen as a successor to the Phoenicians, whose
naval resources they used to maintain Persian presence in the Aegean.
Throughout the fifth and fourth centuries BC the Persians were seen
as the major enemy by the independent Greek city-states. The
Phrygians, originally from Thrace (Thracia: see Map 1) in the late
second millennium BC, occupied west–central Turkey. In the first millennium they were in turn subject to Croesus of Lydia, the Persians,
the Seleucids and, finally, the Romans. Their language and religion,
however, survived well into the first millennium AD.

170. The *Carians* occupied the south-west corner of Turkey. Like
the Phrygians, they were conquered by Croesus and the Persians, but
their coastal situation led them to rebel from Persian rule and look to
Greece for support. In the fourth century, however, Caria flourished
under the independent-minded Persian satrap Mausolus, who made the
harbour of Halicarnassus his capital and incorporated the important
island of Rhodes into his small and very hellenistic empire. His sister
and widow, Artemisia, built for him an enormous marble tomb known
as the Mausoleum, which by *c.* 150 BC was classed by Philon of

Byzantium among the seven wonders of the world. Descriptions of it survive in the work of a Roman architect, Vitruvius (*c.* 30 BC), and in the *Natural History* of Pliny the Elder (AD 23–79).

Like the Carians, the *Mysians*, in the north-west corner of Turkey, succeeded in establishing an independent kingdom under the Attalid dynasty in the third century BC by exploiting Rome's opposition to the power of the Seleucid Antiochus III and by developing the wealth, both mineral and agricultural, of the region. In the second century BC their capital, Pergamum, became an important hellenistic city, famous for her beauty and her intellectual and cultural activities as well as her commercial success. When Attalus III died in 133 BC, he bequeathed his kingdom to Rome, opening the way to total Roman control of Asia Minor.

The *Lydians*, focussed on Sardis and the Aegean coast of Turkey, were always famous for their wealth. This region is claimed as the first to use coinage. Its last, and most famous, king was Croesus, whose kingdom, extending east to the River Halys, fell to Cyrus in 546 BC and became part of the Persian Empire. In 331 BC it fell to Alexander and his successors; in 189 BC it became part of the Attalid kingdom, and in 133 BC a Roman possession.

This list of names in lines 167ff is interesting. The author begins with Solomon's kingdom, but his progression seems to be a geographical one from east to west rather than chronological. He moves via Phoenicia and the islands to central and western Turkey before going on (lines 171ff) to Greece, Macedonia, and ultimately Rome (175ff). The regions and kingdoms of Asia Minor, which flourished particularly in the hellenistic period, receive frequent mention in Sib. Or. III–V; thus disaster is threatened against the Phrygians, Trojans, Carians, and Pamphylians (III.205ff), various cities of Asia (III.343ff), Phrygia again (401ff), Troy (411ff), Lycia (433ff), Caria (470ff), Mysia (484ff); and some of these names reappear in a list of peoples threatened with calamity in III.512ff.

171. *the Greeks, proud and impious*: the description is a stock one, used elsewhere in Book III. The author's sentence is not complete, and something may have been lost after line 171.

172–3. The opening word of the text is suspect and various emendations have been suggested to make an easier transition from the Greeks of line 171 to the Macedonians in this line. Regarded by the Greek city-states as near-barbarians of the north, the Macedonians became a major threat to their independence in the fourth century BC under Philip II, the father of Alexander the Great. Alexander's conquests changed the political face of the Near East from Turkey to India, Egypt in particular becoming progressively hellenised in its government and cultural activities under the Ptolemies. The author of the oracle sees the Alexandrine Empire as one among other empires, in its time *a fearsome cloud of war*, but like the others subject to divine disposal. Compare the comment of Dan. 11: 3f:

> 'Then there will appear a warrior king. He will rule a vast kingdom and will do what he chooses. But as soon as he is established, his kingdom will be shattered and split up north, south, east and west. It will not pass to his descendants, nor will any of his successors have an empire like his; his kingdom will be torn up by the roots and given to others as well as to them.'

175. The successors to the Macedonians (under whom the author includes the Ptolemies and the Seleucids) are the Romans *from the western sea*. They first opposed the Seleucid Antiochus III in Greece and Asia Minor in 191 and 189 BC, defeating him at Magnesia and demanding heavy compensation from him by the terms of the treaty of Apamea (188 BC). In 168 BC they entered Egypt and ordered the Seleucid Antiochus IV out of it. But it was not until 63 BC that Rome, in the person of Pompey, took control of Syria, and it was not until after the battle of Actium in 31 BC, when the future Emperor Augustus defeated Antony and Cleopatra, that Rome took total control of Egypt. *white and many-headed* may be an allusion to the Roman Senate, the governing body of the Republic; cp. 1 Macc. 8: 15; 'They had established a senate where three hundred and twenty senators met daily to deliberate.'

177f. Compare 1 Macc. 8: 12; 'They thus conquered kings near and far, and all who heard their fame went in fear of them.'

180f. *but there will be gold again...*: it is not at all clear whether the author has something particular in mind, or whether he is making a general observation that, for all the Roman Empire's demands for money, wealth will remain to *bring trouble upon men*.

184f. Many commentators note that the accusations of these lines fit the second century AD better than the second century BC, but there is plenty of evidence that the Jews criticised such practices among their neighbours from early times (Lev. 18: 22; 20: 13) and in the hellenistic period (Letter of Aristeas 152; cp. Rom. 1: 26f). The Greek text reads smoothly, and there is no need to suspect interpolation.

187ff. *distress...especially in Macedonia*: the context suggests an event between the Roman victory over Antiochus III and the arrival of the seventh Greek king in Egypt. The reference is thus probably to the Third Macedonian War of 171–168 BC. In 197 Rome had forced Philip V of Macedonia by the decisive battle of Cynoscephalae to leave the Greek cities to their independence, but in 179 Philip was succeeded by his son Perseus, whose territorial ambitions were underlined at Rome by his enemy Eumenes of Pergamum. The resulting war ended with L. Aemilius Paullus' defeat of Perseus at Pydna in 168 BC. A fourth Macedonian war in 149–148 BC ended in the Roman annexation of Macedonia and its incorporation into the growing provincial system.

192f. *until the seventh reign*: with this passage must be compared the oracle addressed to Egypt in lines 315ff: 'a sword shall pass through your midst, and dispersion, death, and famine shall take hold of you in the seventh generation of your kings, and you shall cease'. A similar passage (601ff) refers to a time of divine retribution when men shall throw away their idols 'when a young [Greek *neos*] king, the seventh in succession from the rule of the Greeks, reigns in Egypt'. If one reckons from Ptolemy I Soter, the seventh reign would be that of Ptolemy Neos Philopater (145 BC), or, more realistically, of Ptolemy VIII Euergetes II (145–116 BC), but it is probably better to reckon from Alexander and assume that the reign of Ptolemy VI Philometor (180–145 BC) is meant. His reign saw good relationships between the Egyptian court and the Jewish community in Egypt; under the leadership of Onias, the son of the former Jerusalem high priest Onias (for whose murder in 171 BC see 2 Macc. 4: 30–8), a Jewish military colony was established at Leontopolis in the Nile Delta near Memphis with its own fortress and even a Jewish temple. (See Josephus, *War* I.I.I (33); VII.10.2–3 (423–32); *Ant.* XII.9.7 (387–8); XIII.3.I–3 (62–73).) This Onias held the important rank of *stratēgos* (army general), and after Philometor's death in 145 BC gave military support to his widow Cleopatra against her opponents.

It seems unlikely that such references to the reign of the seventh king could have been published in any meaningful way (even if the 'seventh' king is in some sense an ideal figure) after the reign of the chronologically seventh king, and this oracle, with its description of the rise of the Roman Empire, the Romans' defeat of the Macedonian Empire, their own inevitable decline and fall, and the subsequent restoration and universal role of the Jewish nation (lines 194f) perhaps belong naturally to a generation that was heartened by the resurgent nationalism of the Hasmonaeans in Judah and the support given to the Jewish community in Egypt. Its confident interpretation of current historical events matches that shown in the almost contemporary Book of Daniel.

194f. The oracle ends with a strong statement of the final centrality
of the Jewish people in the divine dispensation. The Jewish Temple had
long been seen as a focus for the nations; cp. Isa. 2: 2–4; Zech. 8: 20–3.

AGAINST EGYPT AND ALEXANDRIA

v.73   These things God ordered me to proclaim in Egypt (74) in the
final age, when men's wickedness will be absolute. (75) But
wicked men suffer wickedness as they await (76) the anger of the
immortal heavenly thunderer, (77) worshipping stones and brute
beasts instead of God, (78) at random fearing different gods who
have no reason, (79) no mind, no hearing – things that are not
fit to be mentioned here, (80) idols, each of them, made by mortal
hand. (81) From their own workmanship and wicked invention,
(82) men have accepted gods of wood and stone, (83) bronze, gold,
and silver; they have made empty, (84) lifeless, dumb, fire-smelted
gods, (85) and have put their trust in them to no purpose. (86)
Thmuis and Xois, Athribis and Koptos will perish, (87) and so will
[the cities] of Heracles, Zeus, and Hermes. (88) And you, Alexandria, famous nurse of cities, (89) will be the victim of permanent
war and [. . .] (90) You will pay for your pride and for your past
deeds. (91) You will fall silent for a great age, and the day of your
return [. . .] (92) and the sweet drink [of the Nile] will no longer
flow for you [. . .] (93) For the Persian will come upon your plain
like hail (94) and will destroy your land and your men with their
wicked skills, (95) surrounding your superb altars with blood and
corpses – (96) men of alien mind, powerful, red-blooded,
ferocious beyond reason, (97) a host numberless as the sand, urging
on your destruction. (98) And then you who have become rich
among cities will become rich in woe. (99–100) All Asia will
weep, falling on the earth, for the loss of those gifts of yours with
which she loved to crown her head. (101) And he who had the
fortune to gain the Persians' land will war with you, (102) and
having killed each man will wipe out all life, (103) so that only
the third part will be left to wretched mortals. (104) From the
west he will leap upon you with a light bound, (105) besieging

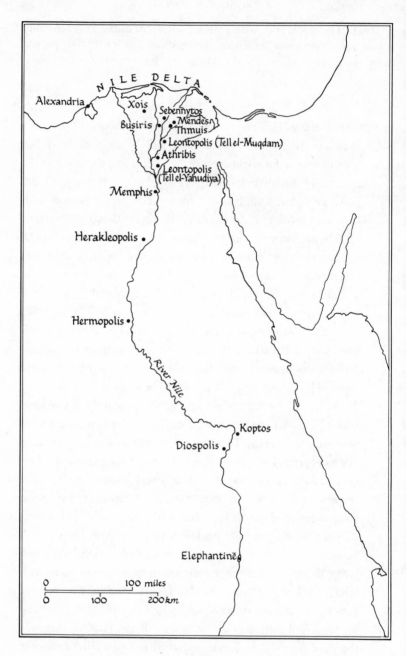

Map 2   Ptolemaic Egypt

the whole land, and making desert of it. (106) But when he has reached the peak of strength and shameless audacity, (107) he will come, anxious to destroy even the city of the blessed. (108) And then a king divinely sent against him (109) will destroy all great kings and the finest men.

This passage from Book v illustrates the new Jewish hostility towards Egypt in general and Alexandria in particular that arose in the first century AD. The writer begins by charging Egypt with idolatry, and threatens retribution upon Alexandria and the cities of the Nile Delta and the lower Nile valley at the hands of the Persians (i.e., the Parthians). The Parthians' leader, however, is revealed to be 'from the west', and his devastation of Egypt is seen as the springboard for an attack on Jerusalem itself. The attack, however, will be thwarted by a divinely sent king who will destroy earthly kings. This sequence – oracles against a nation, the re-appearance of Nero, the arrival of a divine royal figure to save the situation, and a final destruction – seems to be repeated four times in Book v.

74. *in the final age...absolute*: the idea became a commonplace of Jewish and Christian writing. Dan. 12: 1 stresses that 'At that moment...there will be a time of distress such as has never been since they became a nation.' This final period of trouble was described as the 'birth-pangs' preceding the arrival of a messianic figure (cp. Mark 13: 8; Rev. 12: 1–6). The evils of this period are vividly pictured in Jubilees 23: 13ff.

76. *thunderer*: the epithet is used of the Greek gods Zeus and Poseidon in early Greek poetry, but the idea that God speaks in thunder is found also in the Old Testament; cp. Ps. 29: 3; Exod. 19: 19.

77–85. These lines are clearly directed against Egyptian religion. Worship of *idols*, and of *gods of wood and stone, bronze, gold, and silver* was forbidden in the Old Testament; cp. Deut. 29: 16f: 'For you know how we lived in Egypt and how we and you, as we passed through the nations, saw their loathsome idols and the false gods they had, the gods of wood and stone, of silver and gold.' Such gods, made by human hand, are frequently satirised, as in Isa. 44: 9–20; Wisd. of Sol. 13: 10–19; 15: 14–17, in language similar to that used here. The worship of *beasts* does not appear in the Old Testament, though the worship of images of beasts is strongly condemned (cp. the story of the golden calf; Exod. 32). The Alexandrian author of the Wisdom of Solomon, however, refers to 'the insensate imagination of those wicked men, which deluded them into worshipping reptiles devoid of reason, and

mere vermin' (11: 15). The religious importance of animals in ancient
Egypt is obvious from the many mummified animals and amulets found
in Egyptian tombs. In his book *Ancient Egyptian Religion* Henri
Frankfort commented on 'an underlying religious awe felt before all
animal life...The animals never change, and in this respect especially
they would appear to share – in a degree unknown in man – the
fundamental nature of creation...animal life would appear superhuman
to the Egyptian in that it shared directly, patently, in the static life of
the universe' (pp. 12–14).

86. The Greek text of this line makes little sense, and the last three
place-names are the result of conjectural reconstruction of the text.
Thmuis (Tell el-Timai), *Xois* (Sakha), and *Athribis* (Tell Atrib) were
nome (i.e. district) capitals in the Delta region of Lower Egypt. *Koptos*
was a nome capital further up the Nile in Upper Egypt.

87. The last word of the hexameter line is missing, but the
restoration of *polēes*, 'cities', is obvious and convincing. The *cities of
Heracles, Zeus and Hermes* are respectively Herakleopolis (Ihnasya
el-Medina), Diospolis (Thebes), and Hermopolis, all nome capitals of
Upper Egypt. (For illustration and details of these places, see J. Baines
and J. Malek, *Atlas of Ancient Egypt* (Phaidon, Oxford, 1980).) These
Greek names for older Egyptian towns illustrate the hellenistic influence
on Egypt in the Ptolemaic and Roman periods.

90. *your past deeds*: the phrase is vague, but the author may have
in mind the various attacks made upon the Jewish population of
Alexandria (see above, p. 40).

91. *the day of your return* is a phrase derived from the Greek epic
poet Homer. It was used in the *Odyssey* of men returning from the
Trojan War, but here it is apparently used of the long-delayed or totally
unexpected restoration of Alexandria after her coming destruction.
However, the phrase is followed by a lacuna in the Greek text, leaving
the precise meaning uncertain.

92. Presumably the author means that the River Nile will dry up.
Again, the line is incomplete and after it there is a gap in the text.

93–8. There are a number of minor uncertainties in the text in these
lines, and editors enlist the help of an excerpt and appended exegetical
paraphrase found in Codex Parisinus 1043. From this source comes the
restoration of the word *Persian* to the text. The Persians had invaded
Egypt under Cambyses in 525 BC, and the Persian rule of Egypt had
lasted, with some intermissions, until almost the end of the Persian
Empire and Alexander's invasion of Egypt in 331 BC. By the end of
the first century BC, however, the name 'Persian' could be used to refer

to the Parthians (as when the poet Horace complains that he hates Persian luxury in *Odes* 1.38). The Parthians had been Rome's major enemy in the East since the beginning of the first century BC (see A. R. C. Leaney, *The Jewish and Christian World 200 BC to AD 200*, pp. 15–20). Both powers claimed Armenia. In 55 BC the Roman general Crassus suffered a humiliating defeat by the Parthians, who in 40–39 BC invaded Syria and briefly supported Antigonus on the throne of Judah. Possibly a memory of this Parthian invasion of the west lies behind the present oracle. In AD 35, in a peace settlement, the Emperor Tiberius persuaded the Parthians to accept Tiridates III as their king; in AD 63 further trouble was averted when Rome in effect ceded Armenia to Parthia. In AD 113 Trajan temporarily regained Armenia, but after his death in 117, Armenia returned to Parthian rule.

Parthia, then, was an obvious enemy for the Sibylline author to invoke against Egypt. In the civilised hellenistic world, the Parthians would certainly be seen as *men of alien mind,...ferocious beyond reason*. Our author seems to present their arrival as one of the major acts of chaos that precedes the end of things, much as the author of Daniel presents Antiochus (Dan. 11: 42f). A similar idea appears in 1 Enoch 56: 5f:

And in those days the angels shall return
and hurl themselves to the east upon the Parthians and Medes:
they shall stir up the kings, so that a spirit of unrest shall come
   upon them.
and they shall rouse them from their thrones,
that they may break forth as lions from their lairs,
and as hungry wolves among their flocks.
And they shall go up and tread under foot the land of His elect
   ones,
and the land of His elect ones shall be before them a threshing-floor
   and a highway.

99–100. *those gifts of yours*: Ptolemaic Alexandria had much to offer to the world. It was the home of literary and scientific learning, famous for such mathematicians as Euclid, Eratosthenes, Apollonius of Perge, and such poets as Theocritus, Callimachus, Apollonius Rhodius, and many others. Its great library was founded by Ptolemy I, and destroyed, or more probably only partly destroyed, by fire when Egyptian forces blockaded Caesar in Alexandria in the winter of 48–47 BC.

101. *and he who had the fortune to gain the Persians' land*: the text of this line has been reconstructed with the help of the excerpt and prose

exegesis of the Codex Parisinus 1043. The reference appears to be to the Emperor Nero (AD 54–68), who had been popular with Parthia and according to Suetonius (*Nero* 40, 47) had contemplated escaping to Parthia from his difficulties at Rome. Suetonius tells of impostors who traded on the popular belief that Nero had not died by suicide but lived on, one of these impostors gaining support from Parthia. From this, with help from commonplace ideas about the division between East and West, seems to have developed an expectation that Nero would return from the east to conquer Rome. Nero's career is cryptically described in Sib. Or. v.137–54, 214–27. Sib. Or. v.33f says explicitly that 'he shall return, making himself equal to God' (compare the accusation made against Antiochus IV in Dan. 11 : 36; 2 Macc. 9 : 8–12), and lines 361–80 speak of the ruin and destruction Nero will bring upon the earth at the last time 'from the west' (cp. line 104). The present passage, then, appears to be describing the eschatological disaster that will come upon Egypt and Alexandria in terms of a popular legend about the return of the Roman Emperor Nero with the support of the Parthians.

107. *to destroy even the city of the blessed*: the idea that one of the final woes before the end will be a heathen attack on the city of Jerusalem is well established in the Old Testament (e.g., Zech. 14 : 2; cp. Luke 21 : 20). One is again reminded of Dan. 11 : 40–5 where, in the final sequence leading up to the time of the end, Antiochus campaigns against Egypt and other lands, 'amongst them the fairest of all lands'. Just as Antiochus had previously attacked the Temple and desecrated it, so too Nero is accused (Sib. Or. v.150) of having captured the Temple and burnt the worshippers there. (Vespasian was originally sent to Judaea on Nero's orders; Nero, however, died two years before the fall of Jerusalem in AD 70.)

108. *a king divinely sent against him*: in v.408ff 'an obscure and unholy king' who has destroyed the Temple is also followed by a divine royal figure, pictured in terms reminiscent of Dan. 7 : 13f (see above, p. 40). In v.155ff, after a description of the disasters brought upon creation by Nero, earth and sea and Babylon (i.e., Rome) and the rest of Italy are destroyed by a great star from heaven (such stars in Jewish tradition being identified with angels or even messianic figures). In Sib. Or. III.286f the author speaks of God sending a king to bring to an end the Jewish exile; in III.652f: 'From the sun God shall send a king, who shall make the whole earth cease from evil war', a figure probably to be identified with the Ptolemaic seventh king who will bring in a new age (see above, p. 48). This picture of an eschatological royal figure

seems to draw upon both Egyptian and Jewish tradition. The Old Testament background of Jewish Messianism has been much discussed, but there can be little doubt that at its heart lie Jewish ideals of kingship, vividly expressed in such psalms as Ps. 72, and never fully realised in any one historical king.

109. *will destroy all great kings and the finest men*: a stock line of the Sibylline author, used at line 380 of the destruction that follows the return of Nero. The background of such an expectation can be seen in the royal psalms; thus in Ps. 2, kings and rulers of the earth are warned that the Lord has promised his newly-enthroned Israelite king that he will crush all rebellious kings. In Ps. 72.8ff the prayer on behalf of the king is,

> May he hold sway from sea to sea,
> from the River to the ends of the earth...
> and all kings shall pay him homage,
> all nations shall serve him.

In apocalyptic literature, the realisation of such hopes is transferred to the time of the end.

Eupolemus

Eupolemus, author and diplomat

The fourth-century AD Christian historian and theologian Eusebius uses Book IX of his *Praeparatio evangelica* to demonstrate that 'the most illustrious of the Greeks themselves have not been unacquainted with the affairs of the Hebrews', and to prove his point he quotes from Porphyry (a third-century AD philosopher), Hecataeus (a third-century BC historian from Abdera), Clearchus of Soli (fourth to third century BC), and others. Above all he uses a first-century BC historian, Alexander Polyhistor (105–30 BC), who drew on a number of Jewish writers – Eupolemus, Artapanus, Molon, Philo, Demetrius, Theodotus, Ezekiel – and quoted from them extensively, thus preserving them for posterity. His work perhaps met a growing interest in the Jews at Rome in the first century BC. From Eupolemus, Polyhistor preserves a short passage about Moses, a longer passage summarising history from Moses to Solomon, and describing the foundation and building of the Temple, and probably a shorter piece on the fall of Jerusalem to Nebuchadnezzar. (He also preserves a piece from a Samaritan writer which he, or some predecessor, has falsely attributed to Eupolemus.)

A century before Eusebius, Clement of Alexandria had mentioned Eupolemus as showing (along with other Jewish writers such as Philo, Aristobulus, Josephus, and Demetrius) that Moses and his people existed long before the Greeks. Clement quotes three other passages from Eupolemus, in one case revealing his source as Alexander Polyhistor.

Josephus similarly mentions Eupolemus as a writer along with Demetrius Phalereus (whom he is perhaps confusing with a Jewish historian called Demetrius) and the elder Philo, but he mentions them in the company of various Greek historians. Josephus thus conveys the impression that Eupolemus was a Greek rather than a Jewish writer, and, noting that Eupolemus, Philo, and Demetrius were not far from the truth, excuses their inadequacies on the ground that they were unable to understand the Jewish records accurately. Josephus may have been anxious to play down the work of his hellenistic Jewish predecessors in order to enhance his own reputation. The fragments of Eupolemus that survive do not suggest that he was a Gentile, but that from within the Jewish tradition he was representing the Jewish tradition for a largely non-Jewish readership.

1 Macc. 8: 17 speaks of a Jewish diplomat named Eupolemus son of John son of Accos sent on an embassy to Rome in 161 BC. According to 2 Macc. 4: 11 his father John had been responsible for the diplomatic relationships established between Antiochus III and the Jews a generation earlier (cp. Josephus, *Ant.* XII.3.3 (138–44)). Eupolemus thus possibly belonged to the priestly family of Hakkoz (Ezra 2: 61) (this family had been excluded from the priesthood at some time after the exile, at least temporarily). Eupolemus ('good at war') is a Greek name; to judge from the names of his father and grandfather, he was perhaps the first member of his family to acquire a Greek name. 2 Macc. 4: 13, 15 notes that by the third decade of the second century BC 'Hellenism reached a high point' and priests 'placed no value on their hereditary dignities, but cared above everything for Hellenic honours'. The author's bias is evident; but hellenistic influence in Jerusalem is unquestionable.

It is not certain, but it is likely, that Eupolemus the writer, and Eupolemus the diplomat, perhaps of priestly family, are identical. An educated man, from a family with diplomatic and priestly background, would be well placed to write the work of which fragments are preserved in Polyhistor.

The writings of Eupolemus

Eusebius, following Polyhistor, attributes to Eupolemus a writing 'On the Jews'. This title, however, is a reconstruction from a dubious text, and the passage that follows it is almost certainly not to be attributed to Eupolemus, but to an unknown writer from Samaria. At a later point, Eusebius introduces the lengthy section describing events from Moses to Solomon by saying that it derives from Eupolemus' work 'On the prophecy of Elias' (i.e., Elijah). This does not appear to fit the content very well but, as we have only part of the original, we cannot be sure. Eupolemus' work certainly shows great interest in the prophets, and Elijah, or the expectation of his return (cp. Mal. 4: 5) may have been of importance to Eupolemus; 1 Macc. 4: 46 and 14: 41 suggest that the expectation of the coming of the prophet or a 'true prophet' (Elijah?) was important in the Maccabaean period. Clement of Alexandria, however, appears to refer to the same work of Eupolemus by a third title, 'On the kings of Judah', which was also the title of a slightly earlier work by a certain Demetrius at the end of the third century BC. Clement is perhaps applying to Eupolemus' work what he thought to be an appropriate title. The original title and intention of Eupolemus' book thus remain in some doubt.

A survey of the authentic fragments of Eupolemus, however, reveals his basic interests. He is concerned with chronology, calculating that from Adam to his own day lay a period of 5149 years, and that 2580 years has passed since the Exodus from Egypt. Perhaps this interest was not unconnected with his desire to show that the Jews, with their wisdom and culture, were a much more ancient people than the Greeks. Eupolemus was also concerned to demonstrate the wealth and imperial power of David and Solomon, and especially their control over countries in his own day ruled by the Ptolemies and the Seleucids. There are various references showing Eupolemus' awareness of contemporary political affairs. Above all he was concerned to underline the importance of the sanctity of the Temple and to describe it in all its glory. He emphasises the importance of prophets in Judah's history; and, throughout the history, the main concern of leaders, kings, and prophets is for the Tabernacle or Temple.

Apart from the fragments preserved by Polyhistor, Clement, and Eusebius, it has been suggested that Eupolemus was responsible for the report in 1 Macc. 8 of the embassy to Rome in 161 BC on which he served, and that his history was used, directly or indirectly, by the authors of 1 and 2 Maccabees, at least for events up to the death of Judas. In particular, the story of the concealment of the Ark by Jeremiah, preserved in a letter probably dated somewhere between the death of Antiochus IV in December 164 BC and the death of Judas Maccabaeus in May 160 BC (2 Macc. 1: 10 – 2: 18), appears in a fragment probably attributable to Eupolemus (see below, p. 70), and it is at least possible that Eupolemus had a hand in the composition of the letter, which was sent 'From the people of Jerusalem and Judaea, from the Senate, and from Judas, to Aristobulus, the teacher of King Ptolemy and a member of the high-priestly family, and to the Jews in Egypt' (2 Macc. 1: 10).

Whether or not Eupolemus had any hand in writing reports or letters that later appeared in some form in the Books of the Maccabees, the period of his major activity is clearly indicated by his presence on the embassy in 161 BC and by his chronological work, which reckons 'from Adam to the fifth year of King Demetrius, the twelfth of Ptolemy's reign in Egypt' (Clement of Alexandria, *Stromateis* 1.141.1). The fifth year of Demetrius is probably that of Demetrius I Soter, which would be autumn 158–157 BC, but the synchronism with Ptolemy VIII Euergetes II (who was in exile at the time) is a year out, and may have been added later. Eupolemus, then, was probably at the height of his powers and activity between *c.* 165–155 BC; there is no reference to Eupolemus on the next embassy sent to Rome in 143 BC (1 Macc. 12: 16), when the envoys appear to include Antipater, the son of

Eupolemus' fellow envoy Jason in 161 BC. By 143 BC Eupolemus was too old, or out of favour, or dead.

Eupolemus was clearly an educated man, fluent in Greek but also loyal to the Jerusalem Temple and all it represented. He was thus both acceptable and useful to the Maccabees when establishing diplomatic links abroad. We hear of other men of similar abilities in Jerusalem in the third to second centuries BC. If the Letter of Aristeas is accurate upon the point (which is not certain), the Septuagint translation was made by Greek-speaking priests from Jerusalem (see above, pp. 11–34). Demetrius, who wrote on the kings of Judah, and Philo the elder, who wrote a poem on Jerusalem in bad Greek hexameters, may have been Palestinian rather than Alexandrian in origin. The Wisdom of Jesus son of Sirach was translated into Greek by his grandson, who arrived in Egypt from Jerusalem in 132 BC (see *Ecclesiasticus*, CBC, p. 7). Second-century BC Jewish men of letters could write in Greek just as their contemporary Jewish statesmen could have their monuments built in Greek style, as is shown by the tombs of the Maccabees described in 1 Macc. 13: 25–30, or by the early first-century BC tomb of Jason in Jerusalem.

It is not entirely clear whether Eupolemus was writing for fellow Jews (whether of Jerusalem and Judah or of the diaspora) or for Greek-speaking Gentiles, or both. As a diplomat, Eupolemus was probably well aware of the need to present his people in a favourable light abroad, and his writings certainly reached a gentile readership, as is clear from the lengthy quotations of them preserved in Alexander Polyhistor. Josephus, as we have seen, is able to convey the impression that Eupolemus was more Greek than Jewish, and this perhaps means that by Josephus' time Eupolemus was better known in a Greek literary context than in a Jewish one. He is certainly one of the most interesting Jewish writers known to us from the mid second century BC.

MOSES AND THE LAW

Euseb. *P.E.* IX.26.1   Eupolemus says that Moses was the first wise man, and was the first to impart the alphabet to the Jews; and that the Phoenicians received it from the Jews, and the Greeks from the Phoenicians; and that Moses was the first to write down laws for the Jews.

Eusebius is quoting Eupolemus indirectly from the selection of passages on the history of the Jews gathered from a number of authors by Alexander Polyhistor. The same passage is also quoted by Clement of

Alexandria. How far back Eupolemus' history went is not clear, but another fragment preserved in Clement suggests that it went back to Adam. This present section emphasises Moses' place in the cultural history of mankind in general and of Judaism in particular. It underlines especially the centrality of the Law in Jewish tradition.

1. In describing Moses as *the first wise man*, Eupolemus was perhaps making two points. First, he was ranking the Jewish lawgiver above famous sages of the Greek world – men like Thales of Miletus and Solon of Athens. Hecataeus similarly described Moses as 'outstanding for his wisdom'. Secondly, he was ranking Moses above other figures from early Jewish legend and history such as Enoch (Gen. 5: 21–4), who was seen by many in the second century BC as the earliest wise man. Another passage ascribed (wrongly) by Eusebius to Eupolemus comments that Abraham traced back the first discoveries in astronomy and astrology to Enoch, whose 'son Methuselah learned all things though the angels of God'. Jub. 4: 17f says that Enoch 'was first among men born on earth who learned writing and knowledge and wisdom'. Eupolemus thus appears to be claiming Moses as the founder of civilisation and learning.

the first to impart the alphabet (literally, 'letters'): Eupolemus continues to underline the importance of Moses. Writing had been known for at least two millennia before Moses, cuneiform script being used in Mesopotamia and hieroglyphic script in Egypt. The alphabet seems to have originated in the area of Syria, Palestine, and Sinai in the second half of the second millennium BC (see the note on *Apion* 1.2 (6–12) below, p. 174). The precise place of origin was much debated in ancient times, as also now. Hecataeus of Miletus (*c.* 500 BC) opted for Egypt, Herodotus (*c.* 450 BC) for Phoenicia, and Diodorus Siculus (first century BC), quoting an unknown Cretan writer, notes that the Phoenicians took it from its original discoverers, the Syrians. The earliest recognisable examples of alphabetic usage discovered so far are inscriptions showing pictographic signs from Serabit el-Khadem in Sinai (perhaps fifteenth-century BC) and inscriptions on a dagger at Lachish and on a javelin-head from near Bethlehem (perhaps twelfth-century BC). These scripts are called 'Proto-Sinaitic' and 'Proto-Canaanite' respectively; from the latter probably derive the Phoenician and ultimately the Greek script. (See further, pp. 174f.)

Eupolemus presents Moses as a mediator of the alphabet to the Jews. He probably had in mind Exod. 32: 15f, according to which Moses brings down from the mountain the two tablets, written on both sides: 'The tablets were the handiwork of God, and the writing was God's writing.' But Eupolemus is also emphasising that Moses and the Jews were responsible for the wider distribution of this divine blessing to the Mediterranean world of the Phoenicians and the Greeks.

the first to write down laws for the Jews: this appears to be for Eupolemus the climax of Moses' achievements, for which his wisdom and literary skill were essential qualifications. In similar terms, Hecataeus of Abdera (late fourth century BC) had described Mneves (the first Egyptian Pharaoh) as 'the first to persuade the masses of Egypt to adopt written laws' (Diodorus Siculus, *World History* 1.94.1). The fact that Eupolemus was writing just after Antiochus IV's suppression of the Jewish laws may give Eupolemus' emphasis on the Law, the lawgiver, and the Temple extra point. He closely relates Law and Temple in his description of Solomon's Temple, where he makes it clear that Solomon was following the Law's prescriptions for the Tabernacle (Exod. 25–31). Later, Josephus further underlines the importance of the Jewish Law, and asserts the primacy of Moses among the world's lawgivers (*Apion* II.15 (154–6)).

FROM MOSES TO DAVID

Euseb. *P.E.* IX.30.1   In a work of his entitled 'On the prophecy of Elijah' Eupolemus says that Moses prophesied forty years; then came Jesus the son of Naue, thirty years. He lived one hundred and ten years, and pitched the holy Tabernacle in Shiloh. After him
2   Samuel became prophet. Then by the will of God Saul was chosen
3   king by Samuel; he reigned twenty-one years and died. Then his son David came to power; he conquered the Syrians who occupied the region of the Euphrates and Commagene, and the Assyrians in Galadene and the Phoenicians. He campaigned also against the Idumaeans, the Ammonites and the Moabites, the Ituraeans,
4   Nabataeans and Nabdaeans. In addition he campaigned against Souron King of Tyre and Phoenicia, whom he compelled to pay tribute to the Jews. With Vaphres King of Egypt he established friendship.

It is not clear whether Alexander Polyhistor omitted material between Eupolemus' reference to the giving of the Law and the death of Moses, but he may not have omitted very much, in view of the way in this passage Eupolemus seems to pass quickly over the period from Moses to David. David is memorable only for his conquests, his relationships with Egypt and Phoenicia, and his proposal to found a temple (see the next section). It is worth noting that in the decade 170–160 BC Judah's relationships with the kings of Egypt and Syria, and their attitude to the Jerusalem Temple, were matters of great importance to the Jews.

1. '*On the prophecy of Elijah*': the extant fragments of Eupolemus do not cover the words or deeds of Elijah, but they do refer frequently to Shiloh, and it has been suggested that Eupolemus' original reference was to Eli, the priest of Shiloh (1 Sam. 1: 10). However, the extant fragments say little of Shiloh either, and another suggestion is that Eupolemus' work, with its chronological interest, was focussed on the expected coming of the prophet Elijah before the end, as predicted in Mal. 4: 5f (cp. 1 Macc. 4: 46; 14: 41). *Moses prophesied forty years*: this emphasis on Moses as a prophet (cp. Deut. 18: 17f) is interesting. Eupolemus speaks of other prophets – Samuel, Nathan, and Jeremiah. Moses introduces Joshua, Samuel introduces Saul, Nathan prophesies to David, and Jeremiah to Jonachim. For the forty years of Moses' activity, cp. Exod. 7: 7; Deut. 34: 6f. *Jesus the son of Naue* is the form of the name given in the Septuagint for the Hebrew 'Joshua the son of Nun'. According to Josh. 24: 29, Joshua lived for 110 years, and Eupolemus may have calculated the *thirty years* of his leadership from comparison of Josh. 14: 7 and Num. 14: 32f. *pitched the holy Tabernacle in Shiloh*: cp. Josh. 18: 1. Eupolemus ignores all Joshua's other achievements, and mentions the Tabernacle because it points forward to the Temple.

2. *Samuel* is mentioned solely as the prophet who introduces *Saul*. The length of Saul's reign is not clearly given in the Old Testament; the Hebrew text (1 Sam. 13: 1) appears to be corrupt, and the verse is omitted in the best Septuagint texts. Eupolemus may have invented the figure of *twenty-one* years, or drawn it from some unknown source; Josephus similarly allows Saul twenty years (*Ant.* x.8.4 (143); but forty years in *Ant.* VI.14.9 (378)).

3. *his son David*: this would be an extraordinary mistake for anyone learned in the scriptures to make, and the reading therefore is probably original and deliberate. Possibly Eupolemus is trying to avoid showing Saul and David in a bad light; indeed, he may be trying to redeem the reputation of Saul, traditionally suspect because he failed to establish a dynasty and died by his own hand. But in the Maccabaean period, when heroism against the Jewish enemy was the order of the day, Saul may have been more acceptable on account of his bravery against the Philistines. One scribe, offended by the apparent error, corrected the

text here to read 'son-in-law'. *he conquered...*: Eupolemus makes David's conquests reach Commagene, in the far north of Syria, whereas in fact they reached only Aram-Zobah north-east of Damascus towards Tadmor. (See Map 4.) David's empire would thus on Eupolemus' showing include the heartland of the Seleucid Empire under Antiochus IV and his successors. The reference to *Assyrians in Galadene* is difficult; the Assyrians lived east of the River Tigris, and perhaps for *Assyrians* here we should read 'Syrians'. *Galadene* might then be Gilead (though elsewhere Eupolemus correctly names this Galaaditis), or, by correction, Gabalene (the region of Byblos) on the Phoenician coast. There is no specific reference to Davidic victory in this region in 2 Sam. 8. *Idumaeans*: in the hellenistic period Idumaea lay immediately south and south-west of Judah. The name is a Greek one, deriving from the biblical country of Edom, whose original territory lay south-east of the Dead Sea. David's conquest of Edom is recorded in 2 Sam. 8: 12–14. The *Ammonites* and *Moabites* were also conquered by David (2 Sam. 8: 12). Their territory lay north of Edom, east of the Jordan and the Dead Sea. (See Map 5.) In Eupolemus' time this land was known as Ammanitis and Moabitis, which is how they are named in the letter from Solomon to Souron King of Tyre (see below). The *Ituraeans* (cp. Luke 3: 1) lived in the Beka valley in Syria; their capital was modern Baalbek. The *Nabataeans* occupied the region previously held by the Edomites. They are mentioned in Greek historians with reference to events from the late fourth century BC onwards. In the second century BC they appear briefly as allies of the Maccabaean Jonathan (1 Macc. 9: 35). The *Nabdaeans* are unknown, unless they come from Nadabath (1 Macc. 9: 37) or can be identified with 'the Arabs called Zabadaeans' (1 Macc. 12: 31) who lived between Damascus and the River Eleutherus. All these names reflect the political geography of the second century BC, and show that Eupolemus is not simply copying from the list of David's conquests in 2 Sam. 8. Thus Eupolemus makes no mention of David's major enemies, the Philistines, in the second century BC politically non-existent. David is presented as controlling all Syria and Transjordan; this clearly reflects the military interests of the Maccabees (cp. 1 and 2 Maccabees).

4. *Souron King of Tyre...Vaphres King of Egypt*: Eupolemus contrasts these two kings; one is defeated in war, the other is an ally. Possibly Eupolemus identifies Souron with the Seleucid Empire, and Vaphres with the Ptolemaic (there is no evidence that Egypt was an ally of Judas or Jonathan, but at least she was an enemy of Syria). He thus presents Judah as a major power, able to call upon the resources of the Syrian

and Egyptian Empires. It was in fact Hiram of Tyre who helped
Solomon build his Temple (cp. 1 Kings 5: 1–12, 18; 9: 11–14, 26–28),
and it is not clear why his name is replaced by that of Souron. Possibly
Souron is either a transliteration of the Hebrew *zori* ('Tyrian'), or
derived from the Greek word 'Syrian'. *Vaphres* resembles the name
borne by Pharaoh Apries (Herodotus, *Histories* II.161) or Hophra (Jer.
44: 30), whose army perhaps assisted Jerusalem in 588 BC (cp. Jer. 37:
5) and in whose kingdom Jeremiah and other Judaean exiles later found
shelter (Jer. 43: 5–7).

PREPARATION FOR BUILDING THE TEMPLE

Euseb. *P.E.* IX.30.5   When he wanted to build a temple for God, he
[David] prayed to God to show him a place for the altar. Indeed,
an angel appeared there to him, standing over the place where the
altar was later established in Jerusalem, and forbade him to found
the Temple, because he was stained with human blood and had been

6   a man of war for many years. The angel's name was Dianathan.
He ordered David to delegate the building of the Temple to his
son, but to prepare himself the materials for the work – gold, silver,

7   bronze, stones, cypress, and cedar wood. Hearing this, David had
ships built at Elana, a city of Arabia, and sent miners to the island
of Ourphē which lies in the Red Sea and has gold deposits. From

8   there the miners brought the gold to Judaea. When David had ruled
for forty years, he handed over power to his twelve-year-old son
Solomon, in the presence of Eli the high priest and the twelve tribal
heads, and handed over to him also the gold, silver, bronze, stone,
and cypress, and cedar wood.

If the selection made of Eupolemus' writings by Alexander Polyhistor
and Eusebius is representative, then clearly the Temple was very
important to him. From this point onwards, everything we have from
Eupolemus relates to the building of the Temple. His version follows
in outline the account in 1 Chron. 22, according to which David
prepared the materials – stone, metal, and wood – for Solomon's later
use. Eupolemus totally ignores the political struggle for the succession
depicted in 2 Sam. 9 – 1 Kings 2, and presents an idealised account:
as soon as he comes of age, Solomon receives the throne, with the

support of the high priest and the twelve tribal leaders, and immediately continues David's preparations for the Temple by writing to the kings of Egypt and Tyre.

5. According to 2 Sam. 7, David's desire *to build a temple* did not meet divine approval. He later built an *altar*, however, at the instigation of Gad the prophet, in order to avert the plague that resulted from his attempt to conduct a census of the tribes of Israel (2 Sam. 24). The *angel* comes from the Chronicler's version of the story, according to which David 'saw the angel of the LORD standing between earth and heaven, with his sword drawn in his hand and stretched out over Jerusalem' (1 Chron. 21: 16); in Eupolemus, however, the angel is much less hostile. *because...*: these reasons are also taken from the Chronicler, cp. 1 Chron. 22: 8; 28: 2f. Eupolemus develops the story further; David does not build even the altar, but is merely instrumental in indicating where it would stand in Jerusalem. *Dianathan* is an unlikely name, and it is tempting to think that the original name here was that of Nathan the prophet (cp. 2 Sam. 7; 12: 1–15; 1 Kings 1), though the prophet originally associated with this story of the altar-building is Gad (2 Sam. 24: 11ff; 1 Chron. 21: 9ff). Like the Chronicler, Eupolemus is anxious to explain why it was that the actual building of the Temple was done by Solomon, but equally anxious to credit the real impetus to David.

6. *he ordered David*: i.e., the angel ordered David; or perhaps, if we emend the previous sentence to say that the angel's message came 'through' (Greek *dia*) Nathan, *he* refers to Nathan. *gold, silver, bronze, stones, cypress, and cedar wood*: 1 Chron. 22. 2–4, 14–16 refers to hewn stones, iron for nails and clamps, bronze, cedar wood, gold and silver, and appropriate craftsmen. Eupolemus concentrates on the precious materials; he makes Solomon cover the Temple with gold 'from floor to ceiling', covering two pillars with gold 'a finger's thickness', and making 70 golden lamps. According to Eupolemus, Solomon used altogether 4,600,000 talents of gold. Eupolemus ignores iron, perhaps with 1 Kings 6: 7 in mind ('no hammer or axe or any iron tool whatever was heard in the house while it was being built'); according to Exod. 20: 25, the use of chisels (presumably of iron) would profane the altar. *cypress* and *cedar* are mentioned together in 2 Kings 19: 23 (RSV) as trees of Lebanon; cypress was used for the carved doors and the floor (1 Kings 6: 15, 34 (RSV)), and cedar for lining the walls and for the beams (1 Kings 6: 15, 36). For 'cypress' in these passages, however, the NEB translation gives 'pine', which may be more

accurate, following the Septuagint translation. But cypress was much used for timber in the Mediterranean area, and its appearance in Eupolemus' list is not surprising.

7. *Hearing this*: Eupolemus credits the shipbuilding to David (not Solomon, as 1 Kings 9: 26). As Eupolemus had followed the Chronicler in making David prepare gold for the Temple, he now makes David provide for its transportation from *Ourphē* (Ophir of 1 Kings 9: 28; cp. 1 Chron. 29: 4). Ophir is listed among Arabian place-names in Gen. 10: 29; according to 1 Kings 9: 28; 10: 11 it was a source of gold, almug wood and precious stones, which were brought by sea in Hiram's fleet to Ezion-geber 'near Eloth on the shore of the Red Sea' (1 Kings 9: 26). Ophir's location is generally sought somewhere on the coasts of South Arabia, East Africa, or India. Eupolemus describes it as an island in the Red Sea, perhaps on the basis of 1 Kings 9: 26–8 and of the fictional utopian island of Panchaia on the Arabian coast, the fabled wealth of which, according to Euhemerus (*c.* 300 BC) included all the precious metals. *Elana* or Aila is the hellenistic name for the Old Testament Eloth (or Elath; Septuagint Ailath) at the head of the Gulf of Aqabah. (See Map 3.)

8. *forty years*: cp. 2 Sam. 5: 4 f. *twelve-year-old son*: this is the age given by the Greek translation of Codex Alexandrinus at 1 Kings 2: 12. Similarly, the Chronicler speaks of Solomon as 'a boy of tender years' (1 Chron. 22: 5; 29: 1), and Josephus (*Ant.* VIII.1.1 (2), 7.8 (211)) makes him fourteen years old. The narrative of 1 Kings 2, however, implies that Solomon was a mature adult at his accession. Eupolemus may be suggesting that Solomon's concern for the Temple began appropriately at the same time as his accession to the throne and his entry upon adult life. In a similar way Luke marks Jesus' entry upon adult life with his appearance in the Temple (Luke 2: 42–52). *Eli* was not *high priest* of Jerusalem but priest of the sanctuary of Shiloh (cp. 1 Sam. 1) several generations before Solomon. The high priests of Solomon's Temple were Zadok and Abiathar, the latter being banished shortly after the beginning of Solomon's reign (1 Kings 2: 27). Eupolemus, by ignoring Zadok (where the Chronicler emphasises him) and naming the most important of Abiathar's ancestors, may be reflecting the history of his own time in which the last representative of the Zadokite priesthood had been ousted from Jerusalem by Menelaus (see 2 Macc. 4: 23f). As a writer and diplomat concerned to relate to the non-Jewish world, he may have had some sympathy with less exclusive attitudes within the Judaism of his day. *twelve tribal heads*: Eupolemus may have derived the Greek word for *tribal heads*

from its single appearance in the Greek Old Testament at Deut. 31:
28. The function of the tribal heads (cp. Deut. 1: 12f; 33: 21) was
largely judicial and military. Possibly, however, Eupolemus was
following 1 Esdras 7: 8, which records that at the dedication of the
Second Temple 'they offered...twelve goats for the sin of all Israel
corresponding to the twelve patriarchs of Israel', where the Greek
word translated 'patriarchs' is *phularchoi*, 'tribal heads', as used in the
present passage by Eupolemus.

SOLOMON'S CORRESPONDENCE WITH VAPHRES

Euseb. *P.E.* IX.30.8   David died, and Solomon ruled; and he wrote
to Vaphres, king of Egypt, the following letter:

31.1   King Solomon to Vaphres, King of Egypt, friend of my
father, greeting!

You should know that with the aid of God Most High
I have inherited the kingdom from David my father, who
commanded me to build a temple to God who created the
heaven and the earth. At the same time he ordered me to
write to you to send me men from your subjects to help me
until all the necessary work has been completed as was
commanded.

32.1   King Vaphres to Solomon, great king, greeting!

It gave me great pleasure to read your letter. I and my
whole government here have set aside a special day to mark
your succession to a man who was both noble and approved
by so great a God. On the subject of your letter, your request
for manpower from us, I have sent you eighty thousand men;
the details of their number and origin are as follows: from
the Sethroitic nome, ten thousand; from the Mendesian and
Sebennutic nomes, twenty thousand each; from the nomes
of Busiris, Leontopolis, and Athribis, ten thousand men each.
Take care to provide them with the necessities of life, and
see that in other respects affairs be well organised, and that
the men may be repatriated when they have done their duty.

The letter to Vaphres and his reply are paralleled by another pair of
letters (not given here) between Solomon and Souron of Tyre. These

letters, which use conventional hellenistic formulas, are not authentic originals, but were probably composed by Eupolemus on the basis of 1 Kings 5: 2–9 and 2 Chron. 2: 1–16, which tell of Solomon's approach to Hiram of Tyre and his answer. The Old Testament, however, does not tell of any similar request from Solomon to Egypt. Eupolemus has invented this; his aim is to demonstrate to his second-century BC readers that the ancestors of the Ptolemaic and Seleucid kingdoms were respectively friendly and subservient to the interests of Jerusalem.

31.1 *Vaphres*: see above, p. 64. The description *friend of my father* is later more accurately applied to Souron of Tyre (cp. 1 Kings 5: 1; 2 Chron. 2: 3). The author uses the conventional hellenistic epistolary formula of *greeting*. For *You should know* (the imperative is used in the Greek; literally, 'know that...') cp. the letter from Tattenai (Ezra 5: 7f) or Sisinnes (1 Esdras 6: 8ff). *with the aid of God Most High*: Solomon's piety is stressed. The title *God Most High* may have been taken from Gen. 14: 19, together with the phrase *who created the heaven and the earth*. The phrase *who commanded me* again emphasises David's originating role.

32.1 *Vaphres to Solomon, great king*: the importance of Solomon's position is underlined, the Egyptian king appearing as Solomon's deferential vassal. *a special day to mark your succession*: such commemorations were common practice under the Ptolemies. The famous Rosetta Stone is a copy of a decree passed by Egyptian priests assembled in 196 BC to commemorate the coronation of Ptolemy V Epiphanes. Similarly royal birthdays were commemorated; cp. 2 Macc. 6: 7; Mark 6: 21. *On the subject of your letter*: Eupolemus uses an epistolary formula almost identical with that used by Paul in 1 Cor. 7: 1. *eighty thousand men*: Souron of Tyre in his letter says that he will send the same number; this gives a total of 160,000 workers, a figure perhaps rounded up from 1 Kings 5: 13–16 and 2 Chron. 2: 17f, which speak of 70,000 hauliers and 80,000 quarrymen, with 3300 or 3600 foremen. 1 Kings appears to think of Israelites, 2 Chronicles of resident aliens, and Eupolemus of workmen drafted from Egypt and Phoenicia. *Sethroitic nome*: a nome was an administrative district of Egypt. The *Sethroitic* (a generally accepted emendation for the Greek text's 'Sebrethitic') *nome* was the fourteenth Lower Egyptian nome, in the north-eastern Delta region. *Mendesian*: Mendes was the Greek name of Djedet, the capital of the sixteenth Lower Egyptian nome, now Tell el-Rub'a in the central Delta. But in the hellenistic period, nearby Thmuis (Tell el-Timai) became the nome capital (see the note on Sib. Or. v.86; p. 52), and this is probably the reference here. *Sebennutic*: Sebennytos (modern Samannud) on the left bank of the Damietta branch of the Nile was capital of the twelfth Lower Egyptian nome, and the home of the historian Manetho. West of the town lie the remains of a hellenistic temple. *Busiris* (modern Abusir) lies south of Sebennytos. *Leontopolis* (modern Tell el-Muqdam) on the right bank of the Damietta branch of the Nile was the capital of the eleventh Lower Egyptian nome. There was another Leontopolis at Tell el-Yahudiya, where Onias IV, son of Onias III (cp. 2 Macc. 3–4), built a temple for the Jewish military settlement under his command *c.* 145 BC. *Athribis* (an emendation from the Greek *bathribitou* or *bathrioitou*) is Tell Atrib, also on the right bank of the Damietta branch of the Nile. It was capital of the tenth Lower Egyptian nome. *the necessities of life*: in the letter to Souron, Eupolemus makes Solomon say that he has arranged for the provision of grain and wine from the administrative districts of Galilaea, Samaritis, Moabitis, Ammanitis, and Galaaditis, oil from Judaea, and meat from Arabia. *repatriated*: in the Letter of Aristeas, the high priest and his colleagues request Ptolemy II Philadelphus to make arrangements for the safe return of the Jewish translators when their work is done. Some scholars have suggested a direct dependence here on the Letter of Aristeas, but the Letter cannot be dated so early (see p. 17), and any similarities are probably to be explained by conventional epistolary usage.

JEREMIAH AND THE FALL OF JERUSALEM

Euseb. *P.E.* IX.39.2 Then came Jonachim. In his time prophesied Jeremiah the prophet. He, sent by God, caught the Jews offering
3   sacrifice to a golden idol named Baal, and he revealed to them the impending disaster. Jonachim tried to have him burnt alive, but Jeremiah said that with this wood the captive Jews would cook food for the Babylonians and dig out the canals of the Tigris and the Euphrates. Nabuchodonosor, the king of the Babylonians, hearing Jeremiah's prophecies, invited Astibares the king of the Medes to join him in a military campaign. Enlisting Babylonians and Medes, and gathering 180,000 infantry, 120,000 horses, and 10,000 chariots, he first overwhelmed Samaritis, Galilee,
5   Scythopolis, and the Jews dwelling in Galaditis, and then took Jerusalem and captured alive the Jewish king, Jonachim. He removed and sent to Babylon the Temple gold, silver, and bronze,

but not the Ark and the tablets inside it, which were kept by Jeremiah.

Eusebius quotes this paragraph as being preserved by Polyhistor. He does not name Eupolemus as the author, but four of the manuscripts credit the passage to Eupolemus, and his authorship is strongly suggested by the style and contents. Particularly evident are Eupolemus' major interests – prophecy and the Temple; one notes also his interest in numbers and place-names. Eupolemus makes it clear that while the city was destroyed and the king and Temple treasures removed, in accordance with Jeremiah's prophecy, the all-important symbols of Judaism, the Ark and the tablets of the Law inside it, survived the disaster.

2. *Jonachim* is a name not otherwise attested. Jeremiah prophesied in the time of Jehoiakim, who had Jeremiah's scroll (but not Jeremiah himself) burnt in a brazier (Jer. 36), and in the time of Jehoiakim's son Jehoiachin, who was deported to Babylon in 597 BC together with the Temple treasures (2 Kings 24: 13), and also in the time of Zedekiah, in whose reign Nebuchadnezzar destroyed the Temple (2 Kings 25: 9). Eupolemus' names generally seem to be at least one remove from the biblical originals (cp. Hiram and Souron, Ophir and Ourphē), and this raises questions about Eupolemus' sources and closeness to the biblical tradition. There is no record of Jeremiah catching the Jews *offering sacrifice to a golden idol named Baal*, though he certainly accuses them of following the Baalim (2: 23), burning sacrifices to Baal (7: 9), swearing by Baal (12: 16), and giving their sons as whole-offering to Baal (19: 5). (Baal, meaning 'lord', was the name of the main Canaanite god.) Eupolemus' point, however, is that religious syncretism always brings disaster upon Israel.

3. *burnt alive*: this is not related of Jeremiah. Eupolemus may have been thinking of the Maccabaean martyrs (cp. 2 Macc. 7).

4. *hearing Jeremiah's prophecies*: the pagan Babylonian king, unlike the Jewish king, respects Jeremiah. The name *Astibares* was apparently invented by the romantic historian Ctesias of Cnidus, the doctor of Artaxerxes II (404–359 BC). The original name of the Median king was Huvakshatra, which Herodotus gives as Cyaxares. According to the Babylonian chronicles, it was Nebuchadnezzar's father Nabopolassar who made an alliance with this king; Nebuchadnezzar married his daughter. There is, however, no certain evidence that the Medes helped Nebuchadnezzar sack Jerusalem. *180,000 infantry...*: Eupolemus may have in mind the Persian rather than the Babylonian armies, and

perhaps derived the total from Herodotus, who gives the full strength of the Persian army in 479 BC as 300,000. Cavalry and *chariots* were important elements of the Persian army; Herodotus describes their tactics at the battle of Plataea in *Histories* IX.49. *Samaritis...Galaditis*: the names in *-itis* are the hellenistic names for Samaria and Gilead. *Scythopolis* ('city of Scythians') was the hellenistic name of ancient Bethshan, though how it got this name is not known. (See the note on 2 Macc. 12: 29 in *The First and Second Books of the Maccabees*, CBC.) If Nebuchadnezzar's army was coming by the usual route south from Syria, Samaritis would not be the first place captured; possibly Eupolemus is suggesting that Samaritis was rightly the first place to suffer.

5. *took Jerusalem*: Eupolemus gives no details of the fall of Jerusalem or the exile of the king; indeed, he appears to be conflating the first and second occasions on which Nebuchadnezzar took Jerusalem (597 and 587 BC). He concentrates on the Temple, the *gold, silver, and bronze* fittings of which he has already detailed (4,600,000 talents, 1232 talents, and 18,050 talents respectively) (cp. 2 Kings 24: 13; 25: 13–17). For Eupolemus, however, the important point is that *the Ark and the tablets inside it* (i.e., the stone tablets on which were written the ten commandments; cp. 1 Kings 8: 9) were preserved by Jeremiah. This is legend; Jeremiah himself prophesied that 'men shall speak no more of the Ark of the Covenant of the LORD; they shall not think of it nor remember it nor resort to it; it will be needed no more' (Jer. 3: 16). But a similar legend appears in 2 Macc. 2: 1–8, where Jeremiah is responsible for hiding the tent, the Ark, and the incense altar in a cave on Mount Nebo, the place to remain unknown 'until God finally gathers his people together and shows mercy to them' (2 Macc. 2: 7). It has been suggested that this passage also owes its origin to Eupolemus. But whether this is so or not, Eupolemus' purpose seems to be to indicate that in spite of the destruction of the Temple in 587 BC, continuity was assured by the secret preservation of the Ark and of the commandments.

Josephus

The life and career of Josephus

Josephus was born Joseph ben Mattithiah (in the Greek form, Matthias), in the year that Gaius Caligula became emperor at Rome (AD 37–8). The main autobiographical details are given in the opening and closing chapters of the *Life*, which was written *c.* AD 95 to meet the attack of a rival historian, Justus of Tiberias (see below, pp. 90f). Josephus claims that his mother (or, on one reading of the text, his great-great-grandmother) was from the Hasmonaean royal family, and that his father's ancestors were priests from the leading priestly family: his great-great-grandfather Matthias had married a high priest's daughter; his own father Matthias (born AD 6) was a man of noble birth and character in Jerusalem. Josephus goes on to describe how as a boy of fourteen he was consulted by the chief priests and city leaders, and how as a young man he systematically made trial of the teachings of the Pharisees, Sadducees, and Essenes, and finally of the hermit Bannus, who lived in and off the desert and emphasised the value of ritual ablutions – a figure apparently not unlike John the Baptist. In thus stressing his royal and priestly connections and his educational attainments, Josephus, with typical vanity, presents himself as a model young man.

However, Josephus' ability cannot be denied. Aged twenty-six, he took part in an embassy to Rome (Josephus makes it sound an almost single-handed venture) on behalf of some Jewish priests sent by the procurator Felix to answer charges before Caesar. Josephus was shipwrecked in the Adriatic, but survived and reached Rome. With the help of Nero's consort, Poppaea, he won the release of the priests and returned to Judaea. Whatever the part actually played by Josephus, it is clear that Rome greatly impressed and influenced him, as it would any young man of twenty-six, and we can believe him when he says that on his return to Jerusalem he tried to dissuade the more seditious of his countrymen from revolt by pointing to the military skill and fortune of the Romans. From then on, Josephus was, even if he did not always admit it, a man of two cultures and allegiances, with continuing loyalty to his own Jewish people, evidenced particularly by his later apologetic writings, and with an enormous respect for the

Roman Empire, which had been divinely ordained, he believed, to rule the world, and whose rule the Jews had to learn to accept (*War* III.8.3 (351–4), VI.4.8 (267–70)).

It is at this point that Josephus became more deeply involved in politics. Social unrest, inflamed further by insensitive Roman administration and anti-Jewish feeling in the surrounding hellenistic cities, had led step by step to public opposition to Roman rule. According to Josephus, the point of no return was reached when the priests were persuaded to suspend the sacrifices offered in the Temple since Herod's time on behalf of Rome and the emperor (*War* II.17.2 (408)). The failure of a Roman army under Cestius, the governor of Syria, to seize Jerusalem, and its subsequent ambush and defeat at Beth-horon (see Map 5), brought more support for the rebels, and, according to his account in *War* II.20.3–4 (562–8), Josephus was appointed by a public meeting at Jerusalem as a general to Galilee and Gamala to prepare for war and to organise the defence. Josephus portrays himself as a model general, training Galilaeans in the art of Roman warfare, and heroically defending Jotapata, until he is captured and joins the Romans, recognising that God is on their side.

In his later writings, the *Antiquities* and the *Life*, Josephus is at pains to show that the Jews were driven to war by the incompetence of Roman governors and the pressure of Jewish extremists. In the *Life*, Josephus presents himself as one who at heart desired peace with Rome (*Life* 4–5 (17–23); 7 (28–9); 13 (72); 14 (77–9); 35 (175)). In particular, he says that before the war he opposed the extremists, and on that account was forced into temporary hiding, and that he was sent by the leaders at Jerusalem to Galilee not so much to prepare the defence against Rome as to suppress the more violent opposition to Rome. He describes how this policy failed, his colleagues left him, and his opponent John of Gischala plotted with the Jerusalem authorities to have him removed. This forced him to become more obviously anti-Roman, and ultimately led to his capture after being besieged in Jotapata by the Romans.

Was Josephus an ardent anti-Roman general, delegate of the revolutionary party, or a secret Roman sympathiser, delegate of the aristocratic moderate party? According to the *War*, he was appointed general by a public assembly in Jerusalem in the heat of the nationalist fervour arising from the defeat of Cestius; such an assembly would hardly have appointed a man known to be lukewarm. Having acted at Rome on behalf of Jewish priests, Josephus must have appeared as a prominent nationalist to the people of Jerusalem. The account of

Josephus given in the *Life* almost certainly owes something to the fact that he was writing in Rome where for the sake of his comfortable position and pension he might find it prudent to play down his early opposition to Rome.

On the other hand, it is also possible that diplomatic experience had given Josephus some sympathy and respect for Rome, and we are told (*War* II.21.2 (594)) that John of Gischala spread the rumour that Josephus was a secret Roman sympathiser. Josephus seems almost deliberately to have allowed himself to be besieged in Jotapata, possibly calculating the chances of changing sides. But while it is tempting to see Josephus as he portrays himself in the *Life*, certainly at the outbreak of the rebellion his activities would have been interpreted by the Romans as opposition, and Josephus must have known that. By far the most likely explanation of his position is that, like other members of the aristocratic and priestly families of Judaea, he was involved in the rebellion whether he wished to be or not, and like many other people before and since caught in the middle, he was soon forced to take sides. A man of his position and experience had no chance of evading responsibility. In Galilee, which was less rebellious than is often alleged, and where indeed some cities such as Sepphoris were pro-Roman in sympathy, again the circumstances in which Josephus found himself probably forced him to be cautious, and his actions were clearly open to more than one construction. Josephus was a man who knew how to exploit his opportunities; indeed, he boasts of this ability. The story of his survival from the suicide pact at Jotapata, his capture by the Romans, and his escape from death by having the presence of mind to forecast Vespasian's coming elevation to the principate all illustrate perfectly Josephus' skill at survival in difficult circumstances. His narrative also illustrates his skill at justifying his actions in retrospect; in this way he explains that he was no traitor, but rather a prophet announcing God's will. He joined the Romans at this point, he says, because God had already indicated to him in dreams the coming Jewish disaster and the Roman destiny; Fortune had gone over completely to the Roman side (*War* III.8.3 (354)).

Opportunist survivor Josephus may have been, but he was not necessarily insincere or cowardly. From now on, Josephus' life was spent, first as a prisoner, and then as a citizen of Rome, and one senses that after the difficulties of his position in Judaea and Galilee, his new position brought him relief and happiness as well as prosperity, mixed with genuine sorrow at what had happened to his people. He seems to have believed quite sincerely that the Jewish nation was destroyed by its own nationalist extremists, and that there was no reason why a Jew could not practise his Judaism under the divinely ordained Roman rule. It is this belief that makes Josephus an important apologist for Judaism in the Graeco-Roman world. Josephus faces both ways; he wishes to demonstrate the respectability of the Jewish religion to the gentile world, and the benefits that come from accepting the *pax Romana* to the Jewish people in both Judaea and the diaspora. Josephus, like Paul before him, was both a Hebrew of the Hebrews and a Roman citizen, and saw no inconsistency. He was proud on both counts.

After his capture at Jotapata and his prediction of Vespasian's future as emperor (*War* III.8.8–9 (392–408)), Josephus was kept imprisoned, but apparently given preferential treatment. Vespasian procured a captive from Caesarea as a wife for him, but she left him, or more probably he left her, when he was released. He went with Vespasian to Alexandria, where he married again. From Alexandria he returned to Jerusalem, this time on Titus' staff as an interpreter and Roman spokesman to the besieged Jews. He urged the Jews manning the walls to spare the city and population by surrender. His argument that 'you are fighting not just the Romans but God', and that 'God has deserted the sanctuary and now stands on the side of your enemies' (*War* v.9.4 (378, 412)) naturally infuriated the defenders, and on one such occasion Josephus was knocked unconscious by a stone. After the fall of Jerusalem, Josephus apparently declined to accept the booty offered him by Titus, apart from some copies of the scriptures, but successfully requested the release of relatives and friends, including three prisoners being crucified (though two of them died). He did, however, accept an estate on the plain in lieu of his own Jerusalem property, but rather than risk staying in Judaea he went to Rome, where Vespasian, now emperor, gave him his own private house as home and made him a Roman citizen. He survived various Jewish attacks on his character, receiving favours even from Domitian, who exempted his Jewish estates from tax.

Josephus tells us only the bare details of his domestic life. In Rome he divorced his Alexandrian wife, by whom he had three children, 'because her behaviour did not please me' (*Life* 76 (426)), and married a well-born Jewess from Crete who gave him two sons, Justus and Simonides, who was surnamed Agrippa after Josephus' patron King Agrippa II (the Agrippa of Acts 25: 13 – 26: 32).

It was while in Rome that Josephus wrote the *War*, the *Antiquities*, the treatise *Apion*, and the *Life* (see below). The date of his death is uncertain; he was certainly alive in the thirteenth year of Domitian's reign (AD 93–4) (*Ant.* xx.12.1 (267)), while in *Life* 65 (359) he refers to King Agrippa II as no longer alive. Agrippa's death is usually dated AD 93, but some scholars accept the evidence of Photius, a ninth-century Byzantine scholar, that Agrippa died in AD 100. However, inscriptional evidence from the Hauran suggests that Agrippa's rule had ended before Domitian's death in AD 96. The question is further complicated by the suggestion that Josephus prepared a second edition of the *Antiquities* after Agrippa's death (see below, pp. 91f). It is perhaps safest to date Josephus' death somewhere between AD 95 and 105. After his death, according to Eusebius (*Historia Ecclesiastica* iii.9), a statue of Josephus was erected in Rome, and his works were placed in the public library.

The text of Josephus' writings

The earliest known manuscripts of the Greek text have been preserved at Paris, Milan, Venice, and Rome, and date from the tenth to the twelfth centuries AD. The large number of surviving medieval Latin manuscripts witnesses to Josephus' popularity in the West in the Crusading period (perhaps because Josephus was a major source of information about Palestine) and the earliest printed editions of Josephus were in Latin. The Greek text was first printed in Basle in 1544, containing in one volume the *Antiquities*, *Life*, *War*, and *Apion*, together with 4 Maccabees, then ascribed to Josephus. For modern editions and translations, see the Note on Further Reading, pp. 192f.

Two reference systems are used in modern texts of Josephus. The older system, which appears to be a combination of systems used by the mediaeval Latin and Greek texts, divides Josephus into books, chapters, and sections (e.g., *Ant.* ii.1.1). Niese's edition (1887–95) further subdivided the text into numbered paragraphs, and in this book both systems are used in combination (e.g., *Ant.* ii.1.1 (1–3)).

'The Jewish War'

Josephus tells us that in its present form the *War* is his Greek version of an earlier account (probably in Aramaic) addressed to Jews beyond the Euphrates. He confesses that he uses literary assistants to help with the language (*Apion* i.9 (50)). This Greek version was perhaps published in Rome between the building of the Temple of Peace in AD 75 (*War* vii.5.7 (158)) and the death in AD 79 of Vespasian, to whom Josephus says he presented a copy (*Apion* i.9 (50)), or perhaps in the reign of Titus (AD 79–81), who gave the work his official approval (*Life* 65

(363)). It has recently been argued that *War* VII, with its praise of Domitian (VII.4.2 (85–8)) and a style closely similar to that of *Antiquities*, may belong to Domitian's reign, though Josephus' introduction to *War* I seems to suggest that his work originally ended with Titus' return to Italy and his Triumph, which are described in the middle of Book VII. On the other hand, Josephus may have intended the heroic account of the fall of Masada, in the second half of the book, as a counterbalance to the picture of the Roman triumph in the first half, and as a final reminder of the tragedy of it all.

Book I and most of Book II are taken up with the history of the Jews from the Maccabaean struggle to the beginning of the war in summer AD 66. Josephus marks the point with Agrippa II's great speech against the war (*War* II.16.4 (345–401)), which is immediately followed by the cessation of sacrifices on behalf of Rome (II.17.2 (409)). The rest of Book II details the events of AD 66, including Josephus' activities in Galilee. Book III begins with Nero's appointment of Vespasian to the command in Syria, and describes his campaign in Galilee, the siege of Jotapata and the capture of Josephus, the capture of Tiberias and Tarichaeae, and the destruction of the Jewish fleet on the lake of Galilee. Book IV begins with the fall of Gamala and Gischala, and then turns to the political in-fighting of the Jewish factions in Jerusalem. Books V and VI describe the capture and destruction of Jerusalem, Book VII the subsequent operations in Palestine, the Triumph in Rome, and the siege and capture of Masada. Inserted into the history of the war are a number of excursuses – on Herod's buildings (1.21.1–12 (401–28)), the main Jewish sects (II.8.2–14 (119–66)), Galilee, Samaria, and Judaea (III.3.1–5 (35–58)), and Jordan valley (III.10.7–8 (506–21)), Jericho and the Dead Sea (IV.8.2–4 (452–85)), Jerusalem (V.5.1–8 (184–247)), the Roman army (III.5.1–8 (70–109)) and the siege of Jotapata (III.7.3–36 (141–339)). These passages stand out for their interest and value, and reveal Josephus' observation, knowledge, and narrative skill.

Josephus' purpose in writing is reasonably clear. His Preface criticises those who had written about the war from hearsay or with partiality, especially those glorifying the Romans at the expense of the Jews, and he claims to present a more accurate, less biassed account. However, he states that he is writing for subjects of the Roman Empire (Preface (3)) (and so he calls his work *The Jewish War*, which is how most Roman subjects would think of the event; the Jews would speak of 'the war' or 'the Roman War'), though his aim is 'not so much to flatter the Romans as to comfort the conquered and to deter the rebellious' (III.5.8 (108)). It is in keeping with this that Josephus consistently presents the

Romans as ruling their empire in the best interests of their subjects (with some sad lapses, especially in Judaea and Samaria) and the Jews as their own worst enemies, divided into factions and at the mercy of their own extremists. In short, Josephus writes to explain why such an unnecessary disaster took place, and to demonstrate to each side that its opponents were not so brutal, godless, and uncivilised as they were usually thought to be. He is also concerned to present his own part in the war in the best light possible (see above).

The question of the reliability and accuracy of Josephus' account needs careful consideration. Josephus himself claims fairness and accuracy (Preface 2 (6)), and claims that his accuracy was vouched for by Titus and King Agrippa II (*Life* 65 (363–7)), though the letter he quotes from Agrippa notes that Agrippa could reveal still more of the story. Josephus also disarmingly professes to proclaim his bias by admitting his personal grief at what had happened to his country, thus attempting both to satisfy the literary conventions and to counter the Jewish accusation that he was a traitor. Yet for all Josephus' mixed motives, he was certainly well placed to give reliable information. He was in turn a diplomat, a general in Galilee, and a respected prisoner and observer on the Roman side, able to interview Jewish deserters about events in Jerusalem (*Apion* 1.9 (49)). He became a confidant of Titus, and observed his Triumph in Rome. In his later works (*Life* 65 (342, 358); *Apion* 1.10 (56)) he refers to the 'commentaries' of the Roman generals, and, though he nowhere actually states that he used them in compiling his work (perhaps because he is emphasising his own status as eye-witness), he may well have had access to them. He probably had well-informed Roman sources to help in matters of military detail, though he used an earlier account of the Roman army by the Greek historian Polybius as the basis for his own description in *War* III.5.1–8 (70–109). For his description of Palestine he could draw on his own observation; his description of such places as Masada, Herodium or Caesarea is largely supported by the archaeological evidence. On the other hand, he could err in details and exaggerate numbers; and there are some inconsistencies between the *War* and the *Life* regarding the sequence of events in Galilee or the nature of Josephus' own position in Galilee.

One writer has recently commented that 'it would have been an extraordinary feat for Josephus to record the unvarnished truth about anything', and we must always scrutinise Josephus' motives in writing, especially in matters concerning Jewish politics or his own position. But it is also true that Josephus has taken extraordinary pains to compile an informative account of Jewish life and history, based, at least for his own day, on first-hand knowledge. As R. J. H. Shutt observed (*Studies in Josephus* (S.P.C.K.: London, 1961), p. 35): 'Josephus wrote the truth as he saw it: the fact that in his view the power and fortune of the Roman Empire were of paramount importance does not in itself render his work untrustworthy.' Alongside Josephus' account, that of the Roman historian Tacitus (*Histories* v) is revealed as almost totally lacking in accuracy and charity. Josephus must be taken seriously, as well as cautiously. It should also be noted that for much of the period covered, Josephus is often our only source.

'Antiquities of the Jews'

The *Antiquities* is a much larger work. It was the product of Josephus' mature adult life, completed in his fifty-sixth year, the thirteenth year of Domitian's reign, AD 93–4 (*Ant.* xx.12.1 (267)). Josephus conceived the idea of writing it while still engaged on the *War*; he was encouraged to overcome his hesitations and complete the task by his patron Epaphroditus (*Ant.*, Prologue 2 (5–9)). This work thus took up nearly twenty years of Josephus' life, and clearly Josephus thought it of great importance. He aimed to give an account of 'our whole past history and the organisation of our state, translated from the Hebrew literature' (Prologue 2 (5)), including such topics as the origin of the Jewish people, their history, the work of Moses, and the Jews' military record. He intended to write a more theological treatise 'on customs and causes' later (Prologue 4 (25); *Ant.* iv.8.4 (198); see below, pp. 88f).

For Jewish history up to the time of the Maccabees, the work is mainly a paraphrase of the historical books of the Old Testament. Little use is made of the prophetic or Wisdom books. Throughout, the narrative is expanded by non-biblical material and traditional Jewish exegesis, but when Josephus reaches the hellenistic period he becomes dependent on new sources – official records (though their authenticity in some cases has been questioned) and various hellenistic writers such as Berosus and Manetho (see below, p. 88) and Herod the Great's court historian Nicolaus of Damascus. Books i – ii.8.2 cover Genesis, Books ii.9.1 – the end of Book iv the career of Moses, Book v Joshua, Judges, and Ruth, Book vi Saul, Book vii David, Books viii–x the monarchy from Solomon to Nebuchadnezzar's capture of Jerusalem and the story of Daniel. This seems to have been designed as the mid-point of the work. Book xi describes the period from the rise of Cyrus to the death of Alexander the Great; Book xii runs to the death of Judas

Maccabaeus, Book XIII to the death of Queen Salome Alexandra (ruled 76–67 BC); Book XIV to the end of the Hasmonaeans. Books XV–XVII cover Herod and his immediate successors, Books XVIII–XX the Roman administration to the procuratorship of Gessius Florus. (Books XIII–XX cover in fuller detail much of the history already described in *War* I–III.) In *Ant.* XVIII–XX, Josephus is an important independent source for Roman history of the first century AD, supplementing Tacitus, Suetonius, and others. So Josephus notes at the end of *Antiquities* (XX.12.1 (259–60)) that the work 'contains the tradition, from man's first origins to the twelfth year of the principate of Nero, of what has happened to us Jews in Egypt, Syria, and Palestine, both what we suffered from the Assyrians and Babylonians, and the terrible things that were inflicted on us by the Persians and Macedonians, and after them the Romans'.

Such a mammoth literary and historical task was not undertaken without clear aims in mind. Josephus rejected motives of fame or flattery, urging rather his own involvement in affairs and the need for better public information; in particular, he wished to refute the inaccurate accounts of others. In general, he was writing because he believed that Jewish affairs were of interest to the Greek world, and by way of precedents he pointed to the readiness of the high priest Eleazar to meet the request of Ptolemy II Philadelphus of Alexandria for a copy of the Jewish Law, to be translated into Greek.

In fact, however, Josephus' purpose was more serious than he admits. Although he admired the Romans for their empire, and the Greeks for their literature, he was nevertheless proud of his Judaism even if he regretted the political folly of extremist Jews. The *Antiquities* is above all a massive Jewish apologia to the Graeco-Roman world. Recent studies have shown how the stories of Abraham, Moses, Balaam, Solomon, Esther, and Daniel have been retold by Josephus in order to show that Jewish heroes and philosophers were not so different from Greek ones. Josephus says (*Apion* II.12 (136)) that outstanding Jews can hold their own in wider society. Abraham becomes the philosopher who first proclaimed monotheism and taught the Egyptians mathematics and astronomy (see pp. 147f). Moses studied the nature of God with the eye of reason, wrote in hexameter verse, and led a successful military campaign in Ethiopia. Above all, he is presented as a typical hellenistic 'divine man' (*theios anēr*), whose birth was preceded by oracles and dreams, and whose physical beauty, growth, and intellectual development were far above average (see p. 150). In the story of Balaam,

Josephus 81

Josephus demonstrates how liberal pagan sexuality leads to apostasy, and refutes the pagan charge that the Jews were atheists and misanthropes (see p. 157). Here he had in mind the position of the Jew abroad. Solomon is made to pray to God in Stoic terms very similar to those used in Paul's speech at Athens in Acts 17: 27f (*Ant.* VIII.4.2 (108); VIII.4.3 (111)), and to welcome non-Jews to the Temple (VIII.4.3 (116)). (Josephus approved of the Stoics because, like him, they made much of the idea of providence. See p. 170.) The story of Daniel and his prophecies is used to demonstrate that the world was governed by God's providence and not, as the Epicureans argued, by chance, and, secondly, to point to the coming of the Roman Empire (pp. 166–71). The story of Esther is retold to make the story more attractive to the Greek reader, and in particular to give him less excuse for anti-Jewish propaganda; so the dramatic, romantic, and erotic elements are enhanced, Esther becomes a heroine, and the anti-Semitism of the wicked Haman is exaggerated while Jewish dislike of Gentiles is played down (*Ant.* XI.6.1–13 (184–296)). To demonstrate the acceptability of the Jews in the hellenistic world, Josephus includes a highly suspect account of a visit by Alexander the Great to Jerusalem, during which Alexander prostrates himself, sacrifices to the Jewish God, honours the high priest, reads with pleasure a prophecy from the Book of Daniel (Dan. 8: 21) forecasting his own destruction of the Persian Empire, allows the Jews to observe their own laws, and exempts them from tribute every seventh year (*Ant.* XI.8.5 (329–39)). The acceptance of the Jews at Alexandria is demonstrated by the story, taken over from the Letter of Aristeas (see above, pp. 11–34), of the translation of the Jewish scriptures into Greek for Ptolemy II Philadelphus (*Ant.* XII.2.1–15 (17–118)). In the second half of *Antiquities*, Josephus is at pains to demonstrate that all foreign rulers – Cyrus, the Persians, Alexander, the Ptolemies, the early Seleucids, and the Romans – had respected the Jews and allowed them freedom of worship; and, in response, the Jews had been for the most part loyal subjects. Josephus probably felt that this was an important point to make in the principate of the suspicious Domitian, and it may also be that the emphasis on the providential death of the Emperor Gaius Caligula, who tried to have his own statue placed in the Jerusalem Temple, was a pointed warning to Domitian to avoid imposing the imperial cult upon the Jews (XVIII.8.1–9 (257–309)).

Much recent work has been done on Josephus' theological understanding of the history of Israel in *Antiquities*. In particular, it has been urged by H. W. Attridge that for Josephus 'history is a series of examples substantiating the belief that God exercises providential concern that justice be done'; as Josephus says in his Prologue:

> 'The main lesson to be learned from history by the willing inquirer is that those who follow God's will and do not dare to transgress the excellent laws that have been laid down for them will meet with unbelievable good fortune in life, and their reward from God will be prosperity. But to the extent that they depart from the careful observance of their laws, things possible will become impossible, and their good designs will turn to total disaster.' (Prologue 3 (14))

So Josephus stresses the place of divine retribution in human affairs. Of Noah he says: 'God, loving the man for his righteousness, indicated to him that his prayers would be fulfilled' (*Ant.* 1.3.8 (99)). Josephus enjoys demonstrating the 'extraordinary reversals of fortune' (*paralogoi peripeteiai*) that happen to people – perhaps most obviously, for example, in the case of Isaac (*Ant.* 1.13.1–4 (222–36)). The key to this presentation is Josephus' belief in the providence (*pronoia*) of God, a theme that he underlined when describing his own escape from death after the siege of Jotapata (*War* III.8.7 (387–91)). Thus Abraham submitted to God's will and took Isaac away to be sacrificed because 'everything that happened to those favoured by God came by divine providence' (*Ant.* 1.13.2 (225)). The theme of divine providence is stressed in the stories of Jacob (II.2.1 (8)), Joseph (II.5.1 (60)), and the rebellion of Korah (IV.3.2 (47)). In *Ant.* X.11.7 (277f) Josephus uses the prophecies of Daniel to demonstrate

> '...the errors of the Epicureans, who dismiss providence from life and reject the idea that God controls events...they say rather that the cosmos runs itself without there being any hands on the reins or external supervision. But if it were uncontrolled in this way, it would be dashed to pieces by its mindless impetus and would be totally destroyed...if it is the case that the cosmos proceeds in some automatic way, we should not have seen everything turning out in accordance with his [Daniel's] prophecies.'

This stress on providence links Josephus with the Stoic philosophers of the hellenistic world, whose belief it was that 'the world is administered by the providence of the gods' (Cicero, *De Natura Deorum* 2.73f).

This stress on God's providential care that justice should be done in the end is of a piece with Josephus' care to show the virtues of the Israelite leaders and heroes, and he does this in categories familiar to and approved by the Greek world. So Samuel, when presented by Jesse with his eldest, most handsome son as candidate for the throne, says to Jesse: 'No, you look on the beauty of the lad and considered him worthy of the throne; but I have not made the throne a prize for bodily beauty but for virtue of soul, and I am looking for a person outstanding in piety and righteousness, bravery and obedience.' There is both criticism and approval of Greek virtues expressed here, but the picture is certainly drawn in terms the Greek world would recognise. The ideal figure was of course Moses, who not only grew in wisdom and stature and favour with God and man (see *Ant.* II.9.6 (230–1)), like the young Jesus portrayed in Luke 2: 52, but also found favour 'above all by his control of his emotions' – a very Stoic virtue – and by his distinction both as a general and as a prophet (*Ant.* IV.8.49 (327–31)).

Josephus is equally concerned to portray the results of rejecting the divine providence and Law. Cain, for example, went from bad to worse (*Ant.* I.2.2 (60–1)): 'He took his punishment, however, not as a warning, but as a means of increasing his wickedness', and Cain goes on to explore every sensual pleasure, enrich himself by violence, and instruct others in craftiness. In the story of Balaam, the Israelites are corrupted by the Midianite women to prefer pleasure to God (*Ant.* IV.6.10 (143)), and when at the end of the story Zambrias goes further and argues that the Law promulgated by Moses is tyrannical, he meets a swift end at the hands of Phinehas. In Josephus' view, it is men like the sons of Eli, 'insolent to men and impious to God', who are tyrannical. Their death does not surprise Eli, 'for he had been previously warned by God what would happen, and he had warned his sons' (*Ant.* V.11.3 (358)).

Thus in *Antiquities* Josephus uses events in Israel's history to demonstrate God's providential care for the moral order of things, and, one might suppose, to demonstrate God's care for Israel. It is perhaps surprising, therefore, that Josephus appears to play down Israel's special relationship with God. For example, in the patriarchal stories, the theme of the covenant with Abraham and his successors is absent. In *Antiquities* it is the loyalty of the Israelite to God and his laws that gives Israel a special place in God's providence, not God's previous choice of Abraham or covenant with him. The saga of Abraham and his successors begins with Abraham's own advanced 'intellectual theological ability and development', and this leads, in accordance with the will and help of God, to his emigration to Canaan. After his battle with the kings and the rescue of Lot, 'God praised his virtue and said, "You shall not lose the rewards that you deserve for such good deeds"' (*Ant.* 1.10.3 (183)). And, similarly, Israel's special position among the nations of the world is the result of her special virtues, for which she is rewarded by gaining God's assistance against her enemies. Josephus' view of Israel's situation is put into the mouth of the seer Balaam (*Ant.* IV.6.4 (114)):

'Fortunate is the people to whom God grants possession of innumerable blessings, and to whom he assigns his providence as an ally and leader. For there is no race of men who will be judged superior to you, by virtue of your natural excellence and your earnest search for the best behaviour innocent of all wickedness. You will leave your possessions to children even better than yourselves, for God looks with favour on you alone of all men...The land, therefore, to which he sent you will be yours to hold, subject for ever to you and your children, whose fame will fill the whole earth and sea; and there will be enough of you in the world to provide settlers from your own race for every country...the land of Canaan will hold your present small number, but understand that the inhabited world lies before you as an eternal home.'

It is clear that Josephus does not particularly emphasise the biblical promise of the possession of the land of Canaan. The emphasis is rather on Abraham sending out his sons and grandsons to found colonies (an idea very much at home in the Greek world), and Josephus probably has his eyes on the Jewish diaspora, which had in his day made its presence felt in Rome and in Alexandria and throughout the Roman world, as can be seen from the Acts of the Apostles. It may be that Josephus is avoiding too much emphasis on the idea of the Jewish right to Palestine in the light of the destruction of the Temple and its aftermath in AD 70; he prefers to emphasise Judaism as a way of life that leads to virtue by means of its excellent laws (cp. *Apion* II.38–9 (276–86)).

A number of other features demonstrate Josephus' apologetic concern: for example, his emphasis on the antiquity of the Jewish people with a history and historical records that go back far behind Homer (Prologue 1 (16–17)), and on their possession of a political constitution (*diataxis tou politeumatos*) and on the existence of a lawgiver, Moses, the Israelite equivalent of Lycurgus at Sparta or Solon at Athens. But here Josephus underlines that the Israelite Law was not anything extraordinary or uncivilised: it had its roots in a perfectly rational view of the world and of the deity. Moses

> '...thought it most necessary for one intending to govern his own life well and to legislate for others first of all to study the nature of God, and then, having studied his works in a rational manner, to imitate this most perfect model as far as possible and try to follow it...he did not follow the example of others and begin with contracts and reciprocal rights but led people's minds to God and the creation of the world, and persuaded them that we men are the finest of God's earthly works.'

Josephus contrasts the Jewish lawgiver with other lawgivers who based their work on fables; Moses' work was based on the perfection and majesty of God and his love for men, and was 'consistent with the nature of the universe' (see Prologue 4 (18–26)). (Philo made a similar point about the harmony of Law and creation in *De Opificio Mundi* 3.)

There can be little doubt that Josephus was modelling his *archaiologia*, as he calls it, on the work of Dionysius of Halicarnassus (*c.* 60 BC – the early first century AD), who wrote his *Archaiologia Rōmaikē*, a history of Rome from its beginnings to 264 BC, in twenty books. Dionysius appears to have written partly out of admiration for Rome and partly out of admiration 'for all virtuous men and all who enjoy the contemplation of noble and grand deeds' (1.6.5). His view of history was that its object was to please and instruct rather than to tell the truth. In the *War*, Josephus, like Polybius before him, rejects the idea of writing ancient history for the readers' pleasure in favour of writing contemporary history for the readers' instruction (*War* I, Prologue), but in *Antiquities* he notes that, while the author's chief aim is the truth, in recounting ancient history a certain elegance is needed so that the reader may acquire the information 'with a certain degree of gratification and pleasure' (*Ant.* XIV.1.1 (2)), though he is careful to say, when introducing the laws of Moses (*Ant.* IV.8.4 (196)), that 'It has all been written down just as he left it; we have not added anything by way of ornament, nor anything that Moses did not leave for us.' This claim of accuracy and of neither adding nor subtracting anything (cp. *Ant.* I, Prologue I (17), and Deut. 4: 2) is a regular convention followed by other hellenistic historians including Dionysius, and does not prevent Josephus from interpreting what he found. One further point of contact with Dionysius might be mentioned. On several occasions, when dealing with the miraculous, Josephus copies a phrase similarly used by Dionysius, and instructs his readers to make up their own minds on the truth of the story (see, e.g., the story about Alexander in *Ant.* II.16.5 (348); p. 151). This may be Josephus' nod to Greek rationalism, but it must also be noted that Josephus does not reject miracles, which he interprets as revealing the providence and power of God. Thus when the sea retreats before the Israelites, Moses sees it as 'a clear manifestation (*epiphaneia*) of God' (*Ant.* II.16.2 (339)), and he thanks God for the marvellous (*paralogon*) salvation that God has shown them; after the disaster to the Egyptian forces it is called a miraculous (*paradoxon*) salvation (*Ant.* II.16.4 (345)). This is in keeping with Josephus' view that things do not happen of their own accord (*automatōs*) but by the providence of God.

'Against Apion'

Josephus wrote an urgent piece of apologetic in two volumes which Jerome called *Against Apion* (from the main opponent attacked in the work) and which Origen and Eusebius called *On the antiquity of the Jews* (from the contents of the first volume). *Antiquities* is a lengthy rehearsal of Jewish history, *Apion* a brief defence of Judaism, focussed on certain key points and specific opponents.

In Book I, Josephus is primarily concerned to counter gentile disbelief in the antiquity of the Jewish people, a disbelief based on the lack of reference to the Jews in the Greek historians. Josephus responds by pointing to the comparatively recent appearance on the historical scene of the Greeks themselves, and to the erroneous and contradictory statements of the Greek historians, whose lack of official archives on which to draw as source material is contrasted with the carefully preserved official records of the Jews. Josephus goes on to list references to the Jews in historians from Egypt (Manetho), Phoenicia (the archives of Tyre, Dius, and Menander of Ephesus), Babylonia (Berosus), and from Greece (Herodotus, Aristotle, Hecataeus of Abdera, and others), after which Josephus deals with several versions of the story, found in Manetho and other writers, that the Jews were expelled from Egypt as lepers and undesirables.

In Book II, Josephus focusses on the anti-Jewish polemic of the rhetorician, grammarian, historian, and politician Apion. The Emperor Tiberius had called Apion 'the cymbal of the world', reminding us of Paul's comment in I Cor. 13 that a man without love is no better than a clanging cymbal. According to Josephus, Apion wrote a five-volume history of Egypt, and he served on the Alexandrian delegation to Caligula at the time of the dispute over Jewish rights in

Alexandria (*Ant.* xviii.8.1 (257)). Josephus says of him that, though not an Alexandrian by birth, he was given Alexandrian citizenship, and that by way of return he attacked the Jewish community, knowing how much the Alexandrians disliked it (*Apion* ii.3 (29)). Josephus corrects Apion's presentation of Moses, his dating of the Exodus to the seventh Olympiad (752–749 BC), his derivation of the word 'sabbath' from the Egyptian word for an unpleasant disease, and his assertion that the Jews were Egyptian in origin. A long section is devoted to Apion's attack on the Jewish claim to Alexandrian citizenship for Jewish residents. This was indeed an important issue and had occasioned the sending of rival Jewish and Alexandrian delegations to the Emperor Caligula in AD 38 (see below, pp. 182–8). A final section is given to Apion's misrepresentation of the Jewish Temple and Law. Stories that the Jews worshipped an ass's head or sacrificed a Greek each year are scornfully dismissed. Josephus answers Apion's slurs that the Jews were 'never rulers of an empire but ever slaves of different nations' and that they produced no famous artists or scholars, and his complaint that they refused pork and practised circumcision. Josephus regards Apion's death from gangrene after a necessary operation of circumcision as nothing less than fitting (*Apion* ii.13 (143–4)).

The last section of the work is more positive. Josephus stresses the antiquity and achievements of Moses. 'Our lawgiver...if one may use a forced expression, produced a "theocracy" for a constitution, handing over authority and power to God.' Moses did not present a philosophy for the few, but a way of life for the community; he ensured that all men should know the Law, and so produced (according to Josephus' idealistic picture, somewhat belied by his history of the Jewish War) 'a most beautiful harmony in the character of men' (*Apion* ii.19 (179)). 'In our society, all behave alike, all speak alike about God, consistently with the Law and in the stated belief that he oversees everything' (*Apion* ii.19 (181)). Such a law could not be improved. Josephus goes on to describe the Jewish conception of God, the Temple and the cult, the laws governing marriage, children, burial, parents, and aliens. He underlines the humanitarian nature of the Law and details the penalties for serious infringements and the promises of future reward. He ends with a long section comparing Jewish and Greek attitudes to law and religion, a final burst of praise for the Law, and a dedication to his patron Epaphroditus.

This is perhaps one of the most important of Josephus' writings, and the sincerity of the apologia seems clear. He is genuinely proud of his Jewish heritage, and to demonstrate its acceptability in the Graeco-

Roman world he confidently asserts that it attracted Greek philosophers, who, 'while apparently preserving their ancestral traditions, in behaviour and philosophy followed Moses' (*Apion* II.39 (281)). Josephus is anxious to counter the damage done to the reputation of the Jews by racist stories, as popular in the ancient world as in the modern, and to present the Jewish history, literature, and religion – especially the Law – as attractive to his educated Graeco-Roman contemporaries. Josephus may have felt such a defence was much needed in the difficult days of Domitian, and he underlines that, while the Temple stood, sacrifice was offered daily for the Roman emperor. It is impossible to say how far into society this apologia reached and how effective it was, but at least it has survived.

To the student of hellenistic literature, *Apion* is particularly important because it has preserved much information about obscure authors and their writings, and sometimes even quotes at length from them. Josephus quotes directly from Hecataeus of Abdera (a late fourth-century BC historian who wrote on Egypt), Manetho (a third-century BC Egyptian historian), Berosus (a third-century BC historian of Babylon), Clearchus of Soli (a fourth- to third-century BC scholar; see p. 180), and others; and he quotes indirectly a great many others such as Theophrastus, a fourth-century BC pupil of Aristotle, and Polybius of Megalopolis, the second-century BC Greek historian of Rome. Among those mentioned are Megasthenes, a fourth- to third-century BC Ionian who wrote on India, and Euhemerus of Messene, a fourth- to third-century BC philosopher (see pp. 181, 31, 39).

The precise date and occasion of *Apion* are not certain. The opening sentence and the final paragraphs reveal that it followed the *Antiquities*, completed AD 93–4. *Apion* has sometimes been identified, in whole or part, with the work 'About God and his being, and about the laws' that Josephus planned to write in four books (*Ant.* XX.12.1 (268)). The *Apion* discusses the Law, but says little about God and his being except briefly at II.22 (190–2), and it may well be that Josephus was distracted from his original purpose, of a large, more theoretical, work of apologia, by what he felt to be the more urgent need to reply to criticism of his *Antiquities* and current anti-Jewish feelings. A further suggestion has been that in *Apion* II.13 (137–42) (food laws and circumcision), II.2 (20–7), 38 (282) (sabbath), II.8 (103–9), 23 (193–8) (sacrifices and Temple), and in *Ant.* III.9.1 – 12.3 (224–86) and IV.4.3–4 (67–75), 8.5–43 (199–301), Josephus incorporated material that was originally designed for a 'treatise on customs and causes' announced in *Ant.* I, Prologue 4 (25) and given its title in *Ant.* IV.8.4 (198), and for the 'treatise on sacrifices' announced in *Ant.* III.8.6 (205). (It is also possible that in Josephus' mind the projected works on 'customs and causes' and 'About God and his being, and about the laws' were the same project.) If these suggestions are right, then we have extant everything of any importance that Josephus wrote or published, and there are no lost works to lament.

Apion was written, Josephus says, partly as a response to people who criticised his *Antiquities*, and presumably we must allow a reasonable amount of time to elapse for criticisms of that lengthy work to appear. If the Epaphroditus to whom the book is dedicated was the freedman and secretary of Nero who was killed by Domitian in AD 95 (Dio Cassius, *Roman History* LXVII.14), then *Apion* would have been written within a year of the publication of *Antiquities*. If, however, Epaphroditus is the scholar Marcus Mettius Epaphroditus, who lived in Rome until Nerva's reign (AD 96–8), the chronology is easier. This was probably Josephus' last work (unless he revised the *Antiquities* for a second edition, as some scholars argue; see below pp. 91f) before his death.

The 'Life'

The *Life* is perhaps the most difficult of Josephus' writings to assess. I have already noted that the earlier *War* and the *Life* differ in their accounts of Josephus' position and career in Galilee, and I may here turn to other matters.

The work is an autobiography, arranged and proportioned as follows: 1 (1–6), Josephus' ancestry; 2 (8–12), his education; 3–6 (13–27), his early life; 7–74 (28–413), his command in Galilee; 75–6 (414–29), his life under the Romans; 76 (430), conclusion. In pattern, the work is not unlike Tacitus' biographical sketch of his father-in-law Agricola, which similarly devotes a long middle section to the central part of the subject's career. Josephus is particularly concerned to vindicate himself against the attack of another historian, Justus of Tiberias, who had challenged the accuracy of Josephus' account, and in particular had charged him with responsibility for causing the revolt of Tiberias from Rome (65 (336–67)). In reply, Josephus says that his brief from Jerusalem was not to foment revolt but to restrain the more rebellious, prepare official forces for defence, and to wait upon the Romans' next move. He describes the political situation in Galilee at the beginning of the war, carefully noting that while at Tiberias there were those who favoured war or revolution, Sepphoris and Gamala were pro-Roman. Josephus then plunges into a complex narrative in which he emphasises his own popularity among the Galilaeans, and blames the revolt of Tiberias, the disaffection of the Galilaeans, and various plots against his own life and reputation on John of Gischala, Justus of Tiberias and his father Pistus. A large part of the narrative deals with the attempt of the Jerusalem authorities (according to Josephus, at the instigation of John of Gischala) to relieve Josephus of his commission. The attempt finally failed, but it is not easy to get at the truth of the matter. Here too Josephus is trying to justify his activities, or, perhaps, cover his lack of success. Josephus throughout represents himself as a restraining moderate, trying to prevent Galilee and Tiberias from open hostility to Rome; yet Josephus admits to preparing defences in Galilee, claims to have sacked pro-Roman towns, and met Roman forces in battle. He says that his political opponents were jealous of his personal success and standing with the Galilaeans and charged him with wanting to 'be a tyrant' (i.e., assume sole control of Galilee (58 (302)), and that on one occasion he was charged with plotting to betray the country to Rome (26 (129); 27 (132–5)). What emerges is that Josephus did act as a Jewish military leader preparing for war against Rome in Galilee, that his relationships with pro-Roman towns such as Sepphoris and Tiberias were bad, and that his enmity with Justus is in some way connected with this. (*Life* 35 (174–8) appears to suggest that Justus was secretly pro-Roman, and that Josephus knew it.) But in Rome in the last decade of the first century AD Josephus presents matters in such a way as to suggest that he was a moderate Jewish leader, and that the moral responsibility for the revolt of Tiberias lay with the revolutionary party there, with whom he associates Justus.

Josephus addresses a long digression in the *Life* to Justus (65(336–67)), and, to judge from the animosity shown, Josephus regarded Justus' charge as a serious threat. Justus' claim that Tiberias rebelled under military pressure from Josephus might have undermined Josephus' standing with the emperor and jeopardised his pension. Josephus therefore denies his own responsibility and asserts local responsibility for Tiberias' revolt, attempting to undermine Justus' claim to loyalty to Rome, and, on stronger grounds, challenges the accuracy of Justus' account; Justus (unlike Josephus himself) had not been personally involved in the fighting against Rome, either in Galilee or in Jerusalem, had not had access to the *commentarii* (official records) of the Roman generals, and had delayed publication of his work until all eye-witnesses were conveniently dead. Josephus clinches his case by claiming for his own account, the *War*, the *imprimatur* of both King Agrippa II and the Emperor Titus.

The *Life*, then, encloses a lengthy, partisan apologia within an autobiographical framework, and Josephus' personal vanity is clear throughout. He proclaims his youthful intelligence and piety (2 (7–12)), his moral virtues in middle life (15 (80)), his preservation by divine providence (15 (83)), his obedience to divine instruction (42 (208–11)), and his veracity as a historian (65 (336–9)). He never hesitates to boast of his skill as a general, or to find plausible motives for dubious conduct – e.g., the failure of his attack on Sepphoris (67 (373–80)); though he is also capable of some very damaging admissions – e.g., that he sent spoils looted from Syrian towns to his own family at Jerusalem (15 (81)). He ends the *Life* by listing the many favours shown to him by successive Roman emperors and their families. But the whole is unsatisfactory as a literary work. The account of Josephus' doings in Galilee is repetitious and inconsistent, and not a little confusing – perhaps not least because Josephus is trying simultaneously to demonstrate his consistency and loyalty to both Jews and Romans.

The *Life* seems to have been written as some sort of appendix to the *Antiquities*. After saying (*Ant.* XX.12.1 (259)) that he has reached a point where he proposes to end his *Antiquities*, Josephus says (*Ant.* XX.12.1 (266)) that perhaps it might not be out of place to add a short excursus about his family and the activities of his life while his critics and witnesses are still alive. Josephus continues (267): 'But with this I shall end my *archaiologia*, contained in twenty books and sixty thousand lines, and, if God permits, I will remind my readers again briefly of the war and our experiences to the present day, the thirteenth year of the reign of the Emperor Domitian and the fifty-sixth year of my life.' The interpretation of these sentences has caused some discussion. Clearly Josephus intends to add a statement or a short book about his family and his life to the end of *Antiquities*, the contents of which end with the beginning of the Jewish War, and the composition of which was completed in AD 93–4. The *Life* appears to have run on from *Antiquities* with no separate introduction, linked only by the weak connecting particle *de* ('and'). Eusebius later quotes a passage from the *Life* as coming 'at the end of the *Antiquities*'. It has, however, been suggested that *Ant.* XX was given two endings, the original one, dating the work to AD 93–4, being now preceded by a later insertion (XX.12.1 (259–66)), which ends with the reference to the excursus on Josephus' life and family; this insertion belongs to the second edition of the book, issued in response to Justus' accusations and dated after the death of King Agrippa II, usually taken on this view to be after AD 100. But, first, Agrippa's death is most probably to be dated between AD 93 and the death of Domitian in AD 96 (see above, pp. 75f); and, secondly, it is not easy to make a division between paragraphs 266 and 267, as this view demands, for paragraph 267 appears to refer equally to the contents of the *Life* (though in different words), and shows that Josephus' intention to write a brief epilogue goes back to AD 93–4. It has also been noted that the Greek style of the *Life* compares very closely with that of *Ant.* XIX–XX, being rougher than that of the earlier books of the *Antiquities*, and perhaps coming from Josephus' hand, in some haste, without being touched up by an editorial assistant such as Josephus used earlier for the *War* (*Apion* 1.9 (50)). The case for a second edition of *Antiquities* accompanied by the first appearance of the *Life* is thus insecure, and the *Life* perhaps belongs to the end of Domitian's reign or soon after, when Josephus may have felt some unease at his position in Rome.

The ' Testimonium Flavianum'

In *Ant.* XVIII.5.2 (116–19), Josephus noted the popular view that the defeat of the army of Herod Antipas, tetrarch of Galilee and Peraea, by Aretas, King of the Nabataeans, was divine vengeance for Herod's murder of John the Baptist. Josephus describes John as a good man who had taught the Jews to practise righteousness, justice, and piety, and to accept baptism as a sign of their new life. Herod killed John because he feared the possibility of sedition. This picture of John does not tally exactly with the gospel accounts, but shows close enough knowledge to suggest that Josephus might also have known of and written about Jesus of Nazareth.

In *Ant.* XX.9.1 (200), Josephus describes the stoning of James 'the brother of Jesus who was called the Christ', during the high-priesthood of Ananus. The authenticity of this reference is usually accepted, but the fuller account of Jesus in *Ant.* XVIII.3.3 (63–4) – the *testimonium Flavianum*, i.e., the 'witness of Flavius (Josephus)' to Jesus – has met much criticism. The style is Josephan, the passage is cited from Josephus by Eusebius in the early fourth century (*H.E.* 1.11; *Demonstratio Evangelica* III.5.105), and is found in all the manuscript evidence. On the other hand, while Josephus may well have described Jesus as a 'wise man', he is thought unlikely to have added the words 'that is, if one ought to call him a man, for he was a doer of marvellous deeds', and perhaps even less likely to have said, 'This man was the Christ', or that 'he appeared to them on the third day alive again, the prophets of God having predicted these and many other miraculous things about him'. It is often suggested therefore that a Christian interpolator has 'improved' the original account, which perhaps ran much as follows:

> 'About this time lived Jesus, a wise man, a teacher of those who delight in accepting the truth [*or*, the unusual]. He attracted many Jews, and many from the Greek world as well. On the accusation of our leading men Pilate condemned him to the cross, but those who loved him from the first did not cease to love him. The race of Christians named after him has survived to this day.'

This picture is interesting; it emphasises Jesus as a wise teacher (such men were of special interest to Josephus; see *Life* 2 (9–12)) and his attractiveness to both Jew and Greek (another feature with which Josephus would be in sympathy); it notes the love of Christians for their master as central (unless with one scholar we take the sentence to mean merely that his followers were content with him and remained contented, in which case Josephus is sneering at them); and it notes the continuance of the sect under the name 'Christians', a title that according to Acts 11 : 26 first appeared at Antioch in Syria in the middle of the first century AD. Such an account can be credited to Josephus without difficulty. It is however possible that the Christian editor not only added suitable christological material but also omitted what was not to his liking, and that Josephus' account included some reference to Jesus as a trouble-maker, thus explaining his execution. This suggestion is supported by the context, for the *testimonium* is preceded by the account of two riots during Pilate's term of office – the first at the introduction of the Roman army's standards to Jerusalem (*Ant.* XVIII.3.1 (55–9); see p. 110), and the second at the use of the Temple money to pay for an aqueduct (XVIII.3.2 (60–2)) – and followed (after an intrusive account of two scandals at Rome) by an account of Pilate's brutal suppression of a Samaritan disturbance (XVIII.4.1 (85–7)). The episode of Jesus was therefore one section of Josephus' account of the troubles of Pilate's prefecture in Palestine. Josephus may have had some sympathy for Jesus as a wise teacher, but little sympathy for him as a disturber of the peace under Pontius Pilate.

It is hard to be precise about the date and purpose of the interpolated phrases. The fact that they question the use of the word 'man' of Jesus, credit him with miraculous deeds, and stress the prophetic prediction of the resurrection and other miraculous events, suggests the background of the christological controversies of the third century AD. Christian apologetic use of this passage, however, did not stop here. A shorter Arabic variant appears in a tenth-century AD world history of

Agapius of Hierapolis, and it was perhaps composed for use in the Christian debate with Islam. Better known are the additions to the Slavonic translation of the *War*. These additions relate the New Testament history of Herod, John the Baptist, and Jesus, and one passage, on the career, trial, and death of Jesus, clearly uses the opening sentence of the *testimonium*. It has been suggested that the Slavonic version, including these passages, is ultimately dependent on Josephus' earlier Aramaic version of the *War* (*War*, Preface 1 (3)), but it is more likely that these passages are the Slavonic translator's own composition and addition to his early twelfth-century translation from the Greek.

The selected passages

Josephus was a prolific writer, and the Greek text and English translation of his works fill nine volumes in the Loeb Classical Library. Limitations of space in this present volume make selection of passages difficult, and a good case can be made for the inclusion of many passages not found here. However, the theme of this volume is 'Jews in the hellenistic world', and the passages chosen all illustrate in one way or another how Josephus presents Judaism, the Jewish people, and himself to the hellenistic and Roman world around him. In the Preface to the *War*, Josephus presents his credentials and his attitude as an historian, and the theme of history-writing is developed in *Apion* 1, where Josephus comments on Greek and Jewish historians and their approaches (see pp. 171–9). Josephus is particularly concerned to correct the Greek ignorance of the Jews; he demonstrates that Jewish beliefs were acceptable to Greek philosophers (see p. 180), and that the Jewish ancestor Abraham was a man of reason and learning who would have done credit to any Greek society (cp. pp. 144–50). Similarly Moses is presented as a 'divine man' (cp. p. 80), and the Mosaic Law as the constitution (*politeia*) of the Jewish theocracy (cp. p. 161). The prophecies of Daniel are used to show that Jewish history, including the Roman destruction of the Temple, was part of the divine providential scheme for the whole creation (cp. p. 166). That the Jews were different from others, however, is not disguised, and the story of Balaam is retold to emphasise that the Jews cannot without disaster syncretise with other religions (cp. p. 154); indeed, Zambrias, who claims liberty from the tyranny of Moses' Law, is shown to make the wrong choice and so to lose his life (cp. p. 159).

The passages selected from the *War* make points relevant to the political situation of the Jews in the Roman Empire. Herod's readiness to contribute generously to the hellenistic cities of the empire is emphasised (cp. p. 101); the military strength and political generosity of Rome is strongly underlined (cp. pp. 114, 117, and 97), though lapses from normally high standards of administration are not concealed (cp. p. 110). But above all Josephus is concerned to show that the destruction of Jerusalem was to be blamed not on the Romans but on the intransigence of certain factions among the Jewish people (pp. 129–41). Josephus' own position and sympathies are made clear by the Preface to the *War* (cp. p. 97), by his account of a critical moment in his career (p. 121), and also by the speeches that he puts into the mouth of King Agrippa II (pp. 113–17) and Titus (pp. 143f).

Only one passage from the *Life* has been included, because on the whole the brief autobiographical details and the lengthy defence of Josephus' career in Galilee are not particularly relevant to the major theme of the Jews in the hellenistic world. The famous passages on John the Baptist (*Ant.* XVIII.5.2 (116–19)) and Jesus (*Ant.* XVIII.3.3 (63–4) and XX.9.1 (200)) have been omitted for the same reason; they are in any case readily available to the student in other selections of material relating to New Testament studies (e.g., C. K. Barrett, *The New Testament Background: Selected Documents* (S.P.C.K.; London, 1958)). However, both the *Life* and the *Testimonium Flavianum* have been fully described above, pp. 89–94.

JOSEPHUS AND THE JEWISH WAR

War, Preface (1)   The war of the Jews against the Romans was the greatest not only of our contemporary wars but also of almost all wars of which we have record that ever broke out between cities and nations. There exist artificially clever accounts from men who took no direct part but collected useless and

(2)   inconsistent hearsay, and there exist also the false distortions of those who were personally involved but either flatter the Romans or hate the Jews. Their writings show sometimes excessive criticism, sometimes excessive praise, but never the

(3)   accuracy of historical inquiry. For these reasons I, Josephus, the son of Matthias, by birth a Hebrew, a priest from Jerusalem, have decided to relate the story of the war. (At the beginning of the war, I fought against the Romans; later, I was present under Roman compulsion.) I am writing for

subjects of the Roman Empire, turning into Greek what I originally wrote in my own language and sent to the non-Greek-speaking people of the interior.

2 (4)   When this greatest of upheavals, as I called it, began, domestic affairs at Rome were in chaos, and the Jewish revolutionary party, at the height of its power and wealth, took its cue from the troubled nature of the times. In this extremely troubled situation, the dissidents hoped that they would get control of eastern affairs, and the Romans feared

(5)   that they would lose it. The Jews hoped that all their fellow Jews beyond the Euphrates would join them in revolt, while the Romans were under pressure from their neighbours the Gauls. The Celtic world, too, was restive. The period following Nero's reign was full of disturbance. Many were persuaded that the time was ripe to claim sovereign rule, and the soldiers desired change, in hope of plunder.

(6)   I thought it absurd that in such important affairs truth should suffer while I looked on, and that while through my careful work the Parthians, Babylonians, the furthermost Arabs, and our own relatives beyond the Euphrates in Adiabene should have accurate information on how the war began and the misfortunes through which it passed, those Greeks and Romans who had taken no part in the war should remain ignorant of these matters apart from what they learned by being open to flattery or fiction.

3 (7)   Such writers dare to call their works histories, though in them they compound their failure to reveal sound information by missing their target completely, at least in my opinion. They aim to show off Roman greatness, but on all occasions

(8)   play down and disparage Jewish affairs. But I do not see how those who have conquered insignificant people have any claim to be considered great. Such writers have no sensible appreciation of the length of the war, nor of the size of the Roman army involved in it, nor of the stature of the generals who toiled so hard in the siege of Jerusalem. They do not

count for much in the eyes of these writers, I feel, if their success is so disparaged.

4 (9)   I have certainly no intention of exaggerating the deeds of my fellow Jews by vying with those who magnify the deeds of the Romans. I shall rather relate accurately the actions of both sides, though presenting a personal description of events, and allowing my own feelings to express their sorrow at my

(10)   country's misfortunes. It was Titus Caesar who sacked the Temple; but he himself is witness to the fact that the country was destroyed by its own internal divisions, and that it was the Jewish leaders who brought upon the holy Temple the reluctant hands of the Romans and the flames. Throughout the war he showed mercy on the people, who were under the control of the revolutionary factions, and on a number of occasions he was willing to delay the capture of the city and give the defenders time to reconsider their situation.

(11)   Anyone, however, who criticises my accusations against the leaders or their bandit supporters, or my laments over the misfortunes suffered by my country, should make allowances for my feelings, irrespective of the canons of historical practice. For of all the cities under Roman rule, it happened to be ours that reached the heights of good fortune and

(12)   plumbed the depths of misery. Indeed, the misfortunes of all peoples from the beginning of the world are hardly to be compared with those of the Jews. No Gentile can be blamed, and that makes it all the harder to control one's sorrow. Any hard-hearted critic will have to allow the history its truth, and the historian his tears.

Josephus prefaces his history of the Jewish War with an explanation of his reasons for writing, of his own involvement in events, and of the effect the Jewish defeat had on him. He sets himself the difficult task of identifying himself with both the Romans and the Jews – a stance which has its origins in his priestly ancestry and his early diplomatic contact with Rome and which probably does much to explain the ambiguities of his career in Galilee at the beginning of the

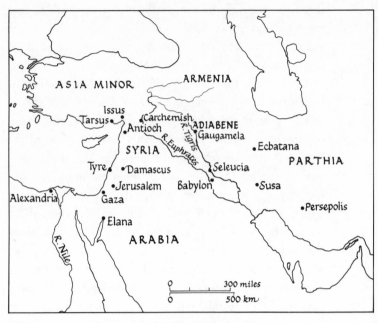

Map 3   Asia, Arabia, Armenia, and Parthia

war and his later accounts of those years. In the remaining paragraphs of his Preface, Josephus aligns himself with earlier historians such as Thucydides and Polybius, who also wrote about their own contemporary history, and he contrasts himself with armchair historians who wrote about the past.

   1. *war of the Jews against the Romans*: this phrase describes the war in factual and almost neutral fashion. Later, however, Josephus speaks of 'my books about the Jewish War' (*Ant.* xx.11.1 (258); cp. *Life* 74 (412); *Ant.* xviii.1.2 (11)), a phrase that more definitely seems to view the war from the Roman side. Another title, *Peri halōseōs*, '*About the capture*' (i.e., of Jerusalem), appears on most early manuscripts of the work, and is also given by the early Christian scholars Origen (*c.* 185–254) and Jerome (*c.* 342–420). Josephus uses the word *halōsis* of the fall of Jerusalem (*War* iv.5.2 (318); cp. p. 128), and the short title may go back to Josephus or be an early shorthand way of referring to the work. *the greatest*: similarly Thucydides begins his work on the Peloponnesian War between Athens and Sparta (431–404 BC) by noting his belief that 'it would be a great war, and more worthy of record than any that preceded it'.

The historians attacked in paragraphs 1 and 2 are unknown, apart from Josephus' political and literary rival Justus of Tiberias, to whom Josephus devotes a scathing section of his *Life* (65 (336–67)), accusing him of disguising the truth, of being responsible for the revolt of the city of Tiberias from Rome, and of publishing, twenty years after the events, a history of the war that lacked first-hand knowledge and contradicted the Roman general's own commentaries. Against Justus, Josephus underlines his own direct involvement in events and the accuracy of his account (see also *Life* 65 (361) and *Apion* 1.9 (47–8), and above, p. 90). *artificially clever accounts*: Josephus in *Apion* 1.10 (53) reacts strongly against critics who suggest that his history is 'a prize competition like those set for school boys'.

2. *hate the Jews*: such hatred is certainly exhibited by the Roman historian Tacitus (*c.* 55–117 AD) in his *Histories*, Book v, though this was not written until the beginning of the second century, long after the composition of the *War* and probably after Josephus' death. Unfortunately, Tacitus' account of the Jewish War does not survive beyond the brief description of Titus' preparations for it (*Histories* v.13), and Tacitus' *Annals* for the years 66–9 are also lost.

3. *I, Josephus*: for his career, see above, pp. 72–6. *for subjects of the Roman Empire*: Josephus says that he originally presented his volumes to Vespasian and Titus and to other Roman participants in the war, and sold other copies to Jews with a Greek education, including King Agrippa II and his brother-in-law Archelaus (*Apion* 1.9 (50)). All these would be able to read and speak Greek. Josephus himself would probably be more fluent in Greek than in Latin, though he tells us that he used literary assistants to polish the prose of the *War* (*Apion* 1.9 (50)). How widely he might have expected his work to be distributed is not clear, but his public readership was almost certainly limited at first to the educated aristocracy of Rome, where professional booksellers (called *librarii*, and later *bibliopolai*) existed from the first century BC. There was no Copyright Act, and, once published, the work could be copied to order. *turning into Greek...my own language*: the first version of *War* was probably a much briefer account written in Josephus' native language, Aramaic, and intended for Aramaic-speaking readers in Parthia, Babylonia, and Arabia, for Jews of Mesopotamia, and for 'our own relatives beyond the Euphrates in Adiabene' (paragraph 6 below). According to *Ant.* XX.2.1 – 4.3 (17–96), the ruling dynasty of Adiabene in northern Mesopotamia east of the River Tigris had recently been converted to Judaism. Josephus says that he wished to inform these peoples about the fate of Jerusalem

and thereby to discourage them from contemplating resistance to the power of Rome (cp. paragraph 6 below, and *War* III.5.8 (108)). Josephus' readership in the East, however, was probably limited to the Jewish community there, who would be able to read his western Aramaic, with which the non-Jewish eastern peoples might have had difficulty. When Josephus turned his narrative into Greek for the benefit of the western world, the motive changed; Josephus wished to correct the distortions of other writers and to improve the mutual relationship and understanding of the Romans and the Jews.

4. *affairs at Rome were in chaos*: Josephus is thinking of the last years of Nero's reign; in AD 61 the Roman settlement of Britain was seriously set back by Boudicca's rebellion; in 64, a fire destroyed or seriously damaged all but four of the fourteen districts of Rome; in 65 the conspiracy led by Gaius Piso reflected the growing disillusionment with Nero; in 68 the Gauls rebelled under Vindex (cp. *War* IV.8.1 (440)), and in 69 the Batavians, a Germanic tribe, under Civilis (Tacitus, *Histories* IV.14ff). In summer 68, Nero died; the following year has become known as 'the year of the four emperors', the last of these being Vespasian, whose success Josephus, fortunately for himself, accurately prophesied (see below, p. 122). But Josephus is in fact finding excuses for Rome; most of these events had little to do with the Jewish revolt. *Jewish revolutionary party*: for Josephus' estimate of their major responsibility for the tragic destruction of Jerusalem, see *War* V.6.1 (248–57) (below, pp. 138–44) and *War* VII.8.1 (252–74).

5. *hoped that all...would join them in revolt*: the Jewish diaspora in the East began with deportations made by the Assyrians (2 Kings 15: 29; 17: 6) and Babylonians (2 Kings 24: 14; 25: 11), and the presence of Jews in the East is evidenced throughout the Persian and hellenistic periods (as can be seen, for example, from a reading of the Old Testament books of Esther, Ezra, and Nehemiah, and the apocryphal book of Tobit). Josephus addressed the first edition of the *War* (see above) partly to these eastern members of the Jewish diaspora. Rome was certainly very conscious of the Parthian presence on the empire's eastern borders; in AD 62 the Roman governor of Cappadocia, Caesennius Paetus, invaded southern Armenia, and was trapped and forced to surrender to the Parthian king, Vologeses. Roman pride was restored by a large show of strength in Armenia in 65, and a compromise whereby the Parthian king came to Rome to receive the crown of Armenia from Nero. (See A. R. C. Leaney, *The Jewish and Christian World 200 BC to AD 200*, pp. 16ff, 97f, for an account of Rome's relationship with Parthia.) One may doubt, however, whether

the Jewish revolutionaries seriously hoped for much support from the East, or the Romans seriously feared that they would lose control there at this period. Josephus is exaggerating the influence of the revolutionaries. *Many were persuaded... to claim sovereign rule*: Josephus has in mind 'the year of the four emperors' (AD 69) when Galba, Otho, Vitellius, and Vespasian in turn seized the principate.

6. *Adiabene*: see paragraph 3 above and *War* v.6.1 (252), p. 139.

7–8. Josephus reveals, as so often, that his sympathies lie with both sides. He makes the strength of the Jewish resistance an indirect compliment to the power of the victorious Roman forces, in opposition to those historians whose belittlement of the Jews is unflattering to Rome.

10. *the Jewish leaders*: Josephus is referring to such men as Eleazar son of Simon, John of Gischala, and Simon son of Gioras. They were the leaders of various revolutionary groups, whose blind nationalism and mutual rivalry were in Josephus' view largely to blame for the fall of Jerusalem (cp. *War* v.1.1–6 (1–46), and below, pp. 129–41). The Greek word for *leaders* (*turannoi*) denotes unconstitutional leaders whose power rested initially on popular support and force of arms and who, once in power, were hard to remove. *Titus Caesar*: after Vespasian's departure for Rome, the siege was concluded by his son Titus, who succeeded Vespasian as emperor (AD 79–81). (See *War* VI.2.4 (124–8); below, pp. 143f.)

12. *no Gentile can be blamed*: Josephus demonstrates his rhetorical skill in this passage. He exculpates the Romans, but balances this by professing that his sympathies lie with his own people. Elsewhere Josephus is ready to admit that the insensitivity and corruption of the later Roman governors of Palestine contributed to the outbreak of war.

HEROD'S GIFTS ABROAD

War I.21.11 (422)   After founding such places, Herod began to show his generosity to a large number of cities outside his kingdom. He had gymnasia built at Tripolis, Damascus, and Ptolemais, a wall at Byblos, halls and porticoes, temples and market-places at Beirut and Tyre, theatres at Sidon and Damascus, an aqueduct for the people at Laodicea-on-sea, and baths and ornate fountains for the population of Ascalon, with colonnades remarkable for their workmanship and size. In other places he dedicated

(423)   groves and meadows. Many cities received in addition land
from him, as though they were partners in his kingdom.
Other cities, like Cos, he endowed with gymnasiarchs,
allocating revenues for an annual appointment in perpe-
(424)   tuity, in order that the honour should never lapse. He
provided a corn supply to all who asked for it. At Rhodes
he offered money repeatedly for shipbuilding, and when
the Pythian temple was burnt down he rebuilt it in grander
(425)   style at his own expense. Surely we need not list his gifts
to the peoples of Lycia or Samos, or his generosity
throughout Ionia wherever individuals required it? Are
not the Athenians, the Spartans, the people of Nicopolis
and Pergamum in Mysia overladen with Herod's gifts? Did
not Herod pave with polished marble the wide street,
twenty stades long (once avoided for its mud), in Syrian
Antioch, and adorn it with a colonnade of equal length
to give shelter from the rain?

12 (426)   These gifts might be said to have been made privately
to successful individual peoples. But the gift to the Eleans
was a gift shared not just with Greece but with the whole
inhabited world, wherever the fame of the Olympian
(427)   Games reaches. For, seeing that these were in decline for
lack of money, and that the one remaining heritage of
ancient Greece was falling into neglect, he not only, *en
route* for Rome, accepted the presidency of the quadrennial
games, but also provided for the continuing remembrance
(428)   of his presidency by permanent financial endowment. It
would be an unending task to catalogue the debts and taxes
that he discharged. For example, he reduced the annual
tribute of the people of Phaselis and Balanaea and the small
cities around Cilicia. But frequently his generosity was
held in check by his fear of exciting envy or appearing to
seek too great advantage in offering more to cities than
their legitimate rulers did.

In the *War*, Josephus clearly approves of Herod the Great, and regards
him (family life apart) as a man blessed with good fortune (*War* 1.33.8

(665)). He begins his account of Herod by describing his suppression of bandits in Galilee (*War* 1.10.5 (204)), and continues with a sympathetic account of Herod's rise to power in which Herod's political acumen and military prowess are prominent and his debt to Rome (in whose Senate Herod was first proclaimed King of Judaea) made clear. This section concludes with a detailed description of Herod's building activities (*War* 1.21.1–12 (401–28)) – the Temple, the Fortress Antonia, Samaria, the temple at Paneion, new buildings at Jericho, the harbour at Caesarea, the rebuilding of Anthedon, the foundation of Antipatris and Phasaelis, the fortresses at Jericho and Herodium. But Josephus underlines that Herod's building-activities and generosity spread far beyond the limits of his kingdom into Syria, Lebanon, the Aegean, Asia Minor, and Greece. A Graeco-Roman reader would note that Herod, at least, made a proper contribution to the city life of the hellenistic world, and that the Jewish people were not, perhaps, as so often alleged, 'haters of mankind' (Tacitus, *Histories* v.5; see below, p. 157). Indeed, Herod's support for the declining Olympian Games was of benefit to the whole inhabited world. Herod thus appears as a typical hellenistic *euergetēs* (benefactor), and as a friend of Rome. Twenty years later, in the *Antiquities*, Josephus is more critical of Herod; he notes that Herod's building of theatres and amphitheatres and the celebration of games were in violation of Jewish Law and custom (*Ant.* xv.8.1–2 (267–79)). He notes also that most of Herod's building-activities were dictated either by the requirements of military security or by his overriding desire of fame: 'Herod yielded to generosity if he saw any hope of future remembrance or present reputation' (*Ant.* xvi.5.4 (153); see also xv.8.5 (292–8)). Perhaps one should add that Herod owed his position to the Romans, and recognised their invincible power and imperial achievement; he wished to belong to the Roman Empire as 'friend and ally'.

(422) *gymnasia* were sports grounds outside the city walls. The main features were a running-track and a *palaistra* (a building equipped for teaching wrestling). Gymnasia were often sited beside a stream and a sacred grove. They were originally designed to teach the young men (*epheboi*) the arts of war, but in hellenistic times their purpose was more generally educational. A gymnasium was founded in Jerusalem 'at the foot of the citadel itself' by Jason the high priest *c.* 175 BC (2 Macc. 4: 12).

Tripolis, on the Lebanese coast, took its name from its three areas separately founded by Aradus, Sidon, and Tyre. In 64 BC Pompey removed its independent ruler and made it part of the Roman province of Syria (*Ant.* xiv.3.2 (39)).

Map 4   The Levant

Damascus was also taken by Pompey in 64 BC. The hellenistic street grid can still be traced on the east side of the old town. 'Straight Street' (Acts 9: 11) forms the main east–west axis of the city. From the first half of the first century AD survives the *peribolos* (precinct wall) round the inner court of the sanctuary of Jupiter.

Ptolemais, modern Akko on the north side of the bay of Haifa, was an important natural harbour in ancient times. It was refounded, and renamed, by Ptolemy II Philadelphus of Egypt in the third century BC, but the hellenistic city has almost entirely disappeared.

Byblos, modern Jebeil, north of Beirut on the Lebanese coast, was inhabited as early as Neolithic times. *Ant.* xv.4.1 (95) suggests that it was one of the coastal cities that Antony gave to Cleopatra. Traces of hellenistic and Roman ramparts, and a Roman temple, basilica, and streets have been found, but which *wall* Herod built is not clear. He probably contributed to the repair of the city wall.

Beirut (ancient Berytus) became a Roman colony in 14 BC. It was much favoured by Herod's family. An inscription of Bernice and Agrippa II (cp. Acts 25: 13) records that 'they raised up the edifice built formerly by their ancestor King Herod, which has fallen to ruin through the ages. It is decorated by them with marbles and six columns.' Josephus records that Agrippa I built there a theatre, amphitheatre, baths and porticoes (*Ant.* XIX.7.5 (335–8)), and that Agrippa II also built a theatre and adorned the city with statues (*Ant.* XX.9.4 (211–13)).

Tyre, 72 kilometres (45 miles) south of Beirut, was famous as a trading-port. Its colourful cosmopolitanism and its threatened destruction are vividly portrayed in Ezek. 26–8. It was besieged unsuccessfully by Nebuchadnezzar and successfully by Alexander the Great, who altered the topography of the island city for all time by developing a causeway for siege purposes. In hellenistic times Tyre had a well-developed southern harbour with a mole 675 metres long and $7\frac{1}{2}$ metres wide ($738\frac{1}{2}$ yards by 8 yards) a paved dry dock, a porticoed street 170 metres long and 11 metres wide (186 yards by 12 yards) columns 7 metres ($7\frac{1}{2}$ yards) high made of stone quarried from Karystos in Euboea (the large island on the east coast of Greece), and a theatre. Jewish affairs seem to have been of importance at Tyre. Julius Caesar offered a bronze tablet to be set up at Tyre (as also at Sidon, Ascalon, and in Rome itself) proclaiming Hyrcanus high priest and ethnarch of Judaea. After Caesar's death, Cassius put a certain Marion in control of Tyre as prince. Marion invaded Galilee, and Herod, in attempting to recover Jewish possessions there, captured some Tyrian soldiers, some of whom he sent home with gifts 'in order to gain from the city goodwill towards himself and ill-feeling towards the tyrant' (*War* I.12.2 (238); cp. *Ant.* XIV.12.1 (298)). Antony sent an edict to Tyre demanding the return of Jewish people and possessions (*Ant.* XIV.12.4–5 (314–22)). Cleopatra coveted Tyre and Sidon, but it seems that Antony was unable to include these in his gift of all the cities between the River Eleutherus and Egypt (*Ant.* XV.4.1 (95)). Jesus visited the region of Tyre (Mark 7: 24); Herod Agrippa I had a dispute with Tyre and Sidon (Acts 12: 20–3). Paul landed at Tyre on his journey to Jerusalem (Acts 21: 3).

Sidon, between Tyre and Beirut, was a Phoenician city known to Homer. It was a commercial city, famous for its purple-dye trade, its glass-making, its bronze work (cp. Homer, *Iliad* XXIII. 740ff), and it seems to have kept a measure of independence under successive empires. A Roman theatre survives, and also the south-east corner of the hellenistic rampart. Paul visited friends here on his voyage to Rome

(Acts 27: 3); from here his ship sailed 'under the lee of Cyprus' (Acts 27: 4) to Myra in Lycia.

Laodicea-on-sea lay on the north Syrian coast and, together with Seleucia, Antioch, and Apamea, was founded by Seleucus I (311–281 BC), who named it (and five other towns) after his mother Laodice. Like other cities on the coast, it had fallen to Pompey. Caesar declared it a free town; after his death Cassius captured it. Herod saw the city when he visited Antony there (*Ant.* XV.3.5 (64–7)). Herod's aqueduct was perhaps a contribution towards the city's restoration. The geographer Strabo (*c.* 64–21 BC) says Laodicea was a well-built town with a flourishing wine-trade (*Geography* XVI.2.9).

Ascalon, once a Philistine city, became autonomous in the hellenistic period, and was careful to maintain good relationships with the expanding Jewish state (1 Macc. 10: 86; 11: 60). In 104 BC it was granted the status of a free city, and minted its own silver coinage. Herod's outstanding generosity to Ascalon may have been due to the fact that Ascalon was his birthplace. After Herod's death, his daughter Salome was given the palace there by the Emperor Augustus (*Ant.* XVII.11.5 (321)). At the beginning of the Jewish war with Rome, the Jews attacked Ascalon and other towns in retaliation for an anti-Jewish pogrom in Caesarea (*War* II.18.1 (457–60)), and the result was the further massacre of 2500 Jews at Ascalon and 2000 at Ptolemais. Josephus may be anxious to indicate that previous relationships between Jews and Ascalon had been good.

groves: it was commonly believed in the Mediterranean world that such places were inhabited by deities, or that their powers (*numina*) could be perceived there.

(423) *Cos* is an Aegean island of the southern Sporades group (see Map 1), at this period a *civitas libera* (a state with some autonomy) in the Roman province of Asia. It was famous as the home of the physician Hippocrates (469–399 BC) and for its temple dedicated to the god of healing, Asclepius. There are many remains of the hellenistic city, including a second-century BC gymnasium, probably the one for whose care Herod provided. Euarestos of Cos was a friend of Herod's son Alexander, and on a visit to Judaea gave evidence on his behalf, but was unable to save him from execution (*War* 1.26.5 (532f)). Herodian contact with Cos was maintained by Herod's son the Tetrarch Antipas (4 BC – AD 39) to whom as friend and guest a Coan called Philon dedicated a monument.

(424) *Rhodes*, a large island off the south-west coast of Turkey (see Map 1), is mentioned in the Homeric Catalogue of Ships (*Iliad* II.653ff)

as having sent nine ships to the siege of Troy. It was famous for its navy, and in the hellenistic period was a prosperous, powerful, and independent state at the centre of the Mediterranean corn- and wine-trade. It was also an important cultural and educational centre, Cicero, for example, having attended the school of Posidonius there in 78 BC. The city had been laid out on the grid pattern, reputedly by Hippodamus of Miletus in 408 BC, but it is not certain that he was still alive at that time. South of the city was the sacred enclosure of the Pythian Apollo (so named because he killed the dragon, Python, that guarded Delphi). Herod visited Rhodes after nearly being shipwrecked on his journey to Rome in 40 BC to seek support for his throne, and had a trireme built for himself to enable him to complete the journey (*War* I.14.3 (280)); his later contributions to shipbuilding there would be an appropriate act of gratitude.

(425) *Lycia* was the south-western region of modern Turkey. In the hellenistic period, it was ruled in succession by the Ptolemies, the Seleucid Antiochus III, and the Rhodians. From 169 BC – AD 43 it was a more or less autonomous confederation of cities, until under Claudius it was united with Pamphylia into a Roman province.

Samos is an island just off the west coast of Turkey. It flourished briefly in the sixth century BC. Its large new temple in honour of the goddess Hera was destroyed *c.* 530 BC; the even larger replacement was under construction until Roman times but never completed. In the hellenistic period Samos was comparatively unimportant; it became part of the Roman province of Asia in 129 BC.

Ionia was the name given to the central western coast of modern Turkey and the adjacent islands, originally settled by the Ionians. This name became in Hebrew *Javan*, which was used by Old Testament writers as a general term for the Greeks. The Ionian Greeks were credited with the development of the practice of colonisation, and with many intellectual achievements.

Athenians: the political glory of Athens lay in the past when Josephus wrote, and under the early Roman Empire Athens was little more than a university town. The account in Acts 17 of Paul's visit is well known. Herod's contribution to Athens is not known, but in his lifetime there were several important attempts to refurbish Athens after the destruction by Sulla in 86 BC. Andronicus of Kyrrhus in Syria built an octagonal water-clock tower; Julius Caesar and Augustus funded a portico to the Roman forum; the Athenians erected a monument to Augustus' right-hand man and son-in-law Marcus Vipsanius Agrippa for his benefactions to the city.

Spartans: again, what Herod built in Sparta we do not know. But since at least the early second century BC there had been current the diplomatic fiction that the Spartans and the Jews 'are kinsmen, descended alike from Abraham' (1 Macc. 12: 21; cp. 2 Macc. 5: 9). The ousted high priest Jason exiled himself to Sparta (2 Macc. 5: 9); his successor bore the Greek name Menelaus, which had been the name of the Spartan king who was the husband of Helen of Troy. According to 1 Macc. 14: 16, 20–3, when Simon became high priest in 142 BC an alliance was made between the Jews and Sparta (though there are some difficulties with this; see *The First and Second Books of the Maccabees*, CBC, pp. 191f). This Jewish claim of kinship with the Spartans may be compared with other similar claims in Jewish hellenistic writings: thus Josephus quotes, from Alexander Polyhistor, a writer with the Greek name Cleodemus and the Semitic name Malchus, who says that the Greek god Heracles married a granddaughter of Abraham (*Ant.* 1.15.1 (240–1)). In *Ant.* XIV.10.22 (247–55) Josephus quotes an alleged decree of Pergamum from the later second century BC, which notes that in Abraham's time the Pergamene ancestors and the Hebrews were friends. These attempts to link the hitherto virtually unknown Jews with Greek history and chronology were the inevitable result of the increasing contact of Jew and Greek in the hellenistic world. Josephus is trying to demonstrate to his non-Jewish readers that the Jews were not so strange a people as they believed.

Nicopolis, 'victory city', on the coast of Epirus in Greece, was founded by Augustus on the site of his army's camp after the battle of Actium (31 BC). According to Strabo (VII.7.6), Nicopolis had a sanctuary of Apollo with a sacred grove, a stadium, and a gymnasium. Paul, spending the winter at Nicopolis, asked Titus to join him there (Tit. 3: 12).

Pergamum in Mysia, 110 kilometres (68 miles) north of modern Izmir, was the capital of an important hellenistic kingdom until, in 133 BC, it was bequeathed by King Attalus III to Rome and incorporated into the province of Asia. It was well endowed with streets and buildings in the best hellenistic style, laid out along the slopes of a high hill. It had an important library, which Antony removed to Alexandria. Pergamum has been described as the most perfectly preserved dynastic capital of Alexander's empire. For an early Christian assessment of Pergamum, see Rev. 2: 12–17.

Syrian Antioch was founded with its port Seleucia by Seleucus I in 300 BC to control the major routes from Syria to the west through Turkey, to the River Euphrates in the east, and to Palestine in the south.

From early on, it had a large Jewish population; later, it was to be an important starting-point for Paul's travels, to invent a name for the members of the new Jewish sect that followed Jesus Christ (cp. Acts 11: 26), and to become a leading centre of this Christianity. It suffered frequently from two forms of disturbance – earthquakes and riots. The axis of the hellenistic city was a great paved and porticoed *wide street* running 15 stades (that is, 2·75 kilometres, or nearly 2 miles) from the Daphne gate in the south to the Aleppo gate on the north side. (Josephus exaggerates its length.) Under the Emperor Augustus, a new building-programme was begun, which transformed the city into a capital worthy of such an important Roman province. An important contribution was the repaving of the street with *marble* by Herod (cp. also *Ant.* XVI.5.3 (148)), and the provision of roofed colonnades on either side (attributed by the sixth-century Antiochene historian Malalas to the Emperor Tiberius, who did much else to beautify the city and was rewarded by having a bronze statue of himself erected at the centre of the city where the main street changes course by a few degrees). The street was 9·4 metres (31 feet) wide, and each of the colonnades was 9·7 metres (32 feet) wide. The *mud* was washed down each year by the winter rains from Mount Silpius on the slopes of which the city was built.

(426) Elis, famous for its horses, lay in the north-western Peloponnese. From about 570 BC the *Eleans* were responsible for the management of the Olympian games at Olympia. According to tradition, the games were founded in 776 BC, and they were held every fourth year until the late third or fourth century AD. They were finally made impossible by Theodosius I's edict in AD 393 that all pagan shrines should be abolished. The games were held in honour of Zeus at his sanctuary by the River Alpheus; Zeus was thought to watch the games from the wooded, conical hill of Kronos overlooking Olympia. By the hellenistic period, the buildings at Olympia included a temple of Zeus and a temple of his consort Hera, the treasuries belonging to the various Greek states, the Philippeum built by Philip II of Macedon, the *palaistra*, a stadium, a hostel, the hippodrome, various guest houses, a council chamber, a magistrate's house, and bath houses. The games took five days. They opened on the first day with sacrifices and oath-taking; on the second day came the chariot, horse, and pentathlon contests. On the third day the boys competed, and on the fourth the men, in foot-races, jumping, wrestling, boxing, and the *pankration* (literally, 'all-in combat'), a kind of wrestling-match with no holds barred. On the last day there were final sacrifices and a banquet.

(427) *en route for Rome*: perhaps in 12 BC, when Herod sought Augustus' help in settling a quarrel with his sons. *Phaselis* was a port on the coast of Lycia known for its pirates; *Balanaea* is modern Baniyas on the Syrian coast between Tripoli and Latakia.

After a famous digression on the three forms of Jewish philosophy, the Pharisees, the Sadducees, and the Essenes (on the latter, see M. A. Knibb, *The Qumran Community*, the second volume in this series), Josephus resumes his account of the political history of first-century Palestine, beginning with the death of Augustus and the accession of Tiberius in AD 14. Josephus, for all his pro-Roman attitude, does not hesitate to show that Roman maladministration was at least partly to blame for the war.

PONTIUS PILATE

War II.9.2. (169) When Pilate was sent by Tiberius to Judaea as prefect, he brought into Jerusalem under cover of night the
(170) images of Caesar called standards. This act caused great consternation among the Jews when daylight came. The residents were dismayed at the sight, feeling that their laws (which forbid the erection of any image in the city) had been trampled upon, and in response to their indignation there
(171) was a mass gathering of the country people. They hastened to Pilate at Caesarea, and begged him to withdraw the standards from Judaea and uphold their ancestral laws. Pilate refused; and the Jews, falling headlong to the ground round Pilate's house, stayed there without moving for five days and nights.

3 (172) The next day Pilate took his seat on the magistrate's dais in the large stadium. He summoned the crowd, as if wishing to give an answer to their request, and then gave an arranged signal to his soldiers to surround the Jews with their
(173) weapons. At the unexpected sight of the three ranks of surrounding troops, the Jews stood in silent shock. Pilate threatened to mow them down unless they accepted Caesar's images, and nodded to the soldiers to bare their
(174) swords. The Jews as one man fell to the ground, and extending their necks cried out that they were ready to offer

themselves to death rather than break the Law. Pilate, utterly astonished at their absolute religious devotion, ordered the standards to be removed from Jerusalem immediately.

In this section, beginning with Pilate, Josephus gives a long catalogue of Roman insensitivity and brutality towards the Jewish people. The emperor Gaius Caligula's attempt to introduce a statue of himself into the Jerusalem Temple is balanced by the patience and understanding shown by his general, Petronius, who nearly paid for his diplomacy with his life. Ventidius Cumanus, Felix, and Festus appear as incapable. Of Albinus, Josephus says, 'There was no kind of villainy that he failed to practise' (*War* II.14.1 (272)), and his successor Gessius Florus made Albinus 'seem by comparison the best of men' (*War* II.14.2 (277)).

(169) *Pilate* governed Judaea from AD 26 to 36 or 37. According to Philo, he was stubborn and cruel, with a record of ruthless and violent behaviour in office (*Legatio ad Gajum* 301–2). Apart from the incident described here, Josephus records of him that he illegally used Temple revenue to finance an aqueduct for Jerusalem, and put down the resulting demonstration with brutality. Luke 13:1 refers to Galilaeans 'whose blood Pilate had mixed with their sacrifices' on some unknown occasion. Philo describes (*Leg Gaj* 299–305) how Pilate fixed gilded shields bearing the names of Pilate and Tiberius (the latter probably described as 'son of the divine Augustus', which is what would have enraged the Jews) to his headquarters at Herod's palace in Jerusalem. The Jews apparently took advantage of Pilate's already precarious standing with Tiberius to appeal to the emperor, who ordered Pilate to remove the shields to Caesarea, where Pilate subsequently dedicated a building to Tiberius. The dedication inscription came to light in 1961, and reveals that Pilate's official title was *praefectus* (*prefect*) of Judaea. Pilate's drastic treatment of an assembly of Samaritans at Mount Gerizim (*Ant.* XVIII.4.1 (85–7)), whose intentions were probably less militant than Pilate feared, led to his recall in the winter of 36–7.

It has been suggested that Pilate's various acts of provocation towards the Jews were connected with the anti-Jewish feeling of his patron in Rome, Sejanus, who was the commander of the Praetorian Guard and Tiberius' right-hand man, and that after Sejanus' fall from grace in AD 31 Pilate's position was weaker, as is shown by the pressure put on him by the Jews to crucify Jesus and to have the shields removed from Jerusalem.

under cover of night: Josephus suggests that Pilate was aware of the trouble his action might cause. *the images of Caesar called standards*: the account in *Ant.* XVIII.3.1 (55–9) speaks of busts, or embossed figures, of Caesar that were attached to the standards. Standards (*signa*) were basically spears decorated with crossbars, ribbons, and discs (*phalerae*), and a plate naming the unit to which the standards belonged. A point on the bottom of the shaft allowed them to be fixed into the ground. In camp they were kept, along with statues of the gods or the emperor, in a chapel under the care of the leading cohort. They were anointed on feast-days, and after a victory they could be offered sacrifice, and they could be grasped by men seeking sanctuary. They were honoured because they embodied the strength or fortune of their unit or maniple (120–200 men, commanded by a centurion). Pilate's troops would not be Roman legionaries, but auxiliary troops raised mostly from the gentile population of the coastal or hellenistic towns of Syria and Palestine. (Later we hear of the 'Italian Cohort' (Acts 10: 1) and the 'Augustan Cohort' (Acts 27: 1) quartered at Caesarea.) Probably one cohort (between 500 and 1000 men) was regularly on duty at Jerusalem, and the trouble on this occasion perhaps arose because Pilate departed from the tactful procedure of his predecessors by allocating to Jerusalem a cohort whose standards were distinguished by likenesses or medallions (*imagines*) of the emperor, perhaps awarded to the cohort as medals for special valour or merit.

(170) *their laws (which forbid the erection of any image...)*: more accurately, *Ant.* XVIII.3.1 (55) states that 'our Law forbids the making of images' (cp. Exod. 20: 4; Deut. 4: 15–18; 5: 8). The Jewish objection to the standards was probably simply that they contravened the second commandment by bringing a carved image or likeness into Jerusalem, and perhaps also that their presence in the Antonia would pollute the high priests' robes, which were kept there. The fact that they were venerated as *numina* and given their own shrine by the Roman army probably added to their objectionable nature.

(171) *Caesarea* was built by Herod in honour of Augustus Caesar near the older site of Strato's Tower between 22 and 10 BC. It was the seat of Roman government in Judaea. Vespasian was proclaimed emperor there. The new city had at its centre a temple of Augustus and Rome, built on a large podium. West of this was the artificially excavated harbour, with its two breakwaters. To the south of it lay a Roman theatre, the first of its kind in Palestine, and to the north an arched aqueduct brought water from Mount Carmel 12 kilometres (7½ miles) away. Other important amenities included the forum, hippodrome, and amphitheatre. Herod 'rebuilt the whole city with

white stone and adorned it with the most splendid palaces. Here above all Herod revealed his natural ability to plan on the grand scale' (*War* 1.21.5 (408)). His masterpiece was the harbour, the massive breakwaters of which, and the outer and inner basins, have been revealed by recent excavations both on land and under water. (For Josephus' full description, see *War* 1.21.6–7 (411–14).) *begged him to withdraw the standards*: in *Ant.* XVIII.3.1 (57) Pilate refuses, on the grounds that this would be to insult the emperor. This appears to be an excuse. Similarly, Pilate was later forced to withdraw the shields from his headquarters in Jerusalem because when challenged he could not show authorisation from Caesar (Philo, *Leg Gaj* 299–305).

(172) *on the magistrate's dais*: the Greek word is *bēma*, as in John 19: 13. *in the large stadium*: the stadium was the running-track about 183 metres (200 yards) long and 27 metres (30 yards) wide, with an embankment, natural or built up on arches, on either side for the spectators. A possibly Herodian stadium has been excavated 500 metres (about 550 yards) east of the temple.

(174) *ready to offer themselves to death*: compare the declaration of the spokesman of the seven brothers in 2 Macc. 7: 2. Philo notes that the Jewish readiness to accept death rather than allow the suppression of their traditions caused Rome to suspect them of intending opposition (*Leg Gaj* 117).

The sequence of Roman misrule illustrated by Josephus reached a climax in Gessius Florus' removal of 17 talents from the Temple treasury, 'as if he had contracted to fan the flames of war' (*War* II.14.6 (293)). This led to the escalation of crowd violence and military retaliation. Bernice, sister of Agrippa II (cp. Acts 25: 13), tried to intercede with Florus, the high priest tried to calm the people, and Florus, Bernice, and the Jewish magistrates all appealed to Cestius Gallus, Roman governor of Syria. He sent an army officer called Neapolitanus on a fact-finding mission to Jerusalem. At the same time, Agrippa II, son of Agrippa I and King of Chalcis, arrived from Alexandria, and tried to persuade the Jews to avoid the fearsome consequences of war with Rome.

A WARNING FROM AGRIPPA

War II.16.4 (358)   'Take the Athenians: for the sake of Greek freedom, they once handed over their city to be burnt. When the proud Xerxes sailed across the land and crossed the sea on foot – yielding nothing to the waves, and leading an army column wider than Europe – they chased him away on a single ship like a runaway slave. They broke the might of Asia round the small island of Salamis. And now they serve the Romans, and the city that once ruled Greece is administered by decrees

(359) from Italy. Consider the Spartans; after their victories at Thermopylae and Plataea, and their Agesilaus, who ventured

(360) deep into Asia, they are happy with the same masters. The Macedonians still idealise Philip and look to Fortune, who with Alexander planted the seeds of their world empire; but they accept the same dramatic change of Fortune, and honour those to whose side Fortune has now crossed.

(361)   Thousands of other peoples, even prouder of their liberty, have yielded. Are you the only people who think it wrong to serve those to whom everything is subject? On what army, on what armour do you rely? Where have you ships to quarter the Roman seas? Where have you financial resources to meet

(362) a war effort? Surely you do not imagine that you are going to war against Egyptians and Arabs? Will you not take careful note of the Roman leadership, or assess your own weakness? Have not our own forces frequently been defeated by neighbouring nations, while theirs remain undefeated in the world?

(363) But they have aimed at more than that. They have not been satisfied with the Euphrates as their boundary in the east, or with the Danube in the north, or with the furthest explored deserts of Libya in the south, or Cadiz in the west. They have sought another world beyond the oceans, and carried their weapons as far as the British, a people not previously known

(364) to historians. Well, then, are you richer than the Gauls, stronger than the Germans, sharper-witted than the Greeks, more numerous than all the world's inhabitants? What is it that gives you confidence to oppose the Romans?'

The speech that Josephus puts into Agrippa's mouth is no doubt largely Josephus' own invention, reflecting Josephus' attitude to the war as much as Agrippa's, though it must be noted that Josephus claimed that the accuracy of his account of the war was vouched for personally by

Agrippa in a private letter to Josephus (*Life* 65 (364), *Apion* 1.9 (51–2)). The argument of the speech is as follows:

(1) The present procurator will not be here for ever. Have patience! It is absurd to go to war with Rome for one man's misdemeanours.

(2) It is too late now to demand liberty: the time to keep the Romans out was when Pompey came (63 BC).

(3) Other great nations have accepted servitude in time of necessity.

(4) Face the facts! Where will you find the resources for a war against Rome?

(5) Other great peoples might rebel with more reason, yet they have accepted their present position, and Rome has no difficulty in keeping them under control.

(6) Whom will you find as your ally – God? But God is on the Roman side.

(7) Failure in the proposed war will mean disaster, not only to Jerusalem, but also to Jews abroad.

The text and commentary here given are of the third and fourth sections of the speech.

(358) *Athenians:* during the second Persian invasion of Greece (480–479 BC) the Athenians evacuated Athens. The small garrison left on the Acropolis was killed, and the temple of Athene burnt. *Xerxes* (Ahasuerus in Ezra 4: 6) succeeded Darius I on the Persian throne. He set out in 481 BC to avenge the Persian defeat at Marathon in 490 BC, and *crossed the sea* (the Hellespont) *on foot* by means of a bridge of boats (Herodotus, *Histories* VII.33–7). *on a single ship like a runaway slave*: the return of the defeated and humiliated Xerxes to Persia offered great scope to the Greek historians for exaggerated disasters. *Salamis* is an island off the coast of Attica just west of the Peiraeus. The Greek leader Themistocles trapped the Persian fleet at the entrance to the straits between Salamis and the mainland and destroyed half of it while Xerxes watched from an overlooking hill. The remains of the Persian fleet retreated home, leaving the army unsupported in Greece, to be defeated at Plataea the following year. (See Map 1.) *they serve the Romans:* Rome conquered Greece in 146 BC. *The city that once ruled Greece* is Athens.

(359) *Spartans*: in classical times Sparta's militaristic constitution, credited to the lawgiver Lycurgus (*Apion* II.15 (154), 31 (255)), and her battle honours gave her a formidable reputation. In 480 BC the Spartan King Leonidas won immortality for himself and his 300 men by holding the pass at Thermopylae against Xerxes' Persian army until a Greek traitor led the Persians through the hills to attack the Spartan rear. All but one of the Spartan contingent was killed. A famous couplet by Simonides (*Anth. Graec.* VII.249) commemorated the event:

> Go, tell the Spartans, thou that passest by,
> That here obedient to their laws we lie.

In the following year the Spartan general Pausanias and his troops played a vital part in the battle of Plataea; the Persian general Mardonius was killed, and the Persian army began its retreat home. *Agesilaus* was one of the more attractive Spartan leaders, and one of the few to be successful abroad. The Peloponnesian War between Athens and Sparta and their respective allies ended in Spartan victory (404 BC), and, for a time, Sparta, led by Agesilaus (444–360 BC), indulged in unusually adventurous operations against the Persians in Asia Minor. But the Spartan fleet was destroyed in a sea battle at Cnidus by the Athenian Conon and the Persian satrap Pharnabazus in 394 BC, and the Spartans withdrew from the Aegean to consolidate their position in central Greece. They came under Roman control in the second century BC, when Sparta was incorporated as a *civitas foederata* (confederate state) into the province of Achaea. Under Roman rule Sparta prospered.

(360) *Macedonians*: Macedonia was a large, mountainous country in north–central Greece, rich in timber and silver. Her power was first felt under Philip II (359–336 BC), who became master of all Greece in 338 BC, when he defeated the Athenians and the Thebans at the battle of Chaeronea. He was assassinated in 336 BC while preparing to lead a Greek force against the Persian empire, a project completed by his son Alexander the Great. Macedon became a Roman province in 146 BC. From 27 BC it was a Senatorial province, from AD 15–44 it was governed by an imperial legate, but after AD 44 it became once again a Senatorial province. The provincial capital was Thessalonica, where Paul met opposition from the Jewish population (cp. Acts 17: 1–15).

(361) *army...ships*: the Jews had no standing army or fleet. For Rome, however, Augustus had organised an army of 28 legions of Roman citizens who served for 20 years, together with auxiliary (non-citizen) troops who served for 25 years. Of these, 3 legions were destroyed in Germany in AD 9, while 2 new legions were raised under the Emperor Gaius or Claudius, and perhaps 3 more under Nero or Vespasian. Not all these, of course, were available for service in Judaea. Vespasian brought 2 legions (the Fifth and the Tenth), and Titus brought the Fifteenth. These, with an extra 23 cohorts of infantry and 6 squadrons of cavalry and other local auxiliaries gave a total, according to Josephus (*War* III.4.2 (64–9)) of some 60,000 troops. Less is known of the Roman fleet. At the battle of Actium in 31 BC Octavian and Antony had 900 ships between them. After the battle Augustus organised a regular navy based on the Italian ports of Misenum and Ravenna. Tacitus notes that there were allied triremes stationed at

suitable points through the Mediterranean, but that they were moved to meet the needs of the moment (*Annals* IV.5).

War III.5.1 (70)   One can only admire the practical foresight of the Romans in this aspect of military service, that is, in the way they prepare their household servants not only for the daily

(71)   duties of life but also for war service. Anyone who examines the general organisation of their army will realise that their enormous empire is held not as the gift of Fortune but as the

(72)   reward of bravery. For their weapon training does not begin when war breaks out, nor do they sit idle in peace-time, stirring themselves to action only when need arises. Like men born to fighting, they neither take time off training nor

(73)   passively await their opportunities. Their exercises lack nothing of the rigours of real battle; every day each private

(74)   shows as much energy in training as he would in battle. Thus they make light work of actual fighting. Their accustomed battle order is not put in disarray by confusion; they are not panicked by fear or exhausted by struggle. Victory is always certain, because they fight against opponents who cannot

(75)   equal them. One might accurately call their manoeuvres

(76)   bloodless battles, and their battle bloody manoeuvres. For they are never easily surprised by the enemy. Whatever enemy country they invade, they never join battle until they have

(77)   fortified their camp. In establishing this, they avoid unconsidered or uneven construction, and they avoid massed and undisciplined labour. If the ground happens to be uneven, they level it, and measure out the camp site as a rectangle.

(78)   A gang of engineers accompanies the army, complete with tools for construction.

2 (79)   They divide up the interior of the camp for rows of barracks. Externally, the surround looks like a wall, equipped

(80)   with regularly distanced towers. On the parapet between the towers they set quick-firers, catapults, and stone-throwers,

(81)   and every sort of artillery piece, all ready for firing. Four gates
         are built, one on each side of the perimeter wall, suitable for
         the entry of baggage animals and wide enough for armed
(82)   sorties when required. Inside, the camp is systematically
         divided by streets. They put the officers' quarters in the centre,
         and in the middle of them the military headquarters, a
(83)   building like a small temple. A city appears in a flash, with
         market-place, craftsmen's quarter, and seats where the officers
(84)   might judge occasional disputes. The number and skill of the
         workmen means that the enclosure wall and everything inside
         it are built faster than one could imagine. If necessary, the
         camp is further encircled by an outer ditch, four cubits deep
         and four cubits wide.

The passage in which Josephus describes the organisation and training
of the Roman army may have been inspired by a similar passage from
the second-century BC historian Polybius (*Histories* VI.6 (19–42)).
Polybius describes the arming of the troops, the formation of the camp,
various camp duties, rewards and punishments, army pay, and breaking
camp. Josephus here describes the soldiers' training, the construction
of the camps, the daily routines and marching-orders, equipment,
cavalry, and the planning and discipline of the army, with the particular
intention 'not so much of glorifying the Romans as of consoling their
victims and deterring the rebellious' (*War* III.5.8 (108)).

(70) *One can only admire...*: in this section Josephus indulges in a
certain amount of rhetoric and gives us very little detailed information
about the training of Roman soldiers. He is much more informative
about the organisation of the camps or forts.

(76) *until they have fortified their camp*: Josephus here appears to be
referring to the semi-permanent camps constructed on campaign rather
than to the more permanent forts built to house a unit, or the large
fortresses built to house the legion's headquarters.

(77) *In establishing this*: Polybius (VI.6 (42)) contrasts Greek and
Roman practice. The Greeks fit their camps to the natural lie of the
land, because they wish to avoid the hard work of digging entrench-
ments, and because they value natural defences more highly than
artificial ones. There is a theoretical description of Roman camp-
construction in a handbook *On camp defences* from the second or third
century AD, doubtfully attributed to Hyginus Gromaticus. The

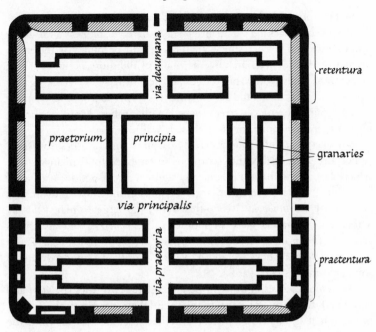

Plan 1 A typical Roman fort

surveyors first select a clear, level site, mark out the site for the
praetorium (the commanding officer's living-quarters) and the *principia*
(headquarters). The *principia* face the enemy, and in front of this
building runs the *via principalis*, the main thoroughfare of the camp,
with the *via praetoria* meeting it at right angles from the front and the
via decumana from behind. Behind the *principia* are the rear lines of
barracks (*retentura*), and in front, on either side of the *via praetoria*, are
the front lines of barracks (*praetentura*). Close beside the headquarters
are the granaries (*horrea*) where the camp's food is stored. These are
carefully built, with raised floors and watertight roofs, to keep out the
damp. The whole forms a square or a rectangle, with gateways in the
middle of each side, and with V-shaped ditches around, about $1\frac{1}{2}$ metres
broad and 1 metre deep (about 5 feet by 3 feet), the outer face being
as vertical as possible, to make it hard for attackers to climb out once
they have jumped in. Inside the ditch is a rampart nearly 2 metres
($6\frac{1}{2}$ feet) high, with wooden breastworks on top. The remains of the
camps set up by the Roman army at the foot of Masada in AD 73 are
still visible.

(79) *barracks*: the Greek word may be used of tents or of more

permanent huts. Leather tents were used in temporary camps built for overnight bivouacking or a brief stay; barrack blocks with stone foundations and timber superstructures would be built for the more permanent forts. *towers* are also the mark of the more permanent fort or fortress, and would be found at the corners and flanking the gateways. The walls would be 3 to 5 metres thick (10 to 16½ feet), made of laid courses of turves strengthened with timber. More important forts might have stone, or stone-based, walls.

(80) *every sort of artillery piece*: Josephus distinguishes *oxubeleis*, 'quick-firers', probably the 'scorpions' mentioned by Roman writers, which shot arrows by a mechanically tightened bow action; *katapeltai*, 'catapults', which were either larger versions of the *oxubeleis* or smaller versions of the *lithobola*, 'stone-throwers', the large Roman *ballistae*. These large catapults were sometimes called *onagri* ('wild asses') on account of their kick. According to *War* v.6.3 (269) those of the Tenth Legion could hurl rocks weighing over 25 kilos (half a hundredweight) some 400 metres (437 yards).

(83) *officers*: this single word here translates two titles (*lochagoi* and *taxiarchoi*) that are not easy to place in their precise rank. In this paragraph it is not entirely clear whether Josephus has in mind the smaller temporary camp erected by the army on the march or on campaign, or the larger, legionary fortress. The walls and towers, and the comparison with a city, suggest the latter, in which case the commanding officer would be the legionary commander, *legatus legionis*. Below him in descending scale of authority would come the senior tribune, the *praefectus castrorum* (an ex-centurion senior quarter-master), six military tribunes (young officers learning their profession), and sixty centurions of varying seniority, one for each of the centuries of the ten cohorts that made up the legion. Each century would be divided into ten watches of eight men (*contuberniae*). In addition there would be various orderlies, clerks, surveyors, engineers, armourers, doctors, and chaplains. A legion would also have auxiliary troops drawn from the local or not too distant native population, consisting of cavalry, infantry cohorts, and a mixed unit of infantry and horsemen, the *cohortes equitatae*.

Which officers Josephus means, therefore, by his *lochagoi* and *taxiarchoi* is not clear. The former could be the centurions, and the latter the superior officers, the tribunes, though the Greek words more commonly used for these two ranks are *hekatontarchai* and *chiliarchoi*, as in Josephus' very next paragraph (*War* III.5.3 (87)).

For a splendid picture of the Roman army in marching order, the reader should see *War* III.6.2 (115–26).

(84) *four cubits*: i.e. approximately 2 metres or 6½ feet.

The following chapters contain an exciting account of Josephus' defence of the Galilaean town of Jotapata against Vespasian's siege. When the town was captured, Josephus hid in a cave with some forty others. His position was revealed by a captured woman, and Vespasian urged him to come out, wishing to capture the Jewish leader alive. Josephus was prepared to surrender, but his companions threatened to prevent this by killing him. Josephus tried to reason with them, but was eventually forced to take the risk of proposing that they all drew lots to decide in which order they should kill each other. They agreed, 'for they thought death with Josephus sweeter than life. But Josephus – should we say by Fortune or by divine providence? – was left at the end with one other…and he persuaded him also to stay alive.'

JOSEPHUS PROPHESIES BEFORE VESPASIAN

War III.8.8 (392) In this manner, then, Josephus survived both the war with the Romans and the war with men of his own
(393) side, and he was taken to Vespasian by Nicanor. The Romans all rushed to see him, and as the crowd pressed round the general there was a confused uproar, some rejoicing at the prisoner's capture, some threatening him,
(394) others nearby pushing to see him. Those further off shouted that the enemy should be punished, but those standing close were affected by the memory of his exploits and amazement
(395) at his change of fortune. Officers previously enraged with
(396) him now without exception forgave him on sight. Titus especially was particularly taken by Josephus' courage in misfortune, and by pity for his youth. Recalling the man's previous fighting spirit, and observing his present captivity among his enemies, he was moved to reflect upon the power of Fortune and the knife-edge balance of war and the
(397) insecurity of human affairs. So he persuaded many Romans to share his sympathy for Josephus, and it was mainly his

doing that Josephus had the good fortune to be preserved
(398)   from death at Vespasian's hands. Vespasian ordered him to
be held in secure custody until he could send him to Nero.

9 (399)   Hearing this, Josephus said that he wished to speak to
Vespasian in private. When Vespasian had dismissed all the
others apart from Titus and two friends, Josephus said:
(400)   'Vespasian, you think that the captured Josephus is a mere
prisoner; but I am here to announce to you much more
important things. I know the Jewish Law, and how a general
(401)   ought to die; but I have been sent by God. Are you sending
me to Nero? Why? Will Nero and those who succeed
him – and precede you – remain in power? You are Caesar
(402)   and Imperator, Vespasian, you and your son here. But now
imprison me more securely, and keep me for yourself; for
you control not just me, Caesar, but the earth, the sea, the
whole human race. Meanwhile, I ask for the penalty of even
(403)   closer confinement if I am taking God's name in vain.' At
the time, Vespasian apparently did not take Josephus' words
very seriously, supposing that he was demonstrating his
(404)   readiness to do anything to save his life. But gradually he
was brought round to believe in them, for God was already
stirring in him hopes of empire and giving him advance
(405)   notice of his future rule by other signs. Vespasian observed
also that Josephus had been accurate in other predictions.
One of the two advisers present at this confidential meeting
commented that if Josephus' prophecy were not just a piece
of trumpery aimed at averting the retribution coming upon
him, it was surprising that Josephus had not prophesied to
the citizens of Jotapata its impending fall, or, indeed, his own
(406)   personal capture. Josephus answered that he had in fact
forewarned the people of Jotapata that their city would fall
after forty-seven days, and that he would be taken captive
(407)   by the Romans. When Vespasian had verified these statements by private inquiries among the prisoners, he began
(408)   to believe the prediction about himself. The result was that,

though he did not release Josephus from prison and chains,
he gave him clothing and other gifts, and he continued to
treat him in the main with kindness and respect, being
supported in this policy by Titus.

Josephus presents himself by turns as a soldier respected for his exploits
and pitied for his misfortunes, but also as a prophet sent by God to
predict Vespasian's elevation to the principate. Josephus sees no
incompatibility between his Judaism and his support for Rome (because
God is on Rome's side), and in the cave he prayed:

'Since you who created the Jewish people are now pleased to break
them, and since all good fortune has passed over to the Roman
side, and since you have chosen my mind to declare what is to
come, I readily hand myself over to the Romans and live, calling
you to witness that I go not as a traitor but as your servant.'

(*War* iii.8.3 (354))

(392) *survived both the war with the Romans...*: i.e., the Galilaean
campaign and the siege of Jotapata, *and the war with men of his own side*:
i.e., the intrigues with John of Gischala and other opponents in Galilee
(*War* ii.21.1–7 (585–631)), and the events in the cave.

Vespasian (Titus Flavius Vespasianus) was born in AD 9, the son of
a tax-gatherer. He commanded the Second Legion in the Roman
invasion of Britain in AD 43, became consul AD 51, and proconsul of
Africa AD 63. In AD 66 he accompanied Nero to Greece, and the next
year was appointed to suppress the Jewish rebellion. In July 69 he was
proclaimed emperor, first by the two legions in Egypt and then by the
legions in Judaea and Syria. He held up the Roman cornships at
Alexandria while his armies marched to Italy, and in December AD 69
the Senate adopted him as emperor. In an industrious and successful
principate (69–79) he restored the Capitol, built the Forum and the
Temple of Peace, and began the Colosseum, increased the army in the
east, and strengthened the Roman frontiers in Britain and Germany.
His last words were ironic: 'Alas, I think I am becoming a god.'

Nicanor (cp. *War* iii.8.2 (346)) was a Roman military tribune
(*chiliarchos*) and friend of the Roman general Titus, son and successor
of the Emperor Vespasian. Nicanor was later wounded when he
accompanied Josephus to discuss peace-terms with defenders on the
Jerusalem wall (*War* v.6.2 (261)).

(396) *Titus* Flavius Vespasianus was Vespasian's elder son, born 30

September AD 39. He served in Germany and Britain, and commanded the Fifteenth Legion in Judaea but took over the direction of the whole campaign when Vespasian went to Rome as emperor. He took Jerusalem in August AD 70, and was voted his own Triumph by the Roman Senate but in fact shared Vespasian's. In his short principate, AD 79–81, he completed the Colosseum and the baths, and organised relief after the eruption of Vesuvius, which destroyed Pompeii in AD 79. According to Suetonius' biography of him, written early in the second century AD, Titus was the 'love and darling of the human race' (*Titus* 1). In the Jewish Talmudic tradition, however, he was described as 'a wicked man, son of a wicked man, son of Esau the wicked' (Bab. Talmud, Giṭṭin 56b). *his youth*: Josephus was born in the first year of Gaius' principate (*Life* 1 (5)), i.e., AD 37–8, so he was now thirty years old.

(398) *send him to Nero*: Nero died 9 June AD 68. Josephus therefore makes his prophecy a year before Nero's death and two years before Vespasian was proclaimed emperor. It was the practice to reserve important prisoners for the emperor's judgement; cp. *War* II.12.6 (243), and *Life* 74 (408), and Paul in Acts 25: 12.

(400) *to announce to you much more important things*: Josephus has already described how, when he was attempting to extricate himself from the cave,

> '...there returned to him a memory of the nightly dreams in which God had forewarned him of the disasters about to come upon the Jews and of the destiny of the Roman emperors. In judging dreams he was capable of divining the ambiguous words of God. As a priest, with priestly ancestry, he was not ignorant of the prophecies of scripture.'   (*War* III.8.3 (351f))

(401) *You are Caesar and Imperator*: *Caesar* was the name of a patrician Roman family that traced its origins back to Aeneas, the founder of Rome. The dictator Julius Caesar adopted Octavian, the later Emperor Augustus, as his son and heir, and Octavian became Gaius Julius Caesar Octavianus. The name Caesar was handed on to Tiberius and his successors, becoming in effect a title. *Imperator* was originally the title bestowed on a victorious general by his soldiers. Julius Caesar was the first to use the title on a permanent basis. From Octavian onwards it was used as a preface to the greater title *Caesar*. For Josephus to address Vespasian as *Caesar and Imperator* therefore was to salute him as emperor.

(404) *by other signs*: Tacitus several times refers to portents and

prodigies preceding Vespasian's accession (*Histories* 1.10; 11.1; v.13). After listing heavenly signs, he refers to a prophecy 'contained in ancient writings of the priests, that at that very time the east would be strong, and men would set out from Judaea to take control of the world. This ambiguity predicted Vespasian and Titus' (*Histories* v.13). Suetonius (*Vespasian* 4) refers to this prophecy in very similar words, and in the following chapter lists various portents: an oak putting out branches when Vespasian's children were born, a dog bringing in a human hand and dropping it under Vespasian's table, an ox bowing before Vespasian, a dream that good fortune would come to him and his family when Nero had a tooth extracted (which happened on the following day). Suetonius goes on to recount Josephus' prophecy. In Rabbinic tradition, a similar prophecy was ascribed to Rabbi Johanan ben Zakkai, a contemporary of Josephus. He escaped from the siege of Jerusalem in a coffin, reached the camp of Vespasian, uttered his prophecy, and asked that the Jewish sages should be saved from the coming destruction.

(405) *Josephus had been accurate in other predictions*: in what sense did Josephus see himself as a prophet? To Josephus, the ancient prophets were privileged historians, 'gaining their knowledge of the earliest and most ancient times through their God-given inspiration, and clearly recording events of their own times just as they took place' (*Apion* 1.7 (37)). As historians they had a privilege not afforded to everyone, and 'the detailed history from Artaxerxes to our own time has indeed been written, but it has not been awarded the same credence as the earlier histories, because the exact line of prophetic succession has not been preserved' (*Apion* 1.8 (41)). Josephus, however, seems to regard himself as in some sense belonging to this succession of prophet-historians. He emphasises at the beginning of the *War* that he is writing about the events of his own time (*War*, Preface 5 (13–16)) – as did the prophets before him. He claims to have had dreams in which God had forewarned him of the coming fate of the Jews and the destiny of the Roman emperors (*War* 111.8.3 (351f)). He seems to have seen himself as a latter-day Jeremiah, who prophesied not only the Babylonian but also the Roman destruction of Jerusalem (*Ant.* x.5.1 (79)), or a Daniel, who also 'wrote about the Roman Empire, and that the Romans would capture Jerusalem and lay waste the Temple' (*Ant.* x.11.7 (276)). Josephus clearly contrasts himself with the false prophets, who were those, like the Zealots, who wrongly claimed divine inspiration to declare the coming messianic redemption of Israel (*War* 11.13.4 (259)).

(406) *he had in fact forewarned the people of Jotapata*: in *War* 111.7.15

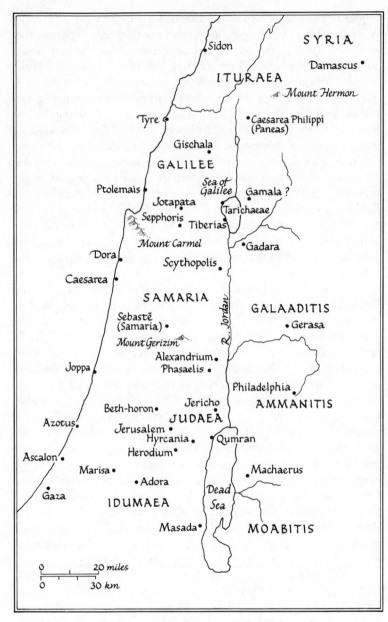

Map 5   Judaea and her neighbours

(193) Josephus recognises that the city could not hold out for long. Josephus entered Jotapata on 21 Artemisios (8 June) AD 67 (*War* III.7.3 (142)); on the forty-seventh day of the siege the Roman earthworks rose above the wall (*War* III.7.33 (316)). In *War* III.8.9 (406) Josephus says that he foretold that the city would fall in forty-seven days; but in *War* III.7.36 (339) Josephus says that Jotapata was taken on the new moon of Panemus (20 July AD 67). Unfortunately, there are only forty-three days, by inclusive reckoning, from 8 June to 20 July.

After the fall of Jotapata in summer AD 67, Vespasian wintered his legions at Ptolemais and Scythopolis, and took Joppa. Tiberias, Tarichaeae, and Gamala fell to Rome, and Titus now approached Gischala, held by the rebel leader John son of Levi and his followers (cp. *War* II.20.6 (575)). 'Anyone could see', says Josephus, 'that he was bent on war as a means of becoming dictator' (*War* IV.2.1 (85)). John of Gischala has already been portrayed as Josephus' treacherous lieutenant in Galilee (*War* II.21.1–2 (585–94); II.21.6–8 (614–32)), and Josephus now describes how John fled from Gischala, entered Jerusalem and won support for resistance. Terrorists from the country also entered Jerusalem, committed various atrocities against the population, and took over the sanctuary, appointing a country nobody as high priest in reaction against the established, urbane, Romanising priesthood. Such terrorists were naturally opposed by the priests, led by Jesus son of Gamalas and Ananus son of Ananus, who mustered a citizen army to blockade these 'Zealots' (on whom see below, p. 134) in the inner court of the Temple. The Zealots, advised by John, who claimed that Ananus was calling in the Romans against them, invited the Idumaeans to help them. Ananus closed the gates against them, but the Zealots let them in by night. A massacre of guards and citizens loyal to Ananus followed.

THE DEATH OF ANANUS

War IV.5.2 (314)   In spite of these massacres, the Idumaeans remained unappeased. They turned to the city, looting every house and

(315)   killing everyone they met. Thinking it a waste of time to pursue the ordinary people, they went looking for the chief priests, and it was against them that their impetus was mainly

(316)   directed. They soon captured them and put them to death, and, standing over the corpses, they ridiculed Ananus for his goodwill towards the people and Jesus for his speech from the

(317)   wall. They went so far in wickedness that they threw out the

corpses without burial, even though the Jews have such respect for burial rites that even those condemned to crucifixion are

(318) taken down and buried before sunset. I might claim with justice that the capture of the city began with the death of Ananus, and that the toppling of the walls and destruction of the Jewish state began from that day, the day when they saw the high priest, the leader of their salvation, done to death in

(319) the middle of the city. For indeed he was in all respects a man of piety and probity, even a holy man; and in addition to his nobility of birth and rank, and the honour that he held, he

(320) loved to claim equality even with the humble. He was an extreme champion of freedom and a lover of democracy, always putting the public good before private profit, and prizing peace above everything. For he knew that one could not fight the Roman power, but, compelled by circumstances, he prepared for war so that if the Jews did not resolve their differences with Rome they might persevere to the end with

(321) some hope. In short, everything would have been resolved if Ananus had survived, for he was an excellent and persuasive public speaker. He had already put down his opponents; under such a general, had they been at war, the Jews would have

(322) caused the Romans considerable trouble. Associated with Ananus was Jesus, who though not as able as Ananus was better

(323) than the rest. But in my view, it was because God had condemned the city to destruction for its pollution and had decided to purify the sanctuary by fire that he cut down those

(324) who loved the place so tenaciously. So those who were recently wearing the sacred garments or leading the world-famous liturgy and were feted by pilgrims to the city from all over the world were now seen thrown out, stripped, as food

(325) for the dogs and the wild beasts. I believe that virtue herself mourned for these men, lamenting that she had been so worsted by evil. Such was the fate of Ananus and Jesus.

Josephus' obituary of Ananus reveals again Josephus' own political view that Jewish acceptance of Roman rule meant peace, rejection of it divine judgement upon Jerusalem.

(314) The *Idumaeans* lived in the Negeb immediately south of Judaea. Their two main towns were Adora and Marisa. They were descendants of semi-nomadic clans who lived in the border areas between ancient Edom and Judah, and were probably related to both peoples. They were not regarded as completely Jewish, though they had accepted Judaism, including circumcision, under the Hasmonaean John Hyrcanus at the end of the second century BC. Alexander Jannaeus had appointed Antipater as governor of Idumaea; Antipater's son, also called Antipater, was father by a Nabataean wife of Herod the Great. After Herod's death, Idumaea became part of the Roman province of Judaea. The Idumaeans clearly supported the revolt against Rome; Vespasian occupied Idumaea in spring AD 68, putting several villages to the fire and sword (*War* IV.8.1 (446–8)).

(316) *Ananus*, fifth and youngest son of Ananus, or Annas (first appointed high priest in AD 6; cp. Luke 3: 2; John 18: 13–24; Acts 4: 6), was appointed high priest in AD 63 by King Agrippa II in the interregnum between the procurators Festus and Albinus. *Jesus*, son of Gamalas (*War* IV.3.9 (160)) was the chief priest next in seniority to Ananus (IV.4.3 (238)). An intimate friend of Josephus (*Life* 41 (204)), he warned Josephus' father of the plot being hatched against Josephus. In his *speech* (*War* IV.4.3 (236–69)) he professed astonishment that the Idumaeans should come to help scoundrels like the Zealots, challenged his hearers to produce evidence that the Jewish leaders were conniving with Rome, and urged them either to assist in suppressing the Zealots or to remain neutral.

(317) *buried before sunset*: cp. Deut. 21: 22f; John 19: 31.

(318) *the capture of the city began with the death of Ananus*: because this marked the collapse of the moderate, constitutional party in Jerusalem, which recognised that the Romans respected the Jewish religion and preferred negotiation to war. Josephus portrays Ananus as a balanced politician, prepared for war but preferring peace. This is in apparent contrast to the 'rash and daring' figure presented in *Ant.* XX.9.1 (197–203) who opposed the Sadducees, had James the brother of Jesus stoned, allowed himself to be bribed to sack Josephus from his Galilaean command (*Life* 38–59 (189–308)), and was himself deposed after a reign of three months in AD 63–4. The reason for the difference may be partly that Ananus matured between 63 and 66, but the more likely reason is to be found in the different aims of Josephus' writings. In the *War* he makes Ananus the mouthpiece of the official Jewish attitude to the revolt against the views of the Zealots and John of Gischala.

(323) *God had condemned*: this is Josephus' overriding theological

explanation for the disaster that overtook the Jews. Daniel had predicted it (*Ant.* x.11.7 (276)); God had foretold it to Josephus himself (*War* III.8.3 (351)). The *pollution* was caused by the murder of the high priest and the unburied corpses just mentioned, as well as by the Zealot occupation of the sanctuary and the illegal replacement of the high priest (*War* IV.3.7 (153ff); cp. *Ant.* XX.8.6 (166)). Josephus comments that by summer AD 66 the city was 'so polluted with a stain of guilt as to make the expectation of some act of heavenly wrath inevitable' (*War* II.17.10 (455)). At the end of the *War* (VII.8.1 (252–74)), Josephus gives a full catalogue of the impieties of the extremists, whose 'fourth philosophy' he regards as a major cause of the war (*Ant.* XVIII.1.6 (23–5)). But Josephus recognised a number of less theological factors: he notes the failings of the Roman governors, especially of Albinus (*War* II.14.1 (271–6)), Gessius Florus (*War* II.14.2–9 (277–308); *Ant.* XVIII.1.6 (25)); the bias of the Syrian auxiliary troops in Judaea (*War* II.13.7 (268)); a dispute at Caesarea between the local Jewish community and their gentile neighbours, which escalated to violence (*War* II.14.4–5 (284–92)); Florus' removal of 17 talents from the Temple treasury and the resultant riot and judicial retributions (*War* II.14.6–9 (293–308)); and the cessation of sacrifices for the emperor, which 'was the starting-point of the war against the Romans' (*War* II.17.2 (409)). Josephus is clearly interested in the physical events that led inescapably to the war; he is also interested (especially in *Antiquities*) in the workings of divine providence. He adopts a view roughly parallel to that of the historian of 2 Kings, who argued that the fall of Samaria was divine retribution for apostasy (2 Kings 17). But how these factors fit together he does not explain. His purpose is more apologetic; he wishes to defend the Jews to the Romans, rather than explain in detail the ways of God to man.

By spring AD 68, Vespasian controlled all Palestine apart from the fortresses of Herodium, Machaerus, Masada, and the city of Jerusalem itself. The death of the Emperor Nero in June 68 (which automatically cancelled Vespasian's command) and the political circumstances of the next twelve months as first Galba, then Otho, and then Vitellius became emperor, caused some loss of tempo in the Roman campaign. In Jerusalem, the Zealots lost the support of most of the Idumaeans, and in addition were opposed by a rival group led by John of Gischala (see above, p. 127). To counter their reign of terror in Jerusalem, in spring AD 69 the priests and people let into the city another freelance partisan leader, Simon son of Gioras. Jerusalem was now split between the

Zealots under Eleazar in the inner court of the Temple, John of Gischala and his supporters in the outer court and part of the lower city on Mount Ophel, and Simon to the west in the upper city and in the greater part of the lower city. The Roman attack was resumed in summer 69, but then delayed while Vespasian, hailed as emperor by his troops at Alexandria, turned his mind towards affairs at Rome and entrusted the continuance of the war to his son Titus, who began the siege of Jerusalem in spring AD 70.

THREE PARTIES IN THE CITY

War V.1.1 (1) Having crossed the desert between Egypt and Palestine in the way we have described, Titus reached Caesarea, where

(2) he had decided to organise his forces. While he was still at Alexandria, helping his father settle the empire that God had newly put into their hands, the rebellion at Jerusalem had come to life again and become three-sided, one party splitting into two factions. In such evil circumstances, one might call

(3) this a good thing, even an act of justice. I have already given an accurate explanation of the Zealots' origins and the appalling results of their attack on the citizens, which was the

(4) real beginning of the capture of the city; and one would not be wrong to call the Zealots a faction born of a faction, the act of a maddened beast attacking its own flesh for lack of other food.

2 (5) It was Eleazar, Simon's son, who originally set the Zealots apart from the general populace in the Temple enclosure. His excuse was indignation at the outrages daily committed by John, whose lust for blood seemed endless, but his real reason was that he could not bear to defer to an even more recently

(6) arrived usurper. He wanted total personal control, and seceded from the Zealots, taking with him Judas son of Chalcias and Simon son of Esron, both powerful men, and in addition Hezekiah son of Chobari, a man not without fame

(7) of his own. Each of these had a substantial Zealot following, and taking over the inner court of the Temple, they piled

(8) their arms on the sacred pediment above the holy gates. As

they were well supplied, their morale was high; for there
were plenty of sacred commodities available for those who
had no religious scruples. But their lack of numbers made
them apprehensive, and for the most part they sat still and

(9)   remained where they were. On the other hand, John's
advantage in numbers was offset by his disadvantage in
position; while he had his enemies above him, he was unable
to attack them without fear of the result, or to remain inactive

(10)   without bitter frustration. Though he suffered more damage
than he inflicted on Eleazar's party, he would not give up.
There were continual sorties and showers of missiles, and the
whole Temple was defiled with slaughter.

3 (11)   The upper city and part of the lower city were held by
Simon son of Gioras. In their trouble, the people had
summoned him in hope of help, but in doing so had brought
upon themselves a tyrant. He now attacked John's party all
the more strongly in view of the fact that it was also under
attack from above. He was attacking them from below, just

(12)   as they were attacking their enemies above them. Though
John was thus caught between two fires, he inflicted as much
damage as he suffered, and what he lost by his position
beneath Eleazar's supporters, he gained by his position above

(13)   Simon's. The result was that he stoutly defended attacks from
below in hand-to-hand fighting, and used his machines to

(14)   repulse those firing down on him from the Temple. For he
was well equipped with quick-firers, catapults and stone-
throwers, with which he not only defended himself against

(15)   attackers but also killed many of the worshippers. For although
Eleazar's supporters were maniacs, ready for any impiety,
nevertheless they let into the Temple those who wished to
offer sacrifice – native Jews after thorough scrutiny, but
foreign visitors with less hesitation. But those let in, though
gaining their entrance by making the Zealots ashamed of their
cruelty, would often become casualties of the party divisions.

(16)   For the missiles from the machines carried over with
considerable force as far as the altar and the sanctuary, and

(17)   fell among the priests and the worshippers, and many who had enthusiastically come from the ends of the earth to gather at this famous spot, sacred to all men, fell in front of the sacrifices, and sprinkled the altar, honoured by all Greeks and

(18)   non-Greeks alike, with libations of their own blood. Local and foreign people, laymen and priests were piled together in death, and the blood from the corpses of every kind formed

(19)   puddles in the sacred courts. Saddest of cities, what comparable disaster did you ever suffer at the hands of the Romans? It was by way of purging the corruption inside you that the Romans entered the city. You were no longer the home of God, nor could you survive once you had become a tomb for the corpses of your own people and made the sanctuary a common grave of the civil war. Your position might perhaps be restored if you were to make atonement to the

(20)   God who destroyed you. But in accordance with the practice of historians, I must control my feelings; this is not the time for personal lament but for the narration of events. So I will go on to the subsequent events of the rebellion.

4 (21)   Those plotting against the city were now divided into three groups. Eleazar's supporters, who had control of the sacred firstfruits, directed their drunken energy against John. His supporters in turn plundered the citizens and were roused to action against Simon. He too relied upon the city for his

(22)   supplies, in competition with the rival factions. Whenever he was set on from both sides, John turned his men some to face one way, some the other. Those who came up to attack from the town he fired on from the colonnades, and those who fired on him from the Temple he drove back with his

(23)   machines. Whenever he was given some relief from those attacking from above (who were often compelled to desist from the effects of drink and fatigue), he would make a foray

(24)   with greater confidence against Simon's party. Whichever part of the city he turned to, he would set on fire the houses full of corn and various supplies. As soon as he retreated, Simon would attack and do the same thing. It was as if they

were deliberately helping the Romans by destroying what the
city had prepared against the eventuality of a siege and
(25)   hamstringing themselves. At all events, the result was that the
whole area around the Temple was burnt out, and the city
became the desert no-man's land of a domestic confrontation.
Nearly all the corn, which might have been enough for
(26)   several years' siege, was destroyed by fire. It was famine that
really brought about the city's capture – a most unlikely
result, had its people not brought it upon themselves.

(1) *Titus*: see above, pp. 123f. Titus had gone with Vespasian to
Beirut, then to Alexandria. From here he returned with 2000 men from
the Third and Twenty-second Legions (cp. *War* v.1.6 (43)) to fill the
gap left by troops sent to support Vespasian's cause in Italy. Titus had
also the Fifth, Tenth, Twelfth, and Fifteenth Legions, and Syrian
auxiliaries. Accompanying him as counsellor was the Roman prefect
of Egypt, Tiberius Julius Alexander, by birth a Jew, the nephew of
Philo, a former procurator of Judaea (AD 46–8) and a friend of Agrippa
II. *Caesarea*: see above, p. 112.

(3) *their attack on the citizens*: this happened after the death of the
high priest Ananus (see p. 129 above; *War* IV.5.3–4 (326–44)). At first,
the Zealots were assisted by the Idumaeans but, according to Josephus,
the Idumaeans became so horrified that they withdrew from Jerusalem.

(5) *Eleazar, Simon's son* is probably the Eleazar son of Gion named
in *War* IV.4.1 (225) as 'the most persuasive' of the Zealots. It was he
who, with Zechariah son of Amphicalleus, called in the Idumaeans
as allies against Ananus and the Jerusalem people blockading the Zealots
in the Temple. Eleazar son of Simon took part in the rout of Cestius
Gallus late in AD 66 (*War* II.20.3 (564)), but the Jews did not trust him
and did not give him any official command when they appointed
generals to conduct the war. *the Zealots*: the name, a literal translation
of the Greek *zēlōtai*, has often been inaccurately used to refer to all
Palestinian bandits of the first century AD whether politically motivated
or not. However, the party actually identifying itself by this name did
not arise until AD 66 (*War* II.22.1 (651); IV.3.9 (160f)). Josephus objected
to their use of the title 'Zealot' 'as if their zeal was in a good cause
and not the excessive pursuit of all that was most wicked' (*War* IV.3.9
(161)). He repeatedly blames the Zealots for their contribution to the
Jewish disaster, notably in the speech put into the mouth of the high

priest Ananus (*War* IV.3.10 (163–92)) and in his own comments on the Sicarii, John of Gischala, Simon son of Gioras, the Idumaeans and the Zealots in *War* VII.8.1 (252–74). The Zealot party seems to have arisen in Jerusalem out of country refugees fleeing ahead of the Roman advance (*War* IV.3.1–4 (121–42)). Josephus stresses the bandit element among them. There was a long tradition of social banditry among the Judaean and Galilean peasantry, who had little respect for the landowners and the city bourgeoisie, and it is not surprising that in Jerusalem they banded together, attacked the city aristocracy, took the Temple, and appointed their own high priest, a man of village origins. (In *War* II.17.9 (444) Josephus uses the word *zēlōtai* of the followers of a Jewish rebel leader Menahem, son of Judas the Galilean (cp. Acts 5: 37), with reference to events in late summer AD 66, but here the word may be used in the wider sense of 'fanatical adherents', for Menahem and his successor, another Eleazar, the son of Jairus, were leaders not of the 'Zealots' but of a separate group, the Sicarii, 'dagger-men' (after their method of political assassination). It was this group that fled to the Herodian fortress of Masada and resisted siege to the end, when they finally committed suicide to avoid falling alive into Roman hands.)

(7) *on the sacred pediment above the holy gates*: it is not clear whether the weapons were placed above the gate between the outer court (the Court of the Gentiles) and the inner Court of Women, or above the gate between the Court of Women and the Court of Israel, inside the inner court area. These two gates were known by various names – the 'Beautiful Gate' (cp. Acts 3: 2), the 'Corinthian Gate', and the 'Gate of Nicanor' – but scholars do not agree which name or names should be attached to which gate. See Plan 2 on p. 142. The Greek phrase suggests stacking arms rather than mounting them for display, so presumably Josephus means that they were sacrilegiously stored in the inner courts as if in the armoury of a barracks. (See Plan 2.)

(9) *John's...position*: John had fled to Jerusalem from the siege of Gischala, and began to build a political following by urging war against the Romans. He sought further power by pretending to be a sincere mediator between the Zealots and the high priest Ananus, but his sympathies were with the former, whom he persuaded to bring in the Idumaeans as allies. John and his Galilean supporters, however, won a deserved reputation for bloodthirstiness (*War* IV.9.10 (558–65)); the Idumaeans withdrew, and the people invited Simon son of Gioras into Jerusalem to defend them from John. Within the Zealot party, Eleazar son of Simon and his supporters broke away from John and occupied

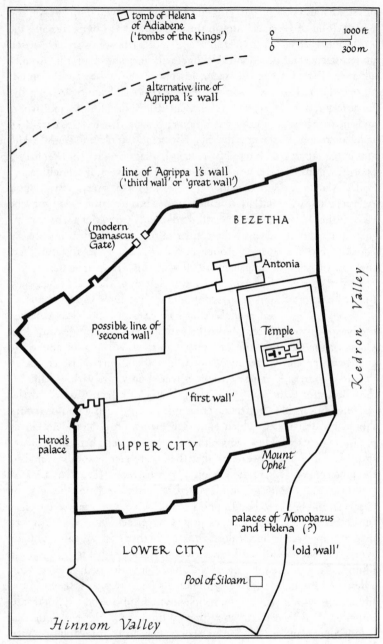

tomb of Helena
of Adiabene
('tombs of the Kings')

0   1000 ft
0   300 m

alternative line of
Agrippa I's wall

line of Agrippa I's wall
('third wall' or 'great wall')

BEZETHA

(modern
Damascus
Gate)

Antonia

Temple

Kedron Valley

possible line of
'second wall'

'first wall'

Herod's
palace

UPPER CITY

*Mount
Ophel*

palaces of Monobazus
and Helena (?)

'old wall'

LOWER CITY

Pool of Siloam

Hinnom Valley

Map 6   Jerusalem AD 66–70 (the double line marks the course of the present
walls of the Old City)

the inner Temple courts (see above), leaving John and his followers holding the outer Temple court and Mount Ophel and the hillside above the Kedron valley on its west.

(11) *Simon son of Gioras* came from Gerasa in Transjordan. Removed from his post as governor of the district of Acrabatene by Ananus, he had joined the Sicarii at Masada for a time before forming his own party of dissidents in the wilderness (*War* IV.9.3–4 (503–13)). He terrorised Idumaea, and when his wife was taken hostage by the Zealots recovered her by threatening to spare no one in Jerusalem itself. 'To the people Simon outside the walls was more terrifying than the Romans, and the Zealots inside more brutal than either' (*War* IV.9.10 (558)), but eventually, 'in order to get rid of John, they decided to welcome Simon and at their own request to bring a second tyrant upon themselves' (IV.9.11 (573)). Josephus dates his admission to Jerusalem in the month Xanthicus (i.e., April–May) of AD 69. *The upper city and part of the lower city*: see the comment on *War* V.6.1 (252) below, p. 140.

(13) *machines*: see above, p. 120. The Zealots had acquired machines abandoned by Cestius (*War* II.19.9 (553)).

(15) *they let into the Temple those who wished to offer sacrifice*: as they did later, at Passover AD 70, thereby admitting John's disguised supporters, who took over the inner courts and eliminated Eleazar's separatist party (*War* V.3.1 (98–105)). *native Jews after thorough scrutiny, but foreign visitors with less hesitation*: the present text makes the natural suggestion that the native Jews were more suspect and more thoroughly scrutinised; but a well-attested variant ('native Jews with some suspicion and with due security arrangements, foreign visitors after careful scrutiny') suggests that strangers were more thoroughly checked than native Jews. Presumably Eleazar and his supporters were on their guard against John of Gischala and his Zealots.

(16) *the altar and the sanctuary*: the altar of burnt-offering lay inside the Court of Priests just east of the porch of the Temple (*sanctuary*). In the somewhat rhetorical passage that follows, Josephus stresses two points: first, that an altar of universal importance (for it was the altar of the one God, whose unity and universality were basic to Josephus' theology) was being stained by the blood of the sacrificers as well as the victims; and secondly, that the Temple was more polluted by civil war among the Jews than by its destruction by the Romans, who entered to purge with fire its internal pollutions.

(19) *tomb...common grave*: the Temple would be defiled by contact with corpses. Thus in his vision of the restored Temple, Ezekiel was

told that the bodies of dead kings interred nearby (or perhaps their monuments) must be moved well away from the Temple to avoid defiling it (Ezek. 43: 6–9).

(20) *I must control my feelings*: see Josephus' comment on this in his Preface to the *War*, above, p. 97.

(21) *sacred firstfruits*: an important commandment of the Law was that 'You shall bring the choicest firstfruits of your soil to the house of the LORD your God' (Exod. 23: 19), and these firstfruits – 'the choicest of the oil, the choicest of the new wine and the corn' (Num. 18: 12; cp. Neh. 10: 35–8) – became the perquisite of the priests and levites, and were stored in rooms in the inner courts of the Temple. This was naturally an important asset to Eleazar and his men.

(22) The *colonnades* ran round the perimeter of the outer court of the Temple.

In the following chapters, Josephus describes the arrival of Titus and the beginning of the siege. The three parties temporarily united and won a minor skirmish, but John of Gischala took advantage of the Passover feast to smuggle armed supporters into the inner courts of the Temple and so took control of it. Jerusalem was now divided between the force under John in the Temple courts and the forces of Simon surrounding them in the upper and lower city. Josephus describes the city and Temple in some detail (*War* v.4.1 – 5.8 (136–247; cp. *Ant.* xv.11.1–7 (380–425)); these descriptions, together with evidence from the Mishnaic tractates Middot, Šeqalim, and Tamid, and from archaeology, are the main source for our knowledge of Herodian Jerusalem.

TWO PARTIES IN THE CITY

War v.6.1 (248) The active strength of the insurgents under Simon's command in the city, apart from the Idumaeans, was ten thousand men. They were led by fifty officers and commanded

(249) by Simon himself. The Idumaeans allied to him had five thousand men under ten officers, whose leaders were reputed

(250) to be Jacob son of Sosas and Simon son of Kathlas. On the other side, John, now in control of the Temple, had six thousand armed men under twenty officers, but they were soon joined by the Zealots (who had put aside their disagreements), two thousand four hundred in number, under the command

of their former leader Eleazar and Simon the son of Arinus.

(251) As we have said, in their mutual struggle each side fought to win the people, and those citizens who refused to take part

(252) in their criminal activities became the prey of both sides. Simon held the upper town and the great wall as far as Kedron valley, and the old wall from Siloam where it came down on the east to the palace courtyard of Monobazus (he was King of

(253) Adiabene, east of the Euphrates). Simon controlled also the fountain and part of the citadel (that is, the lower city) as far

(254) as the palace of Helena the mother of Monobazus. John controlled the Temple and the immediate environs, Mount Ophel and the ravine known as the Kedron. The area between these positions they burnt to clear space for their own fighting.

(255) For the civil war did not come to a halt even when the Romans were camped against the wall. The rivals were temporarily brought to their senses when they made their first sorties, but they went out of their minds again, broke apart, and renewed their fight, as if acting in answer to the prayers of the besiegers.

(256) They certainly suffered nothing worse at Roman hands than what they inflicted upon each other, and after them there was no new form of suffering left for the city to experience. On the contrary, she met with the worst before she was taken, and those who captured her achieved something more than

(257) capture. In my view the civil war destroyed the city, but the Romans ended the civil war – a far greater achievement than the destruction of the walls. One might reasonably blame the tragedy of it on the inhabitants and credit the justice of it to the Romans. But everyone is entitled to his own interpretation of the event.

In this passage, Josephus describes the new relative strength and positions of the two opposing factions in Jerusalem.

(248) *Simon*: see above, p. 137. He appears to have lost a considerable number of men since his campaign against Idumaea with 20,000 men (*War* IV.9.5 (515)), if Josephus' figures are accurate. *Idumaeans*: it seems that not all the Idumaean forces had withdrawn from Jerusalem

appalled by the behaviour of the Zealots, as Josephus had suggested (*War* IV.6.1 (353)). At least some, with two senior officers, joined Simon, whose devastation of Idumaea (*War* IV.9.5–7 (514–37)) had been followed by a Roman annexation that may have driven many Idumaeans back to join the Jewish rebels. *Jacob son of Sosas* and Simon son of Thraceas (called *Simon son of Kathlas* in the present passage) are mentioned as two of the four Idumaean generals leading 20,000 men in *War* IV.4.2 (235).

(250) *John*: see above, p. 127. *Simon the son of Arinus* may be Simon son of Ari, listed among Zealots who distinguished themselves in the fighting when the Romans attacked the Antonia and the Temple (*War* VI.1.8 (92), 2.6 (148)).

(252) *Simon held the upper town*...: not all the places and features named by Josephus are certainly located. The *great wall* is probably the wall built by Agrippa I to enclose a new suburb on the north of Jerusalem; it was of such a size, remarks Josephus (*War* II.11.6 (218); cp. *Ant*. XIX.7.2 (327)), that had it been completed the Roman siege would not have succeeded. This wall has been identified by some with the wall of enormous rectangular blocks running roughly east–west about 500 metres (547 yards) north of the present-day Damascus Gate of Jerusalem, but it is more likely to have followed the course of the present-day northern wall of the Old City of Jerusalem. The *old wall* is presumably the wall bounding Herodian Jerusalem on its west, south-western, and southern sides (John held the eastern side of Jerusalem). The section *from Siloam*...*to the palace courtyard of Monobazus* (the site of which is not precisely known) is probably the stretch along the south-eastern side of the city overlooking the Kedron and Hinnom valleys and their confluence.

(253) *the fountain* is probably the pool of Siloam itself, where the water emerges from Hezekiah's tunnel. The position of *the citadel* (originally the garrison fortress built by the Seleucid occupying force to control access to the Temple; cp. 1 Macc. 1:33) has been much debated, some scholars locating it immediately south of the Temple area, or even within it on its southern edge, others identifying it with the later Roman Antonia. But these identifications do not suit the present passage, for they would locate the citadel in an area held by John. The citadel was probably west of the Temple on the northern side of the lower town. Josephus is thus telling us that Simon held the walls and city of Jerusalem on the west and south in a semi-circle round John. The *palace of Helena* has not been identified. *Adiabene*, the kingdom of *Monobazus* and *Helena*, was the region of ancient Assyria, located

east of the upper Tigris. Josephus tells the story of the conversion of King Izates and his mother Helena to Judaism in *Ant.* XX.2.1–5 (17–53). Helena's husband was called Monobazus; their eldest son, also called Monobazus, abdicated in favour of Izates. Helena visited Jerusalem at the time of the famine in the reign of Claudius (cp. Acts 11: 28) and gave some welcome relief to the people by buying grain from Egypt and figs from Cyprus. Helena was buried in Jerusalem in the 'three pyramids' that she had built for her near the city (*Ant.* XX.4.3 (95); cp. *War* V.2.2 (55), 3.3 (119)). This monument may be identified with the 'Tombs of the Kings' north of the Damascus Gate. The second-century Greek traveller Pausanias takes this tomb and the famous tomb of Mausolus at Halicarnassus (the famous Mausoleum) as his two examples of the many wonderful tombs he knows (*Description of Greece* VIII.16.5).

(254) *John* of Gischala and his supporters held the well-defended Temple courts, with the region of Mount Ophel just to the south, and so inevitably overlooked the *Kedron* valley beneath the Temple's eastern wall. It was a strong position, perhaps most vulnerable on the north, where it was defended by the fortress rebuilt by Herod the Great and called Antonia after his then patron, Mark Antony.

(256) *nothing worse at Roman hands*...: cp. Josephus' comment at *War* V.1.3 (19); above, p. 137. Josephus develops the theme in the following sentences in rhetorical fashion.

(257) *everyone is entitled to his own interpretation*: certainly not every Jew would agree with Josephus' assessment of the blame for the tragedy. He uses a formula borrowed from the historian Dionysius of Halicarnassus.

In spring AD 70 the assault on Jerusalem began in earnest. While John defended the Temple area and Simon the upper and lower cities, Titus began his attack on the north-west section of Agrippa's 'great wall'. This was soon breached, and the defenders withdrew to the 'second wall', the Antonia fortress, and the north wall of the Temple, while the Romans occupied the suburbs enclosed by Agrippa's wall, most of which they demolished. After capturing the second wall, west of the Antonia, the Romans attacked the Antonia itself, the key to the Temple area, and eventually took it on 24 July AD 70. At this point Josephus emphasises Titus' anxiety to preserve the city and Temple: Titus sends Josephus off to tell John

'...that, if he had an inordinate desire to fight, then he had Titus' permission to come out with as many troops as he liked and fight

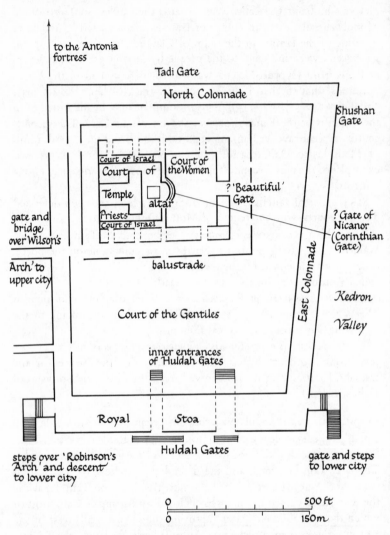

to the Antonia
fortress

Tadi Gate

North Colonnade

Shushan
Gate

Court of Israel

Court of
the Women

Court of Temple

? 'Beautiful'
Gate

gate and
bridge
over Wilson's

Temple

altar

? Gate of
Nicanor
(Corinthian
Gate)

Priests
Court of Israel

Arch' to
upper city

balustrade

East Colonnade

Kedron

Valley

Court of the Gentiles

inner entrances
of Huldah Gates

Royal   Stoa

Huldah Gates

steps over 'Robinson's
Arch' and descent
to lower city

gate and steps
to lower city

0   500 ft
0   150 m

Plan 2   The Herodian Temple and its courts. Parts of the western wall, the
south-western corner, the south wall and the Huldah Gates (the 'Double' and
'Triple' Gates), the south-eastern corner, and the eastern wall of the great
Herodian courts are still standing and visible. The precise course of the northern
wall, however, is not known; some scholars place it further north. The altar of
burnt-offering may have been sited (as on this plan) on the rock today enshrined
in the Dome of the Rock.

without involving the city and the Temple in disaster with him.
In any case, he should cease defiling the sanctuary and giving
offence to God, and it was open to him to offer the suspended
sacrifices with the help of any Jews he chose.'

(War VI.2.1 (95))

In an impassioned speech Josephus asks,

'Are you blaming the Romans for your sins? Right up to this
very moment they have concern for our laws, and are pressing
you hard to pay back to God the sacrifices that you have cut short.'

(War VI.2.1 (101))

Other Jewish deserters appealed to the Jews to surrender, and Titus
added his own plea.

TITUS DISCLAIMS RESPONSIBILITY

War VI.2.4 (124) Titus, extremely distressed, directed another re-
proachful speech at John's supporters. 'Tell me', he said, 'you
most abominable people, was it not you who set this balustrade
(125) in front of your sanctuary? Was it not you who erected the
stone slabs inscribed in Greek and in our own Latin to give
warning that no one should pass beyond the enclosure wall?
(126) Did we not allow you to execute any who passed it – even
if he should be a Roman? How is it, you sinners, that in this
place you now trample over corpses? Why do you pollute the
(127) sanctuary with the blood of non-Jew and Jew alike? I appeal
for witness to my own ancestral gods, and to any deity that
ever graced this place (for I do not believe that any god now
guards it); I appeal to my own army and to the Jews among
my troops, and to you yourselves, to bear witness that it is
not under any compulsion from me that you desecrate this
(128) place. If you will change the battleground, no Roman shall
enter your sanctuary or dishonour it; I will preserve your
Temple for you whether you want me to or not.'

(124) *abominable people*: a similar attitude is expressed by Tacitus
(*Histories* v.4): 'whatever is sacred to us is profane to them; again, they
allow what we think impure'. Much of Josephus' work is directed
against gentile misunderstanding and prejudice; see particularly the

section on *Apion* below, pp. 171–88. *balustrade*: this is described by
Josephus, *War* v.5.2 (193f). Breast-high (or waist-high, according to
Mid. 2: 3a), it ran round the outside of the steps leading to the inner
courts, marking them off clearly from the outer court. On it at regular
intervals were plaques with inscriptions, some in Greek and some in
Latin, warning non-Jews that their entry into the enclosure would incur
the death penalty. One complete example and one fragment of the
Greek inscriptions have been found. Paul was accused of taking the
Greek Trophimus inside the barrier (Acts 21: 28f).

(126) *allow you to execute*: this was an exception to the general rule.
The Roman administration normally kept judicial execution in its own
hands (cp. John 18: 31f). *Why do you pollute the sanctuary...?*: Titus
emphasises that it is the Jews, not the Romans, who are defiling the
Temple; cp. *War* v.1.3 (19), and p. 137 above. Josephus lays the major
blame on the rebellious Jews. According to Josephus, Titus later
rejected the advice of his council that the Temple should be destroyed,
saying that he would not exact revenge on objects rather than men,
nor burn down so marvellous a building (*War* vi.4.3 (241)). Josephus,
however, comments that God had long since sentenced the Temple to
burning, and says that the Jews themselves were ultimately responsible
(*War* vi.4.5 (250f)). Josephus clearly wishes to exonerate Titus, but it
has been argued that, since Roman soldiers were well disciplined, the
fourth-century AD historian Sulpicius Severus is more likely to be right
when he claims that Titus himself ordered the firing of the Temple.
But the best-disciplined soldiers can act beyond orders in the heat of
battle, and Titus may well have preferred to preserve the building intact
if possible as 'an ornament of the empire' (*War* vi.4.3 (241)).

(127) *any deity that ever graced this place*: Josephus repeats his view
that God has deserted the Temple and is on the Roman side.

ABRAHAM

Ant. 1.7.1 (154)   Abraham, who had no child of his own, adopted his
brother Aran's son Lot, the brother of his own wife Sarah,
and at the age of seventy-five, left Chaldaea and emigrated,
at God's command, to Canaan, which he made his home
and handed down to his descendants. He was a man of quick
intelligence on all subjects, trusted by those who listened to
(155)   him, and accurate in his conjectures. This made him begin
to ponder more deeply about virtue than others had done,

and he had it in mind to reform and change the commonly-held view of God. He was thus the first to proclaim boldly that God, the creator of all, was one, and that if there were any other contributors to human happiness, each was making his contribution at the command of God and not

(156) from his own innate capacity. He conjectured this on the basis of the changing conditions of the earth and the sea, and the motions of the sun and moon and all the heavenly bodies; for if these things had their own inherent power, they would have taken thought for their own ordered behaviour. Without such power, it was obvious that even when co-operating for our benefit they helped us not by virtue of their own authority but by the might of him who commanded them, to whom alone may rightly be ascribed

(157) honour and thanksgiving. Such opinions brought on him the opposition of the Chaldaeans and other peoples of Mesopotamia, and he thought it wise to emigrate. By the will and help of God, he occupied the land of Canaan, and, once settled there, built an altar and performed a sacrifice to God.

2 (158) Our father Abraham is mentioned by Berosus, not by name but in the following way: 'In the tenth generation after the flood there lived among the Chaldaeans a certain righteous man, a great man, expert in heavenly matters.'

(159) Hecataeus has given him more than a mere mention, for he has left us a book that he put together about him. Nicolaus of Damascus, in the fourth book of his *Histories*, says this: 'Abraham reigned at Damascus. He arrived as an invader with an army from the land beyond Babylon called

(160) the land of the Chaldaeans. But soon afterwards he emigrated, and together with his people changed his home from this country to the land then called Canaan, now Judaea. With him were his many descendants, whose history I shall tell in another book. The name of Abraham is honoured in Damascus to this day, and a village is shown called Abrahamsville after him.'

In his account of Abraham, Josephus, like other Jewish writers in the hellenistic world, presents a figure with virtues recognisable and attractive to hellenised readers. Abraham is a man of virtue (*aretē*) and enthusiasm (*spoudē*) for God (*Ant.* 1.17.1 (256)). His *aretē* was demonstrated by his refusing to keep more of the spoils of his victory over the Assyrians than was necessary for his servants' maintenance (*Ant.* 1.10.2 (182)), and his piety and obedience to God by his response to the demand for the sacrifice of Isaac. But in particular, Abraham is a man of intelligence, a persuasive theologian, a philosopher and teacher, a skilled practitioner of the sciences, and the first to proclaim monotheism. His inquiring intellect enforced his emigration from Chaldaea, and led to his visit to Egypt, where he refuted Egyptian religious beliefs and introduced the study of arithmetic and astronomy. Abraham is presented as an educated hellenistic gentleman of recognised fame. Similarly, Eupolemus spoke of Abraham as a wise man, as did also Philo (*De Abrahamo* XVII.77–80).

(154) *Abraham*: this form of the name is used here as being that most familiar to English readers. According to Gen. 17: 5f, it was given to the patriarch in place of his original name Abram. Josephus uses the form *Abramos* throughout, and omits the story of his change of name.

(155) *more deeply about virtue*: Josephus here uses a word, *aretē*, that in the Greek world denoted not so much moral virtue as the excellence of which a man or an animal or a thing at its best was capable. In what precisely that excellence consisted was much discussed, especially in the case of man. The 'virtue' of man might be seen, now in manliness of a physical sort, now in the ability to acquire wealth, now in the ability to think or do what is true, or just, or beautiful. Above all, since Aristotle, a man's supreme *aretē* might be found in reason, 'which seems to exercise rule and authority by natural right and to have a conception of things noble and divine, because it is either itself divine or is relatively the most divine part of our being'; 'reason is the true self of man – if a man's true self is the highest or best thing to him' (Aristotle, *Nicomachean Ethics* X.7.1, 8, from R. W. Livingstone, *Greek ideals and modern life* (Oxford, 1935), p. 87). Josephus certainly presents Abraham as a man well endowed with reason; but *virtue* here, to judge from the context, appears to be used not in any technical sense but rather with vague reference to human theological opinions.

that God, the creator of all, was one: the Graeco-Roman world was used to a plurality of gods manifest in various forms. Jewish refusal to accept such gods incurred the charges of atheism and misanthropy (*Apion* II.14 (148)) and sometimes ridicule: thus Apion and others mocked the Jews for worshipping an ass's head (*Apion* II.7 (80); cp. Tacitus, *Histories* v.3f). Josephus denies the charge of atheism, and challenges polytheism by affirming the superiority of Jewish mono-theism, the origin of which he attributes to the Jewish patriarch and philosopher Abraham. In *Apion* II.16 (166–8) Josephus makes Moses represent God 'as being himself one, uncreated, eternally unchanging', and notes that 'Pythagoras, Anaxagoras, Plato, and the Stoic philoso-phers after him all seem to have not-dissimilar ideas about the nature of God.' The unity of God is important for Josephus: 'to share one and the same belief about God, and to have complete agreement in matters of behaviour and customs, results in a most beautiful harmony in the character of men' (*Apion* II.19 (179)). 'In our society, all behave alike, all speak alike about God, consistently with the Law and the stated belief that he oversees everything' (*Apion* II.19 (181)). 'We have one temple for the one God...common to all as God is common to all' (*Apion* II.23 (193)).

The emphasis on God as *creator* is in opposition to those who would deny the existence of a creator God or who would deify the universe itself in whole or part.

(156) *He conjectured this*: the usual argument, employed by the Stoic philosophers (cp. p. 82) and by many others since, is that the ordered nature of the universe reveals the divine intelligence behind it. Josephus also argues from observed celestial phenomena; his argument, however, is that the observed irregularity of the universe shows that it has no inherent divinity, and that since the universe operates harmoniously (in spite of its disorderly nature) for the general benefit of man, there lies behind it a controlling intelligence. Josephus is clearly rejecting the Stoic tendency to pantheism in favour of the Jewish emphasis on a personal deity endowed with purpose and free will.

(157) *the opposition of the Chaldaeans*: according to Gen. 12: 4 Abraham migrated 'as the LORD had bidden him'; there is no reference to local hostility. Philo, however, also refers to Chaldaean opposition to Abraham's beliefs; Abraham's departure from Chaldaea stands for his recognition that the universe is not God. The background of these stories lies in the Jewish diaspora; the differences in belief between Jews and Gentiles had to be explained and justified. In particular, there was Jewish opposition to Chaldaean astrology (cp. Isa. 47; Dan. 2), and Abraham appears in apologetic literature as one with superior know-ledge of the heavens, as here, and in *Ant.* 1.8.2 (168), where he teaches the Egyptians astronomy (see p. 149 below), and in fragments preserved from Aristobulus and Eupolemus (in Eusebius, *P.E.* XIII.12; IX.17–18).

Abraham's reputation for astronomy and astrology is probably based on Gen. 15: 5, where God tells Abraham to look at the heavens and to number the stars. Josephus notes that the longevity of the patriarchs was designed by God partly 'on account of the value of their studies in astronomy and geometry' (*Ant.* 1.3.9 (106)). Abraham is shown as one who rises above Chaldaean astronomy, understanding the stars correctly and worshipping their creator. In the Palestinian Jewish tradition, however, Abraham's knowledge of the stars was suspect, and by one rabbi treated as the idolatry of his early years.

Josephus frequently in *Antiquities* notes that events happen according to *the will...of God*, and more particularly emphasises that things happen according to the providence (*pronoia*) of God. Thus, for example, Abraham accepted the demanded sacrifice of Isaac on the ground that enjoyment of life was entirely dependent upon God's providence (*Ant.* 1.13.2 (225)). Joseph accepted his prison sentence confidently and had swift proof of God's providence in the trust put in him by his gaoler (*Ant.* II.5.1 (60f)). In *Ant.* X.11.7 (278) Josephus strongly criticises the Epicureans 'who dismiss providence from life and reject the idea that God controls events' (see below, p. 170).

(158) *Berosus* was a Babylonian priest of the god Bel. He lived about the turn of the third to second century BC, and dedicated his three-volume history of Babylon (from the beginning of the world to the death of Alexander the Great) to Antiochus I. He wrote in Greek. Josephus quotes a lengthy passage referring to the deeds of Nabopolassar and his son Nebuchadnezzar in *Apion* 1.19–20 (128–53). The identification of *a certain righteous man* with Abraham may derive from Josephus or Jewish tradition rather than from Berosus himself, and from the biblical count of ten generations beween Noah and Abraham (Gen. 11: 10–27).

(159) *Hecataeus*, a contemporary of Alexander the Great, Antiochus I and Berosus, came from Abdera, an important city on the Thracian coast. He is mentioned in the Letter of Aristeas 31 (see p. 21). His large work on Egypt, of which his book on the Jews may or may not have been a part (*Apion* 1.22 (183)), is quoted by the Letter of Aristeas, Diodorus Siculus, and Josephus, and is an important source for the hellenistic view of the Jews, comparatively well-informed and not unsympathetic. The *book* about Abraham, however, may not be authentic; according to Clement of Alexandria it contained some propagandistic verses, falsely attributed to the Greek poet Sophocles (496–406 BC) and preaching monotheism. *Nicolaus of Damascus*, born *c.* 64 BC, became political adviser to Herod the Great, and a prolific writer of plays, philosophy, biography, and history. Josephus used him

as a major source for his account of the reign of Herod. The 144 books of the *Histories* told the story of the world from its creation to the death of Herod. Like Trogus Pompeius (an historian from Gaul, *c.* 20 BC, who based his work on the first-century BC writer Timagenes of Alexandria), Nicolaus credits Abraham with ruling as king for a time in Damascus. Possibly this story originally developed from the tradition that Abraham pursued raiders beyond Damascus (Gen. 14: 15) and that his heir was one Eliezer of Damascus (Gen. 15: 2).

(160) *the land then called Canaan, now Judaea*: the phrase attracts attention, because Judaea was only part of what had once been Canaan. Nicolaus probably knew this, and Josephus certainly did. The aim may be to connect Abraham with Judaea and to avoid connecting him with Samaria and Shechem.

Josephus follows Gen. 12: 10–20 and tells the story of Abraham's visit to Egypt and the concealment from Pharaoh of Sarai's true status. But Josephus changes the motive for Abraham's visit. Abraham wishes to learn about Egyptian religion; 'he would become a disciple if he found their beliefs superior, or, if his own were better, he would try to convert them to a better view' (*Ant.* 1.8.1 (161)). Josephus' Abraham is not narrow-minded; he is as willing to learn as Aristotle (see below, p. 180), and as rational as any hellenistic philosopher.

ABRAHAM AS A MAN OF LEARNING

Ant. 1.8.2 (166)   The Egyptians enjoyed a variety of beliefs and practices, but showed great contempt for each other's accustomed ways. For this reason they were perpetually quarrelling among themselves. Abraham conferred with each party, and rejected the arguments they put for their own positions, demonstrating them to be worthless and devoid of truth.

(167)   Having thus won at these meetings their respect for his extreme intelligence, quickness of perception, and powers of persuasion on whatever subject he set himself to expound, he readily gave them instruction in arithmetic and passed on to (168)   them knowledge in astronomy. For until Abraham's arrival the Egyptians were completely ignorant of these matters, knowledge of which spread from the Chaldaeans to Egypt, and from Egypt to the Greeks.

(166) *perpetually quarrelling among themselves*: for the hellenistic
view of the Egyptians' quarrelsome nature, see below, p. 186. *rejected
the arguments*: Josephus presents Abraham as exposing the failings of
Egyptian religion as he had previously exposed those of the Chaldaean
religion (cp. pp. 144f above).

(167) *his extreme intelligence...powers of persuasion*: compare the
similar description on p. 144 above.

arithmetic: the Egyptians were capable of calculation long before
Abraham's time, as is shown by the evidence of their buildings, and
by such texts as the Moscow Papyrus and the Rhind Papyrus, which
pose mathematical problems with their answers from the early middle
second millenium BC, though it seems that their mathematical expertise
remained at a fairly elementary level. Perhaps partly as a result of this
mathematical poverty, there is little extant evidence of astronomical
ability in ancient Egypt, though it was in Egypt that the division of
the year into 365 days and of the day into 24 hours was first practised.

The Mesopotamian skills in mathematics and *astronomy* were well
known, and it would be natural for Josephus, like others before him,
to think of diffusion from Mesopotamia to Egypt. In the second century
BC, Artapanus and Pseudo-Eupolemus (in Eusebius, *P.E.* IX.17.1–9,
18.1; see above, p. 7) similarly say that Abraham brought astrology
to Egypt.

(168) *and from Egypt to the Greeks*: it seems more likely that
Babylonian knowledge and technical skills reached Greece by way of
Ionia than by way of Egypt, though it is true that there had been
Egyptian influence in the eastern Mediterranean and Levant throughout
the second millennium BC.

From *Ant.* II.9.1 (201) onwards, Josephus tells the familiar story of
Moses. He adds to it an Egyptian prediction that Egypt would suffer
from a king to be born to the Israelites. The young Moses is pictured
as a boy of intelligence and maturity beyond his years, of stature and
beauty and engaging charm. His behaviour at court, where he tramples
on the royal diadem, leads a scribe at Pharaoh's court to recognise the
fulfilment of the prophecy and to urge the death of the child, but Moses
is saved by God's providence. He becomes an Egyptian general,
defeating the invading Ethiopians and marrying an Ethiopian princess.
He is then forced by Egyptian envy to take refuge in Midian. Josephus
now returns to follow the biblical story up to the destruction of the
Egyptians in the sea.

MOSES

Ant. II.16.4 (345) The Hebrews could not restrain themselves for joy at their unbelievable deliverance and the destruction of the enemy. Now that those who wanted to enslave them had been destroyed, they confidently believed that they had been granted freedom, and that God was clearly on their side.

(346) And having in this way escaped danger, and in addition having seen their enemies punished in a manner unparalleled, so far as could be remembered, in the previous history of mankind, they spent the whole night in singing and revelry. Moses composed in hexameter verse an ode in praise of God and in thanksgiving for his goodness.

5 (347) I have therefore handed down each of these stories exactly as I found them in the scriptures. No one should wonder at the unbelievable nature of the record, or that it was to men of old time, innocent of deceit, that the road of salvation appeared, or that it was through the sea, or that (348) it happened through the will of God, or fortuitously. After all, it was in front of men born only yesterday or the day before, the followers of Alexander King of Macedon, that the Pamphylian Sea retreated, offering through its waves a road to men who had no other way. This was when God wished to destroy the Persian Empire, and the story is agreed by all those who have compiled accounts of Alexander's exploits. On such matters, every one must draw his own conclusions.

Josephus typically leaves his readers to assess whether this event was an act of God or a natural event paralleled in more recent history.

(345) *their unbelievable deliverance*: Josephus' view of the miraculous is not entirely clear. Here he does seem to accept the saving event as at least *paradoxos*, 'contrary to belief', and urges his readers to accept it as such, defending himself by saying that he has told the story exactly as he found it in the scriptures. A few pages earlier Josephus noted the retreat of the sea at the touch of Moses' rod as 'a clear manifestation of God' (*epiphaneia*), a word he uses elsewhere to describe such

occurrences as the spontaneous burning of sacrifices on the altar (*Ant.* VIII.4.4 (119)) or a providential and unexpected shower of rain (*Ant.* XVIII.8.6 (286)). He does not believe that things happen fortuitously (*automatōs*), but by God's providence (*pronoia*) (cp. *Ant.* IV.3.2 (47); X.11.7 (278); see above, p. 148). So Moses' miracles proceed 'not from witchcraft or deception...but from God's providence and power' (*Ant.* II.13.3 (286)). But Josephus is also prepared to meet hellenistic rationalism: thus he finds naturalistic explanations for the longevity of the patriarchs (*Ant.* I.3.9 (104–6)), for the sweetening of the waters of Marah (Exod. 15: 23; *Ant.* III.1.2 (8)), and for the supply of quails (Exod. 16: 11f; *Ant.* III.1.5 (25)). In his introduction of the *Antiquities*, Josephus argues that the lawgiver Moses began his work by studying the nature of God and contemplating his work 'with the eye of reason', and that the inquirer will find in the Law 'nothing irrational, nothing out of harmony with the greatness of God and his love for men; for in the Law everything is presented consistently with the nature of the universe' (Prologue 1.4 (24)).

(346) The *hexameter verse* had six feet, the first four of dactyls (one long followed by two short syllables) or spondees (two long syllables), the fifth a dactyl, and the sixth a spondee or a trochee (a long syllable followed by a short). A caesura divided the line in the third or fourth foot. Dactylic hexameters of this sort were used by the Greek epic poets from Homer (and his predecessors) onwards, and later taken up by Roman poets. The metre was used at Alexandria by the Jewish authors of the Sibylline Oracles (see pp. 35–42). The 'Song of Moses' in Exod. 15 was not originally composed in Greek dactylic hexameters but in Hebrew verse, which has a quite different rhythmic structure. Josephus appears to be presenting Moses as a poet worthy to be compared with Homer, whose great epic poems, the *Iliad* and the *Odyssey*, held such a high place in Greek education and tradition. In *Ant.* IV.8.44 (303) Josephus says that Moses read publicly a poem in hexameter verse, which he deposited in a book in the Temple. 'It contained a prophecy of future events, in accordance with which everything has happened and continues to happen.' It looks as if Josephus is here crediting Moses with poems exactly like the Sibylline Oracles.

(348) *the Pamphylian sea retreated*: the geographer Strabo, writing in the early years of the first century AD, says that Alexander, on his way eastwards through Turkey, chose to avoid a roundabout inland route through the Lycian mountains and march northwards along the western shore of the gulf of Phaselis, where the mountains descend sheer to the sea. (See Map 1.) In calm weather this was possible, but

Alexander made the attempt too soon after stormy weather, and the army marched in water, submerged to their navels (*Geography* XIV.3.9). Arrian, writing over a century later but using the accounts of Alexander's general, Ptolemy, notes the difficulties of the route but says that a north wind providentially set in, allowing a swift and easy passage (*Anabasis* I. 26). Josephus seems to have made this story conform a little more to the biblical one for the sake of the parallel.

Another aspect of the parallel is that Moses is directly compared with Alexander as a general (*stratēgos*). Unlike the Old Testament, Josephus emphasises the military aspects of Moses' leadership, demonstrating his generalship against the Ethiopians, the Egyptians, and the Canaanites, and over the Jewish force; in his final eulogy of Moses, Josephus says: 'as a general, he ranked among the leading few' (*Ant.* IV.8.49 (329)).

his own conclusions: see above, p. 141. One scholar describes this sentence as 'a final verbal shrug of the shoulders'. But Josephus is not in fact indifferent; he is both Jew and hellenist, allowing place both to God's *pronoia* and also to scientific and philosophical explanations where available — an attitude equally common today among educated believers.

The first half of *Ant.* IV is largely taken up with the extended accounts of two episodes — the rebellion of Korah, Abiram, and Dathan (Num. 16) and the story of Balaam (Num. 22–4). The book begins with a minor episode, arising from the Israelites' complaint that Moses is a tyrant; in defiance of Moses, the Israelites fight the Canaanites and are defeated. Josephus then describes the rebellion of Korah, who seeks the priesthood for himself and accuses Moses of despotic behaviour in conferring the honour upon Aaron and his family. Moses meets the rebellion by proposing that the choice of priesthood should be left to God, and Korah and his followers are dramatically eliminated by earthquake and fire. After narrating the events described in Num. 18–21, Josephus turns to his next major section, the story of Balak and Balaam.

BALAAM

Ant. IV.6.6 (126) Balak, angry because the Israelites had not been cursed, sent Balaam away without paying him any fee. But Balaam, when he had already set out on his way and had reached the Euphrates' crossing, sent for Balak and the
(127) Midianite leaders, and said: 'Balak, and you Midianite

representatives here, I must help you even if it means opposing
God's will. The Hebrew race is never likely to be overwhelmed
by total destruction, or by war, plague, or famine of the earth's
produce, and they are not likely to be destroyed by any other
(128) irrational cause. For God's providence is watching over them
to preserve them from all harm and to prevent any such totally
destructive disaster coming upon them. They may suffer some
small temporary misfortunes, but after that they will flourish
once more, to the dismay of those who brought their troubles
(129) upon them. If, then, you are anxious to win some temporary
success against them, you might achieve it by acting as follows.
Send to the neighbourhood of the Israelite camp the best-
looking of your daughters, the ones most likely by their beauty
to influence and overcome the good sense of those who see
them. Adorn their figures to improve their good looks, and
order them to go along with the young men when invited.
(130) As soon as they see the young men at the mercy of their desires,
they should desert them; and when the young men urge them
to stay, they must not agree to this until they have persuaded
the men to renounce their ancestral laws and the God at whose
direction they honour them, and to worship the Midianite and
Moabite gods. In this way the wrath of God will come upon
them.' And having proposed this scheme to them, Balaam
departed.

In the biblical account of Num. 22–4, the Moabites and Midianites hire
the seer Balaam to curse the invading Israelites for them, but Balaam,
under God's instructions, blesses them; in Num. 25, the involvement
of the Israelite men with the Moabite and Midianite women leads to
apostasy. Josephus develops and expands the story, not only to
emphasise the point that Israelite passion for foreign women undermines
the authority of the Law and the lawgiver, and leads to idolatry and
apostasy, but also to demonstrate that those who forsake Jewish
exclusivism and the authority of the Mosaic Law in order to conform
to the 'civilised' behaviour of the other nations do not gain the personal
liberty they claim to be seeking. The climax comes in the speech of
Zambrias (see below, pp. 158–60).

(126) *had reached the Euphrates' crossing*: according to Num. 22: 5, Balak sent messengers to Balaam 'at Pethor, by the Euphrates', usually identified as Assyrian Pitru (south of Carchemish) in northern Syria, which is consistent with the information in Num. 23: 7 that Balaam came from Aram (Syria). Josephus clearly accepts this, but the discovery in 1967 at Tell Deir'Alla in Jordan of an Aramaic inscription written in ink on a plastered wall referring to a prophetic figure Balaam reinforces a long-held suspicion that Balaam was originally a more local figure belonging somewhere east of the River Jordan. *sent for Balak and the Midianite leaders*: Balaam has, in spite of his personal inclination to help Balak, pronounced over Israel a blessing, not a curse. He now makes one last attempt to help Balak, by offering some advice. This presentation of Balaam as sympathetic to the Moabite–Midianite cause derives from Num. 31: 8, where the Israelites put Balaam to death along with the five enemy Midianite kings; in Num. 22–4 Balaam is neutral. The hostility of Balaam is developed in later tradition. In the New Testament (Jude 11 and 2 Pet. 2: 15; cp. CBC *The Letters of Peter and Jude*, pp. 92, 123f) and the Mishnah (Abot 5: 22) Balaam has become the arch-enemy of Israel.

(129 *Send...the best-looking of your daughters*: the root of this story probably lies in Num. 31: 16; after the destruction of the Midianites, Moses says to the Israelites: 'Have you spared all the women?... Remember, it was they who, on Balaam's departure (RSV, 'by the counsel of Balaam'), set about seducing the Israelites into disloyalty to the LORD that day at Peor.' The RSV translation explicitly blames Balaam's advice for what the women did, as does the Septuagint translation.

The Midianites follow Balaam's advice. Their daughters, having aroused the passions of the Israelite youth, pretend to withdraw, thus prompting immediate Israelite promises of marriage and possessions. The Midianite girls coyly demand pledges of the men's good intentions, which are promised.

ISRAELITE APOSTASY

Ant. IV.6.8 (137)   'Since you have agreed on this', the Midianite
          women said, 'and since in matters of behaviour and way
          of life your practice is so totally different from everyone
          else's – for example, your food is distinctive, and you do
          not drink the same kind of things as other people – if you

want to live with us you must worship our gods. There
could be no better evidence of the feelings you say you now
have for us and of your future commitment than

(138)   worshipping the same gods as we do. No one would blame
you if you were to turn to worshipping the gods of the
country to which you have come, especially since our gods
are common to everybody and your god is worshipped by
none but yourselves.' The young men ought, therefore, they
said, to share the general beliefs or seek another world in
which to live alone, conforming to their own private laws.

9 (139)   The young men, infatuated by love for the girls, thought
that this was well said, and, surrendering themselves to what
was proposed, flouted the ancestral laws, accepted the
existence of many other gods and determined to sacrifice
to them in accordance with the laws established by the local
worshippers. They were happy to indulge in non-Jewish
food and, for the sake of pleasing the women, they persisted
in doing the precise opposite of what their own Law

(140)   commanded. As a result, the young men's lawless behaviour
soon ran through the whole army, and they fell into worse
sedition than before. There was a danger that their Jewish
way of life would be completely corrupted. For once the
young men had tasted non-Jewish ways of life, they became
totally addicted, and there were cases where leading men
of distinguished and virtuous ancestry were corrupted along
with the others.

Josephus may have in mind a story in Herodotus (*Histories* IV.110–17).
When the Amazons, a warlike race of women, settled in Scythia, the
young men of Scythia were sent to prepare the way for intermarriage.
In due course the young men proposed marriage and peaceful
settlement to the Amazons, who refused on the grounds that their own
way of life in the field was so different from the domesticated ways
of the Scythian women, and the Amazons in turn invited the Scythians
to collect their patrimonies and join the Amazons and live separately
with them. The youths agreed, but the Amazons then claimed that they
feared to live without family protection in the land they had once
pillaged, and they emigrated with their new husbands to new

territories. There are parallels with Josephus' story; in each story the men speak of homes and possessions, the women speak of a cultural division and a fear of the result of settling down with the men, and it is the men who make the break from their parents' way of life.

(137) *your practice is so totally different*: this was a common hellenistic accusation against the Jews. In Esther 3: 8, Haman observes to King Ahasuerus about the Jews: 'There is a certain people, dispersed among the many peoples in all the provinces of your kingdom, who keep themselves apart. Their laws are different from those of every other people; they do not keep your majesty's laws.' Josephus (*Apion* II.7 (79)) says that the Stoic Posidonius of Apamea (135–51 BC) and Apollonius Molon, a rhetorician from Rhodes, 'accuse us of not worshipping the same gods as other people'. Apion himself falsely asserts 'that we swear by God who made the heaven and the earth and the sea to show no favour to any foreigner, especially to the Greeks' (*Apion* II.10 (121)). Tacitus spoke of the Jews as 'atheists and haters of mankind' (*Histories* v.5) and Apollonius Molon of 'atheists and misanthropes' (*Apion* II.14 (148)). Josephus clearly feels the importance of this charge, and announced his intention of following *Antiquities* with a treatise in four books 'on our Jewish beliefs about God and his being, and about the laws – why some things are allowed us by them, and other things are forbidden' (*Ant* xx.12.1 (268)). (This work may be the 'treatise on customs and causes' announced in *Ant*. I, Prologue 4 (25) and *Ant*. IV.8.4 (198). Some scholars think that Josephus did not live to write this work, others that *Apion* was meant to fulfil this aim, and others that the material was not published separately but later integrated into *Ant*. III.9.1 – 12.3 (224–86); IV.4.3–4 (67–75), passages based on the laws of Leviticus and Numbers. See above, pp. 88f.) *your food is distinctive*: Apion 'charges us with sacrificing domestic animals and not eating pork' (*Apion* II.13 (137)). Josephus gives the basic rules in *Ant*. III.11.2 (259–60). In Acts 15: 29 the early Christian Church asked its gentile members 'to abstain from meat that has been offered to idols, from blood, from anything that has been strangled', and this prohibition of eating flesh with blood in it was of basic importance (cp. Gen 9: 4; Lev. 3: 17; 17: 10, and elsewhere). Also forbidden were animals that died from natural causes, or as the prey of other animals, or that had been killed in unprescribed ways, or were classed as unclean (cp. Lev. 11 and Deut. 14). *you do not drink the same kind of things as other people*: there was little prohibited here apart from blood, or from wine from which an oblation had been poured to a pagan deity, or from anything that had become unclean.

(138) *No one would blame you*...: this sentence is the crux of the

matter, and the argument was probably familiar to every diaspora Jew. But to accept this argument meant breaking the first commandment, 'You shall have no other god to set against me' (Exod. 20: 3), and denying the belief that 'God, the creator of all, is one', the first expression of which Josephus attributes to Abraham (*Ant.* 1.7.1 (155); see above, p. 145). The temptation *to share the general beliefs* must sometimes have been very great.

(139–140) The result is a total denial of *the ancestral laws* and *worse sedition than before* (i.e., under Korah) and *a danger that their Jewish way of life would be completely corrupted.* In Balaam's time the laws were hardly yet ancestral, but Josephus is thinking of his own contemporaries. According to Acts 22: 3, Paul claims to have been 'thoroughly trained in every point of our ancestral law'.

Josephus brings the story of Balaam to a climax by developing the character of the man named in Num. 25: 14 as Zimri, an Israelite killed for bringing a Midianite woman into his family. When Moses complains that the Israelites were preferring pleasure to a God-fearing life, Zambrias, as Josephus calls him (following the Septuagint), makes a speech accusing Moses of tyrannically depriving the Israelites of the pleasure of personal liberty and suppressing what is universally agreed to be good.

ZAMBRIAS

Ant. IV.6.10 (141)   Among them was also Zambrias, the head of the tribe of Simeon, who took as his companion Chosbia, Midianitess, the daughter of Souros, one of the local chiefs. At the prompting of the woman, he ignored the Mosaic decrees and applied himself to the religious practices that

11 (145)   would please her...After Moses had spoken, Zambrias stood up and said: 'Very well, Moses, it is for you to practise the laws for which you have been so enthusiastic. You have secured them for the people only through their naivety. If they had not had that character, you would already have been rebuked, and you would have learned

(146)   that the Hebrews are not easily imposed upon. But you will not find me following your tyrannical commands. So far you have done nothing less than wickedly contrive

slavery for us and power for yourself under the pretext of "laws" and "God". You have deprived us of the pleasure of liberty in life, which is the prerogative of men who are

(147) free and own no master. You would become harsher than the Egyptians to the Hebrews if you decided to punish by law each man's wish to please himself. Justice would be better served if you yourself were to undergo punishment for having chosen to suppress what is universally agreed to be good and for having established, in defiance of

(148) universal opinion, your own eccentricity. I myself might reasonably be restrained from my present behaviour if, having first considered it proper, I then hesitated to proclaim it publicly in this assembly. As you say, I have married a non-Jewish wife. You shall hear what I have done from my own mouth – I am a free man – for I have

(149) no intention of hiding the matter. I sacrifice to the gods to whom I think it right to sacrifice, in the belief that I can arrive at truth from many sources, and that I do not have to live as if under some tyranny, making the entire hope of my whole life dependent on one man. There will be no joy for anyone who declares that he has greater control than my own personal will over my actions.'

Zambrias has proposed to demonstrate his own freedom by marrying and worshipping whom he likes, but he is eventually killed by Phinehas, the high priest's son, 'a man in every way superior to the other young men', as punishment for his apostasy. This cautionary tale is clearly relevant to the situation of the Jews living amid Gentiles in the diaspora; Josephus firmly supports the view that Jewish identity is preserved not so much by the existence of the Jewish state as by the observance of the Jewish Law.

(141) *Zambrias*: according to Num. 25: 14, Zimri, the son of Salu, a chief in a Simeonite family. *Chosbia*: Cozbi daughter of Zur, who was at the head of a group of fathers' families in Midian (Num. 25: 15). *the religious practices that would please her*: i.e., the cult of the Baal of Peor (Num. 25: 1–4). The explanation found in many manuscripts, 'by ceasing to offer sacrifice in accordance with the ancestral laws, and by marrying a foreigner', probably derives from an early glossator.

(145) *after Moses had spoken*: Moses met the crisis by calling an assembly, complaining that the people were acting unworthily in preferring pleasure to a God-fearing life, and urging them to repent (142–4).

(146) *You have deprived us of the pleasure of personal liberty in life*: Zambrias' main complaint is that servile obedience to the Law takes away a man's freedom to make independent decisions and to be himself (Greek, *to autoexousion*: the word is used, e.g., by the first-century AD philosopher Musonius Rufus, of being free of all *anangkē*, necessity). Zambrias' plea for *autoexousion* may reflect the Stoic teaching of a man like Epictetus (*Discourses* II.16.42): 'Have courage to look up to God and say: "From now on, treat me as you will. I am of one mind with you; I am yours. I ask for no exemption from anything you think good."' However, the biblical Jewish tradition was that men were free to choose between life and good, death and evil, obedience to the commands of God and the worship of other gods (cp. Deut. 30: 15–20), and Zambrias, in biblical terms, exercises his freedom, claims that he is free to worship other gods, and receives his due reward.

The hellenistic Jewish philosopher Philo, in his treatise *That every good man is free* (*Quod omnis Probus Liber sit*), argued along Stoic lines that true freedom lies in being free from domination by the passions and in accepting God as one's leader (Zambrias therefore would fail on both counts). Philo would have no difficulty with Zambrias' argument that the Mosaic Law entailed the annulment of freedom; soldiers, slaves and children, and law-abiding communities, for all their obedience, can still be free. 'The wise man is free because he does right voluntarily, cannot be compelled to do wrong, and treats things indifferent with indifference.' The paradox of the Anglican collect – 'whose service is perfect freedom' – has a long history. Zambrias represents not so much the hellenistic philosopher as the diaspora Jew making use of a second-hand philosophy to justify his apostasy.

Zambrias is killed, the Midianites are defeated, Joshua is appointed successor to Moses, and the land settlements are made (cp. Num. 26–36). Josephus now turns to Deuteronomy. Moses addresses the people and presents them with 'the laws and constitution written in a book' (*Ant.* IV.8.3 (194)).

THE LAW OF MOSES AND DIRECTIONS FOR THE TEMPLE

Ant. IV.8.4 (196)   Before turning to give an account of other matters, I wish to say something about the constitution. It reflects the worth of Moses' personal qualities and enables those who come across it to learn from it what kind of laws we had from the beginning. It has all been written down just as he left it; we have not added anything by way of ornament,

(197)   nor anything that Moses did not leave for us. What is new is our arrangement of each law according to subject-matter, for the laws he wrote were left in the haphazard arrangement in which he learned them from God. I thought it necessary to explain this detail beforehand, lest any fellow Jew who meets this work should blame me for having made mistakes.

(198)   Here, then, are set out these laws of ours that relate to the constitution. Those which Moses left bearing on our general behaviour towards one another I have put on one side for treatment in my work 'On customs and causes', which, with the help of God, I intend to put together after completing this present work.

5 (199)   'When you have won the land of Canaan and have leisure to enjoy its good things, and decide to start founding cities, you will please God and secure your prosperity by observing

(200)   the following: Let there be one holy city in the most beautiful and best-appointed part of the land of Canaan, a city that God will select for himself by prophetic means. And let there be one sanctuary in it, and one altar, its stones not worked but selected to fit together and when plastered

(201)   pleasing and orderly to the eye. The approach to the altar must not be up steps but up an inclined ramp. There must be no altar or sanctuary in any other city, for God is one, and the Hebrew race is one.'

(196) *constitution*: by using this word (Greek *politeia*) Josephus set the Mosaic Law in a new context. A *politeia* was the civil constitution of the state; the fourth-century BC philosopher Aristotle wrote an

important work entitled *Politeiai* (*Constitutions*), of which the lost *Athēnaiōn politeia* (*The constitution of the Athenians*) was discovered in Egypt in 1890. The statesman Aeschines (*c.* 397–322 BC) referred to three types of *politeia*: tyranny, oligarchy, and democracy (Josephus appears to have preferred the second in its aristocratic form: cp. *Ant.* IV.8.17 (223)). 'Where there are no laws', said Aristotle, 'there is no *politeia.*' Josephus thus presents the Jewish state in terms recognisable throughout the Graeco-Roman world, even if his gentile readers would find the laws of the constitution sometimes a little strange. *we have not added anything*: Josephus refers to the command of Deut. 4: 2. He has already stated that he will follow the scriptural record 'neither adding nor omitting anything' (*Ant.* Prologue 1 (17)).

(197) *according to subject-matter*: Josephus organises his material (mostly from Exodus and Deuteronomy) with care, concentrating on those laws that concern the political constitution and leaving others (mainly from Leviticus and Numbers) to his projected work 'On customs and causes' (for which see above, pp. 88f). (Other material, on circumcision, the sabbath, and food laws, appears in *Apion* II.13 (137–42), 2 (20–7), 32 (234), 38 (282), 8 (103–9), 23 (193–8).) Josephus begins with a statement of the cardinal requirements of Judaism – one city, one temple, one altar, 'for God is one, and the Hebrew race is one' – with legislation on cultic affairs such as blasphemy, tithes, feasts, sacrifices, reading of the Law, and prayers. He turns next to the administration of justice; then to laws relating to the land and the harvests; then to laws of marriage, property, money, and torts; and finally to regulations for war. *in the haphazard arrangement in which he learned them from God*: in the Old Testament, Moses receives separately the ten commandments, the legislation of Exod. 20: 21 – 23: 33, the instructions about the cult in Exod. 25–31, the further cultic instructions of Exod. 34, the cultic instructions of Lev. 1–7, and a large number of individual laws or groupings of laws throughout the rest of Leviticus and Numbers. Deuteronomy is a regrouping of many laws, presented as Moses' recapitulation of the Law on the plains of Moab.

(199) *When you have won... and decide to start founding cities*: this was the typical pattern of Greek colonisation. The Israelite occupation of Palestine was not followed immediately by the building of cities: on the whole, this came later, under the monarchy (e.g., Gezer, Beth-horon (1 Kings 9: 17); Raamah (1 Kings 15: 17); Geba (1 Kings 15: 22); Samaria (1 Kings 16: 24); Jericho (1 Kings 16: 34); Elath (2 Kings 14: 22).

(200) *one holy city*: the reference is to Deut. 12: 5, 11, 14, where

it is commanded that burnt-offerings, sacrifices, tithes, and votive-offerings shall be presented to God only in 'the place which the LORD your God will choose out of all your tribes to receive his Name that it may dwell there'. This, in Judaean circles at least, was taken to be Jerusalem (cp. 1 Kings 8: 44; 2 Kings 21: 7; Zech. 1: 17). *by prophetic means*: Josephus may have in mind Nathan's oracle (2 Sam. 7, cp. 1 Kings 5: 5f), which promises that Solomon would build a house for the Lord, but does not speak of God's choosing Jerusalem, though cp. 1 Kings 14: 21: Rehoboam 'reigned for seventeen years in Jerusalem, the city which the LORD had chosen out of all the tribes of Israel to receive his Name'. *in the most beautiful and best-appointed part*: Apion 1.22 (197) refers to the great beauty of Jerusalem; cp. Ps. 50: 2; 'God shines out from Zion, perfect in beauty', and Ps. 96: 6: 'might and beauty are in his sanctuary'. The beauty was not limited to the sanctuary; cp. Lam. 2: 15: 'Is this the city once called Perfect in beauty, Joy of the whole earth?' *one altar, its stones not worked but selected to fit together*: the Greek words are reminiscent of a phrase in the late-fifth-century BC *History of the War between Athens and Sparta* (IV.4), by the Greek general and historian Thucydides, whom Josephus had read (cp. *Apion* 1.3 (18)). Exod. 20: 25 commands: 'If you make an altar of stones for me, you must not build it of hewn stones, for if you use a chisel on it, you will profane it [cp. Deut. 27: 5f]. You must not mount up to my altar by steps, in case your private parts be exposed on it.' The reference to the altar's being *plastered* may derive from Deut. 27: 4, though here the plaster is to be applied to stones set up on Mount Ebal, not to the altar described in the next verse. Ezek. 43: 17 states that the altar of burnt-offering of the restored Temple was to have steps. Hecataeus, quoted by Josephus (*Apion* 1.22 (198)) speaks of an altar of heaped-up stones, unhewn and unwrought; cp. also 1 Macc. 4: 47, Philo (*De Specialibus Legibus* 1.51 (274)), and the Mishnah, Mid. 3: 4. This last passage also notes that the stones of the ramp and of the altar were quarried without the help of iron tools from virgin soil in the valley of Beth-Kerem, and that 'they did not plaster them with an iron trowel lest it should touch (the stones) and render them invalid' (H. Danby, *The Mishnah* (Oxford, 1933), p. 594).

(201) *in any other city*: Josiah, according to 2 Kings 23, following the demands of the lawbook found in the Temple, defiled high places and destroyed altars outside Jerusalem. In *Apion* II.23 (193), Josephus speaks of 'one sanctuary of the one God'. For Josephus the oneness of God is at the heart of Judaism; Abraham was 'the first to proclaim boldly that God, the creator of all, was one' (*Ant.* 1.7.1 (155)); see above,

p. 145). Moses affirms, in his speech introducing the present passage on the Law, that 'the gracious God is the single source of the good things of creation for all men; for he alone has the power to give these things to those worthy of them' (*Ant.* IV.8.2 (180)). In *Apion* II.16 (164–8), Josephus emphasises the theological unity of Israel's political and religious life in a 'theocracy', which puts all rule and authority into God's hands.

> 'Moses persuaded everybody to look to God as the cause of all blessings...he represented him as one, uncreated, externally unchangeable, in beauty of form beyond all human imagination, made known to us by his power, but unknown in his essential being...Indeed, Pythagoras, Anaxagoras, Plato and the Stoics after him, and almost all the philosophers, seem to have held much the same views about the nature of God.'

DANIEL

Ant. X.11.7 (266)   It might astonish you to hear some of the stories about this man Daniel, but they are worth the telling. Everything turned out well for him in most unexpected ways, as if for one of the greatest prophets. During his lifetime he enjoyed honour and fame among rulers and people alike; now

(267)   that he is dead, he is held in perpetual memory. We still read the books that he compiled and left for us, and from them we have come to believe that Daniel had direct converse with God. He not only made a practice of prophesying future events like other prophets, but he also determined the time of their

(268)   fulfilment. While the prophets foretold the worst and were for this reason hated by both rulers and people, Daniel prophesied success for them. From the welcome nature of his prophecies, he drew upon himself approval from all sides, and from their fulfilment he gained the crowds' trust in his truthfulness and

(269)   respect for his divine power. He left behind writings in which he made clear for us the accuracy and consistency of his prophecy. For he says that when he was in Susa, the Persian capital city, he went out to the plain with his friends, and there arose a sudden earthquake and tremor. His friends fled, and

he was left alone. Terrified, he fell on his face and hands.
Someone touched him, ordering him to stand up and see what
would happen to his fellow citizens many generations later.

(270) He indicated how when he stood up he was shown a great
ram, with many horns springing out of his head, the last of
them being the highest. Then he looked towards the west, and
saw a goat rush through the air from the west, attack the ram,
strike him twice with his horns, throw him to the ground and

(271) trample on him. Then he saw the goat putting out an
enormous horn from his forehead; when it had been broken
off, four other horns sprang up, each turned to one of the
winds. From them (according to Daniel's book) there arose one
other, smaller horn, which God, who showed him these things,
told him would go to war with his people, take their city by
force, disrupt Temple worship, and prevent the offering of
sacrifice for a period of one thousand, two hundred and

(272) ninety-six days. Daniel wrote that he had this vision in the plain
of Susa, and he explained that God interpreted the vision for
him as follows: he said that the ram represented the kingdoms
of the Medes and the Persians, the horns the future rulers, and
the last horn the last king, who would be richer and more

(273) glorious than the others. The goat meant that there would be
a ruler from among the Greeks who would meet the Persian
king twice in battle, defeat him, and take over the whole

(274) empire. The enormous horn on the goat's forehead represented
the first king. The springing up of the four horns when the
first fell out and the turning of each horn towards one of
the four corners of the earth indicated the *Diadochoi* after the
death of the first king and the division of the empire between
them (they were neither the king's sons nor close relatives) for

(275) a rule of many years' duration over the world. From among
them would arise one particular king who would make war
against the Jewish nation and its laws, pillage the sanctuary,

(276) and prevent the offering of sacrifice for three years. And
indeed, our nation came to suffer all this under Antiochus

Epiphanes, exactly as Daniel had foreseen and predicted in his writing many years previously. Daniel wrote in similar fashion also about the Roman Empire, prophesying that Jerusalem would be captured by the Romans and the Temple desolated.

(277)   All this he handed down to us, having committed it to writing at God's revelation. The result was that those who read it and observed events were astonished at the honour in which Daniel was held by God. From the same events they discovered the

(278)   errors of the Epicureans, who dismiss providence from life and reject the idea that God controls events or that creation is governed by a blessed and immortal being with the perpetuity of the whole in view. They say rather that the cosmos runs itself without there being any hands on the reins or external

(279)   supervision. But if it were uncontrolled in this way, it would be dashed to pieces by its mindless impetus and would be totally destroyed – just as one sees ships without their helmsmen foundering in the gale, or chariots without their drivers

(280)   overturning. Those who publicise the view that God has no concern for mankind seem to me to hold the most improbable views, to judge from Daniel's prophecies. For if it is the case that the cosmos proceeds in some automatic way, we should not have seen everything turning out in accordance with his

(281)   prophecies. But I have written on these matters in accordance with my reading. If any one wishes to put a different construction on them, he is free to do so without blame.

Josephus sets his version of the story of Daniel in the period of the exile. He tells the story of Dan. 1–6 in full, but from chs. 7–12 he limits himself to an account of the vision of the ram and the goat and its interpretation in Dan. 8. He emphasises Daniel's prophetic powers and skill at interpreting dreams, noting particularly that what Daniel predicted was actually fulfilled partly under Antiochus IV and partly in events that Josephus himself experienced. From the accuracy of Daniel's prophecies, Josephus demonstrates to his readers the *pronoia* (providence) of God (see above, p. 148), taking the opportunity to attack the Epicurean philosophers, who argued that the world ran by its own momentum (*automatōs*), that the gods had no concern or forethought for human affairs, and that therefore their intentions could not be prophesied or predicted.

(266) *in most unexpected ways*: e.g., the story of Daniel in the lions' den (Dan. 6). *as if for one of the greatest prophets*: the Book of Daniel was probably not completed until *c.* 160 BC and therefore was not included among the prophetic books of the Bible but among the writings (*kethūbīm*). Josephus, however, placing Daniel's life and activity in the sixth century BC, has no difficulty in including Daniel among the goodly fellowship of the prophets. Josephus saw him as *one of the greatest* simply because so many of his predictions appeared to have been fulfilled. *honour and fame among rulers and people alike*: from Nebuchadnezzar (Dan. 2: 48), Belshazzar (Dan. 5: 29), and Darius and all in his royal domains (Dan. 6: 25f).

(267) *We still read...*: clearly the Book of Daniel was commonly accepted by Josephus' time. It was known and read at Qumran. *the books that he compiled*: only one book is known. The Apocrypha contains additions to it – The Song of the Three (including the prayer of Azariah), and the stories of Daniel and Susanna, and of Daniel, Bel, and the Snake. Josephus did not use these stories, and may not have known them. *he also determined the time of their fulfilment*: Josephus is presumably referring to Dan. 8: 14, where Daniel prophesies that the desecration of the sanctuary will last one thousand one hundred and fifty days (from autumn 167 BC to 14 December 164 BC), and to Dan. 12: 11f, where the period from the cessation of the daily sacrifice to the end is given as 'one thousand two hundred and ninety days', and a further reference is made to him 'who waits and lives to see the completion of one thousand three hundred and thirty-five days'. In Dan. 7: 25, the saints of the Most High will be given into the hands of the fourth beast for 'a time, and times, and half a time', i.e., three and a half years; cp. Dan. 9: 27, where the prince who is to come 'shall make a firm league with the mighty for one week; and, the week half spent, he shall put a stop to sacrifice and offering'. Cp. also Dan. 12: 7.

(268) *Daniel prophesied success*: in Josephus' version, Daniel has so far prophesied to Nebuchadnezzar that his empire will be brought to an end (*Ant.* x.10.4 (208)); he has foretold how Nebuchadnezzar's second dream (cp. Dan. 4) would come to pass (*Ant.* x.10.6 (217)), and he has explained to Belshazzar that the writing on the wall presages his end (*Ant.* x.11.3 (239–44)). Such prophecy was perhaps welcome to the Jews; but in the following sections Daniel goes on to prophesy the damage that Antiochus Epiphanes and the Romans would do to the Jewish laws, Temple and sacrifices. This would be welcome only

to those who saw the events of AD 66–70 from the Roman side. As David Daube comments: 'Surely, it is the relationship between the author and the Flavian dynasty that inspires this evaluation.' It is noticeable that Josephus carefully ignores the more hopeful eschatology of Dan. 7–12, in which, after the destruction of the beasts, an everlasting dominion is given to the Son of Man and the people of the saints of the Most High, the angel Michael will appear to guard Israel, and the people will be delivered (cp. Dan. 12: 1–3). Josephus regards prophets who proclaim the imminent salvation of Israel by act of God as misleading and dangerous, and partly responsible for the disasters that have come upon the Jews.

(269) *in Susa, the Persian capital city*: cp. Dan. 8: 2. Susa lay in the region of Elam, east of the River Tigris, north of the Persian Gulf. (See Map 3.) Under the Persian Empire it remained an important city, together with Persepolis (founded by Darius as his capital) and Ecbatana (Darius' summer capital in the cooler north; cp. Ezra 6: 2; Judith 1: 1–14; 2 Macc. 9: 3; in *Ant.* x.11.7 (264) Josephus says that Daniel built a beautiful fortress in Ecbatana). Nehemiah served Artaxerxes I in the palace at Susa (Neh. 1: 1); the story of Esther is also set in Susa. Medieval Jewish legend said that Daniel was buried in Susa, and that to allow equal access to the prophet by both poor and wealthy Jews his remains were suspended from the middle of the bridge across the river.

(270) *a great ram, with many horns*: according to Dan. 8: 3, two horns.

(271) *then...putting out an enormous horn*: cp. Dan. 8: 5, where the goat is equipped with 'a prominent horn' before he attacks the ram. *go to war with his people, take their city by force*: not in Daniel. *one thousand, two hundred and ninety-six days*: in Dan. 8: 14, 'two thousand three hundred evenings and mornings' (i.e., one thousand one hundred and fifty days). Josephus appears to have taken his figure from Dan. 12: 11: 'from the time when the regular offering is abolished and "the abomination of desolation" is set up, there shall be an interval of one thousand two hundred and ninety days', perhaps because the figure of one thousand two hundred and ninety (or ninety-six) is rather nearer than one thousand one hundred and fifty to the three and a half years of Dan. 7: 25 (though cp. *Ant.* x.11.7 (275), p. 165 above, where Josephus refers only to a three-year period for the cessation of sacrifices).

(272) *the ram...the kingdoms of the Medes and the Persians*: a ram or a he-goat is often used symbolically for the leader of a nation (a flock), and the horn symbolises power. The higher of the two horns of Dan.

8: 3 symbolised Persia, which conquered and succeeded Media as the great imperial power. Josephus changes the 'two horns' of Dan. 8: 3 into *horns*, making them refer to the kings of the Medes and the Persians. *the last horn* would thus be Darius III, King of Persia (336–331 BC).

(273) *The goat* in Daniel was the kingdom of Macedonia, and its 'prominent horn' or 'great horn' (Dan. 8: 5, 8) Alexander the Great. In the present passage Josephus speaks of him as *a ruler from among the Greeks* and an *enormous horn*. In the phrase *who would meet the Persians twice in battle* Josephus is probably referring to the battles of Issus (333 BC), by the Gulf of Iskanderun, and Gaugamela (331 BC), east of the River Tigris near Arbela.

(274) *four horns...the 'Diadochoi'*: many writers still use the Greek word *Diadochoi* ('successors') for the rulers who inherited Alexander's empire. They were Ptolemy I of Egypt, Philip Arrhidaeus of Macedonia, Seleucus of Babylon, and Antigonus of Asia Minor. After the battle of Ipsus (301 BC) in which Antigonus was crushed by the other generals, the empire was divided between Ptolemy in Egypt, Cassander in Macedonia, Lysimachus in Thrace, and Seleucus in Babylon. Cp. Dan. 11: 4: 'as soon as he is established, his kingdom will be shattered and split up north, south, east and west. It will not pass to his descendants, nor will any of his successors have an empire like his; his kingdom will be torn up by the roots and given to others as well as to them.'

(275) *one particular king who would make war against the Jewish nation and its laws* is identified in the next sentence as Antiochus Epiphanes; cp. 1 Macc. 1: 10 – 6: 15; 2 Macc. 3: 1 – 9: 29; Dan. 11: 21–45.

(276) *Daniel wrote in similar fashion also about the Roman Empire*: the authenticity of these words has been doubted, but unnecessarily. Josephus sees that the primary reference of Daniel's prophecies is to what the nation experienced under Antiochus Epiphanes, but he also seems to believe that the destructions of Jerusalem and its Temple by Nebuchadnezzar and Antiochus foreshadow the Roman destruction of his own day. Thus, for example, in *Ant.* x.5.1 (79) he says of Jeremiah, prophesying of the fall of Jerusalem in 587 BC: 'This prophet prophesied in addition the terrible things that were going to happen to the city, leaving in his writings reference to the capture of Jerusalem recently inflicted upon us as well as to the Babylonian conquest.' It is of a piece with this that Josephus sees himself as a present-day Jeremiah (cp. *War* v.9.4 (392f)). Josephus, like many other biblical commentators of his own and later times, saw in events of his own day the fulfilment of biblical prophecies. Thus in the reduction in size of the Temple area,

after the fall of the Antonia to the besieging Romans, to a defendable square (*War* VI.5.4 (311)) Josephus probably saw the fulfilment of Dan. 9: 25: 'it shall be built again with squares and moat, but in a troubled time' (RSV). In the death of Ananus the high priest (*War* IV.5.2 (318)) he may have seen the fulfilment of Dan. 9: 26: 'one who is anointed shall be removed with no one to take his part'; in the cessation of the daily sacrifice (*War* VI.2.1 (94)) the fulfilment of Dan 8: 11; 9: 27; 11: 31; and 12: 11; and in the Emperor Vespasian the fulfilment of Dan. 9: 26: 'the horde of an invading prince shall work havoc on city and sanctuary'. In *Ant.* X.10.4 (209–10), where Josephus recounts the dream of Dan. 2, he identifies the kingdom of iron and clay that will destroy the empire of Alexander the Great with the Romans. They in turn will be destroyed by a great stone. Perhaps out of respect for his Roman readers, Josephus declines to explain this stone, but he probably identifies it with the messianic kingdom to come.

(277–8) *the errors of the Epicureans*: Epicurus was an Athenian philosopher who lived *c.* 342–270 BC. He founded a school of disciples who lived with him and followed his teaching, which was often misunderstood to be libertine but in practice tended to ascetic discipline. Epicurus wrote a large number of works, of which only a few fragments remain. At Rome his views were presented in Latin verse by the poet Lucretius (94–55 BC) in his *De rerum natura* (*On the nature of things*). The Epicurean aim was *ataraxia*, the state of being undisturbed, in particular by superstitious fears of divine intervention in the world. Epicurus did not deny the existence of the divine, but argued that 'the blissful and imperishable [cp. Josephus' *blessed and immortal being*] neither for itself knows trouble nor gives trouble to anyone else, so that it is not involved in angry passions or favours. For everything of that kind marks the weak.' Consistently with this, 'the god takes no providential thought for anything. In fact there is no such thing as providence or destiny, but everything happens automatically' (see H. Usener, *Epicurea* (Leipzig and Bonn, 1887), p. 351). To explain this, Epicurus developed the view that the cosmos was formed of atoms that fell through space and collided by making a slight and unpredictable swerve, thus setting in motion the grouping and regrouping of atoms that led to the creation of matter and the free will of man. Epicurus caustically observed that 'if the god attended to the prayers of men, the whole human race would come to a very speedy end, since men are always praying for all kinds of trouble to befall their neighbours'. Josephus' views are nearer the Stoic view that 'the world is ruled by the providence of the gods'. The idea of providence plays a large part in Josephus' presentation of events (see above, pp. 81–3, 148).

Josephus has two lines of argument against the Epicureans. First, if there were no *pronoia* (providence), the world would have destroyed itself, like a driverless chariot or a pilotless ship, but since it manifestly has not, *pronoia* must exist. Secondly, Josephus argues that the existence of *pronoia* is demonstrated clearly by the accurate fulfilment of Daniel's prophecies.

(281) *If anyone wishes...*: Josephus' customary pretence of impartiality; cp. above, p. 141.

GREEK HISTORIANS

Apion 1.2 (6)   In the first place, I am overwhelmed with astonishment at those who believe that in matters of ancient history attention should be given to the Greeks alone, and that the truth should be sought from them, no credence being given to us or to other men. For in my observation, the opposite is the case, at least if we are to avoid idle prejudice and to judge events on their (7) own merit. For in Greek history, everything is of recent origin – dating from yesterday, one might say, or from the day before: I refer to the foundation of their cities, the world of art and technology, and the codification of the laws. Perhaps most (8) recent of all is their concern for history-writing. On the other hand, the Egyptians, the Chaldaeans, and the Phoenicians (to say nothing for the moment of ourselves) have by their own account an historical record rooted in tradition of extreme antiquity and (9) stability. For all these peoples live in places where the climate causes little decay, and they take great care not to let any of their historical experiences pass out of their memory. On the contrary, they religiously preserve it in their public records, (10) written by their most able scholars. In the Greek world, however, the memory of past events has been blotted out by the innumerable disasters that it has suffered. With the perpetual renewal of life, each generation thought that life began with itself, and the Greeks learned the art of writing at a late stage in their development, and with difficulty. Those who would like to think that their use of writing goes back to earliest antiquity solemnly declare that they learned it from the Phoenicians and (11) from Cadmus. But even for that period, they could not show

(12)

any inscription preserved either in a temple or on public monuments; indeed, in later times it became a matter for dispute and controversy whether those who fought at Troy for so many years made use of writing, and the prevailing view is that they had no knowledge of the alphabet now used. In Greek literature as a whole, no authentic history is known to be earlier than the work of Homer. But he seems to have lived later than the Trojan Wars, and it is said that not even Homer left his work in written form, but that it was only later put together by memory from the ballads, and that this circumstance is responsible for the many inconsistencies of the work.

In the opening paragraphs of *Apion*, Josephus declares that he intends to rebut critics of his *Antiquities* who 'disbelieve what I have written about our antiquity and, as evidence that our race is relatively young, offer the fact that it has won no mention among the more famous Greek historians'. He begins by reversing the charge and pointing to the comparatively later arrival of the Greeks, and in the following sections points to the discrepancies between Greek historians, the Greek neglect of public records, and their preference for literary merit over veracity.

(7) *in Greek history, everything is of recent origin*: the accusation was not new. Plato (*Timaeus* 22B) relates a story about the meeting of the Greek lawgiver Solon (sixth century BC) with Egyptian priests, one of whom said to him: 'Solon, you Hellenes are never anything but children...in mind you are all young; there is no old opinion handed down among you by ancient tradition, nor any science which is hoary with age' (Jowett's translation). *the foundation of their cities*: how much Josephus really knew about the early history of the Greek cities is hard to say, but he had read Thucydides, who rather vaguely says that in ancient times Greece had no settled population and the tribes 'did not build large cities or reach any other kind of greatness' (*History* I.2). Nevertheless, he speaks of the existence of towns and cities with and without walls, and piratical raids upon them, apparently before the Trojan War (I.2–8). In ignoring Thucydides and denying the antiquity of the Greek world Josephus does in fact seem to be falling into the 'idle prejudice' he wishes to avoid (6). *the codification of the laws*: Josephus probably has in mind particularly the laws of Athens and Sparta. According to Aristotle (*Ath. Pol.* XLI.2) the Athenian laws were first codified by Dracon (*c.* 620 BC). His penalties were severe, and one later comment was that he wrote all his laws in blood instead of ink.

Most of his laws were repealed by Solon, chief archon (magistrate) in Athens in 594/3 BC, who tried to relieve economic distress by reforms of debts, coinage, and the constitution. The constitution of classical Sparta was traditionally credited to Lycurgus, a legendary figure who, if he existed, perhaps belonged to the eighth century BC. In comparison with these, laws ascribed to Moses could easily appear much older. Josephus was conveniently ignoring the cities, arts, and laws of the Homeric world that he mentions below. *concern for history writing*: in *Apion* I.2 (13) Josephus names the earliest attempts at Greek historiography as those by Cadmus of Miletus (given the same honour by Pliny, *Natural History* V.31 (112), VII.56 (205)) and Acusilaus of Argos, who wrote on genealogies. Josephus dates them to just before the Persian invasion of Greece, i.e., late sixth century BC. These authors are known only by occasional quotations and references.

(8) The *Egyptians* possessed historical records going back to the third millennium BC. On the Narmer palette, from the beginning of this millennium, is depicted an Egyptian king conquering his enemies; the figures are identified by hieroglyphs. In the middle of this millennium a large slab of stone was set up, probably at Memphis, listing the early kings of Upper and Lower Egypt. Another famous list of kings, the Turin Papyrus, dates from the thirteenth century BC. The *Chaldaeans* are not at first sight a particularly good choice for Josephus' purpose, for the Kaldu did not become established in southern Mesopotamia until late in the second millennium BC. The Kesed of Gen. 22: 22 may have been understood as the eponymous ancestor of the Chaldaeans (Hebrew *Kasdīm*). The first clear historical reference to them is in the records of Ashurnasirpal II (885–859 BC), King of Assyria: 'the fear of my dominion extended to the land of Kardumatti (Babylon), and the fear of my weapons overwhelmed the land of Kaldu'. The Chaldaeans, led by Nebuchadnezzar's father Nabopolassar, founded the Neo-Babylonian Empire of the seventh to sixth century BC, and Jeremiah and Ezekiel call Babylon 'the land of the Chaldaeans'. But Josephus may be using the name to embrace the Babylonians of the mid second millennium BC, whose first dynasty (*c.* 1900–1600 BC), which included the famous Hammurabi, was Amorite in origin, and whose second dynasty was Kassite (*c.* 1600–1150 BC). Important texts from third-millennium BC Mesopotamia were preserved in second-millennium Babylonia, such as the Sumerian king-list and the epic of the flood. The *Phoenicians* were the occupants of the cities of the Levant coast, including Arvad (Aradus), Tripolis, Byblos, Beirut, Sidon, and Tyre. In biblical tradition, these people are Canaanites; Josephus follows this by

making the eponymous ancestors of the Phoenician cities Sidon, Amathus, and Aradus sons of Canaan (*Ant.* 1.6.2 (138)). The Greeks from Homer onwards called these people *Phoinikes* and the Romans called them *Punici*, but the Semitic name remained in use: even as late as the fifth century AD the Carthaginians, originally Phoenician colonists, called themselves *Chanani*.

(9) *written by their most able scholars*: in *Ant.* 1.3.9 (107) Josephus reveals which writers he had in mind: 'Manetho, who wrote a record of the Egyptians; Berosus, who compiled the Chaldaean history; Mochus, Hestiaeus, and in addition the Egyptian Hieronymus, fellow authors of Phoenician history'. In *Apion* 1.6 (28) Josephus speaks again of Egyptian and Babylonian care with chronicles, and says that of the nations in contact with the Greeks it was the Phoenicians who made the most use of writing both for daily business and for the record of public affairs. In *Apion* 1.17–18 (106–27) and 21 (154–60) Josephus quotes evidence for Israelite history from Tyrian archives, and in 1.19–20 (128–53) from Berosus, and he argues that the antiquity of the Israelites is well established by Egyptian, Chaldaean, and Phoenician records as well as by a great many Greek writers (*Apion* 1.23 (215f)). It is noticeable, however, that Josephus himself relies more on the compilers and chroniclers of the hellenistic period than on the first-hand sources themselves.

(10) *innumerable disasters*: whether Josephus is thinking of mythical or historical catastrophes, his argument is hardly convincing. Egypt, Phoenicia, and Chaldaea, not to mention Israel, were equally prone to catastrophe. Josephus moves on to a stronger point. *the Greeks learned the art of writing at a late stage*: there is a good deal of evidence that the early development of the alphabet took place in the area of Syria, Palestine, and Sinai in the second half of the second millennium BC. A version using thirty cuneiform letters was known at Ugarit (Ras Shamra) in the fourteenth century BC; a twenty-two-letter consonantal alphabet is evidenced at Byblos in the tenth century BC, and now also from 'Isbet Ṣarṭah near Aphek in Israel. Trade from the Phoenician ports carried this alphabetic script into the Aegean, where it seems to have become well established by the ninth century BC. Recent study has suggested, however, that the Greeks could have first met and used the Semitic alphabet perhaps as early as the eleventh century BC. Different areas developed variant forms, but in general the Greeks turned the Semitic letters *aleph*, *he*, *yodh*, and *'ayin* into vowels (*a*, *e*, *i*, and short *o*), and added some new letters, *upsilon*, *phi*, *chi*, *psi*, and *omega* (long *ō*). Hence Josephus remarks that they learned the art of

writing *with difficulty*. According to a legend preserved by Herodotus (*Histories* v.58), it was *Cadmus*, son of a king of Tyre, who first brought writing to Greece. Herodotus says that the Greeks originally formed their letters the same way as the Phoenicians did, but with the passing of time gradually changed the forms of their letters. He further observes that he saw what he calls 'Cadmeian characters' engraved on tripods in the temple of Apollo at Thebes in Boeotia (v.59).

(11) *made use of writing*: it is possible, but not certain, that Josephus is thinking of the story told in *Iliad* vi.168, where King Proteus, suspecting Bellerophon of an affair with his wife, sent him to the King of Lycia carrying folded tablets inscribed with 'deadly signs' – in fact an order for Bellerophon's execution. *had no knowledge of the alphabet now used*: Josephus is concerned to undermine the trustworthiness of Greek records by arguing that even the earliest Greek literature, the Homeric poems, is comparatively late, owes nothing to the written record, was not at first preserved in writing, is inconsistent in detail and did not become a unity until long after the composition of the separate songs. He is only partly correct. The modern discovery of tablets bearing the Linear B script at Knossos in Crete *c.* 1400 BC and at Pylos in the Peloponnese *c.* 1200 BC shows that a syllabic script was in regular use by educated scribes well before the fall of Troy. The language used is an early form of Greek, and it seems that some of the terms used for military affairs and for royalty were preserved in the poetic tradition used by Homer several hundred years after the Trojan Wars, probably in the eighth century BC. Josephus, like many Homeric scholars of more recent times, takes the observed *inconsistencies* (*diaphōniai*) in the poems to suggest that they arose piecemeal, were handed down by oral tradition, and were only later united. But more recent scholarship has favoured the view that the *Iliad* and the *Odyssey* 'each shows in itself the marks of a controlling and unifying poet' (*Oxford Classical Dictionary*, p. 524b). The minor inconsistencies would be the result both of the poet's harmonisation of the varied traditions he inherited, and perhaps to some small extent of later additions and interpolations. The Homeric poems were, as Josephus says, first transmitted by memory, especially by the Homerides, the guild based on the island of Chios who recited Homer's poetry. (According to a mistrusted tradition, the poems were first written down by a commission appointed by the Athenian tyrant Peisistratus in the sixth century BC.) But the work of Milman Parry in Yugoslavia showed that professional singers used stock formulas to recreate and retell the heroic oral traditions familiar to their hearers, and that in this way the same heroic

tale could be handed on, with minor changes or embellishments, for centuries. It is now well established that an oral tradition is not necessarily less accurate than a written one, a point that has been of equal importance in the discussion of biblical tradition.

THE JEWISH HISTORIANS

Apion 1.7 (37) The privilege of writing is not extended to everyone, and inconsistency is absent from our scriptures. Indeed, only the prophets, through their divine inspiration, have knowledge of the earliest and most archaic periods or set down on paper a clear account of events of their own times

8 (38) as they actually happened. It is therefore natural, indeed inevitable, that we should be spared having thousands of inconsistent and contradictory books. We have twenty-two books only that have any claim to be accepted as trustworthy, and they contain a history of all time.

(39) Of these books, five are the books of Moses, embracing the laws and the tradition from the origins of man to the death of Moses. This period is a little less than three thousand years.

(40) From the death of Moses to the Artaxerxes who was king of Persia after Xerxes, the prophets who followed Moses wrote the events of their own times in thirteen books. The remaining four books contain hymns to God and advice to

(41) men on daily conduct. From Artaxerxes to our own day, the detailed history has been written, but it has not been granted the same credibility as the earlier writings, because the prophetic succession is not certainly established.

(42) Our approach to our scriptures is in fact clear. For in spite of the enormous passage of time, no one has dared to add anything or to remove anything from them, or to change anything. From the moment of birth, it is instinctive with every Jew to consider the scriptures to be the oracles of God, and to live by them, and, if necessary, gladly to die for them.

(43) Prisoners have often been seen enduring the rack and every sort of death in the theatres for the sake of not uttering a word

(44) against the laws and the writings that belong with them. Is

there any Greek who would endure this for the same cause?
No, a Greek would not undergo the slightest pain, even if the
whole of his nation's literature were at stake.

Having pointed to the comparative lateness of the Greek historical
tradition, to the discrepancies between Greek historians, and to their
dependence on style rather than accurate records, Josephus contrasts
with them the Jewish scriptures, especially the historical writings. In
the paragraphs immediately preceding this excerpt, Josephus emphasises
that the scriptural records were scrupulously preserved by priests whose
pedigree was zealously guarded.

(37) *The privilege of writing is not extended to everyone*: Josephus has
already noted that the priests compile and keep the genealogies and
marriage records; here he explains that history-writing is the privilege
of the *prophets*, aided by divine inspiration. Thus from Moses to
Artaxerxes, history was written, as it happened, by a succession of
prophets; after Artaxerxes, because there was a 'failure' in the
succession, existing Jewish histories are accorded less respect. Josephus
seems to take it for granted that the prophets are above all authors;
there is no reference here to their oral proclamation of the word of
the Lord. Moses wrote the Law, and the prophets continued the
tradition by writing the subsequent history (cp. the Mishnah, Ab. 1:
1). Josephus is particularly emphatic that the prophets wrote the history
of the *events of their own times*. In the Preface to the *War* (5 (15)) he
declares that it is his own praiseworthy purpose to write a history of
his own times, and, consistently, sees himself as a prophet (see above,
p. 125).

(38) *inconsistent and contradictory books*: Josephus commented severely
on the discrepancies between Greek historians, which were due, he
alleged, to the Greek failure to keep proper records and to their vanity
as literary men (*Apion* 1.3–5 (15–27)).

(39) *five are the books of Moses*: Josephus is ready to apply literary
criticism to Homer, but not to Moses, crediting him with the first five
books of the Jewish scriptures, Genesis–Deuteronomy. Josephus sees
Moses not just as a lawgiver but also as an historian and a prophet,
whose books contain history. In *Ant.* IV.8.49 (329) Josephus' final
assessment of Moses is that as a prophet he had no equal: 'in whatever
he said one seemed to hear God himself speaking'. *a little less than three
thousand years*: compare the results of Archbishop Ussher, who used
the internal evidence of the Pentateuch to date creation at 4004 BC and
the date of the Exodus at 1492 BC.

(40) *Artaxerxes* I (465–424 BC) succeeded *Xerxes* (486–465 BC),

whom Josephus identifies with the King Ahasuerus of the book of Esther. See also Ezra 4: 6f. *the prophets who followed Moses...thirteen books*: again, Moses is placed in the category of prophet, and the prophets are seen as historians. (So too in later Jewish scholarship the historical books of the Bible placed between the Pentateuch and the prophetic books became known as 'the former prophets'.) The thirteen books are probably to be identified as Joshua, Judges (with Ruth), Samuel, Kings, Chronicles, Ezra–Nehemiah, Esther, Job, Isaiah, Jeremiah (with Lamentations), Ezekiel, the book of the twelve minor prophets, and Daniel. *The remaining four books* are probably Psalms, Song of Songs, Proverbs, and Ecclesiastes. The scriptural books are here divided into three groups, as is done also in the Prologue to Ecclesiasticus and in Luke 24: 44. The division may have arisen from the different origin and nature of the materials and have been reinforced by their use in the context of worship. In the synagogue, the basic reading came from the Law (cp. Acts 15: 21), and a supplementary reading came from the prophets. The Psalms (*hymns to God*) were clearly the first component of the third group (cp. Luke 24: 44) and derived from the worship of the Temple.

(41) *From Artaxerxes...the detailed history has been written*: of what writings is Josephus thinking? In *Apion* 1.22 (183–204) Josephus quotes at length from Hecataeus of Abdera, who lived under Alexander the Great and Ptolemy I and wrote a book on Egyptian affairs (*Aegyptiaca*). Josephus says that he wrote 'a book entirely about the Jews', from which he quotes. Josephus used the Letter of Aristeas (see pp. 11–34) as an important source, but it was hardly a *detailed history* of the whole period. For the second century BC, Josephus used 1 Maccabees. For the career of Herod the Great, Josephus used as a source, particularly in *Ant.* XV–XVII, the work of Herod's counsellor and ambassador, Nicolaus of Damascus (*c.* 65 BC to the early first century AD). Nicolaus wrote a biography of Augustus, an autobiography, and a world history in 144 books. Josephus also knew the important historical works of non-Jewish authors such as Polybius, Diodorus Siculus, and Strabo. *because the prophetic succession is not certainly established*: Ps. 74: 9; Mal. 4: 5f; and Zech. 13: 4–6 are usually taken to point to the general absence of prophets in the society of the Persian period. 1 Macc. 4: 46; 9: 23; 14: 41; and the Prayer of Azariah 15 (see The Song of the Three in the NEB Apocrypha) reveal a second- to first-century BC belief in some quarters that prophets were markedly absent from Judah in the Maccabaean period, but could be expected to return at some future point. The Testament of Benjamin 9: 2 looks forward to the visitation

of 'an only-begotten prophet'. Mal. 4: 5f looks forward to the return
of Elijah, a theme taken up in the early second century BC by
Ecclesiasticus 48: 1–12. Josephus stresses the dangerous contribution to
first-century AD politics from false prophets – an Egyptian false prophet
(*War* II.13.5 (261–3)), Theudas (*Ant.* xx.5.1 (97–9); cp. Acts 5: 36) – and
the misunderstanding of prophecies (*War* VI.5.4 (312–13)). The only
post-canonical prophet worthy in Josephus' eyes of standing in the
prophetic succession appears to be Josephus himself (see above, p. 125)!

(42) *to add anything or to remove anything*: Josephus is doubtless
thinking of the Deuteronomic command in Deut. 4: 2; compare in
the New Testament Rev. 22: 18. This is a natural consequence of
regarding the scriptures as *the oracles of God*.

(43) *enduring the rack*: in *War* II.8.10 (152) Josephus describes the
Essenes' resistance to Roman torture for the sake of the Law. He may
here have had in mind also the martyrdom stories of 2 Macc. 6: 18–31;
7: 1–42. The same theme is vividly presented in the New Testament
Letter to the Hebrews (11: 32–8).

ARISTOTLE AND THE JEW

Apion I.22 (175) It is easy to perceive that the Greeks – and not just
the most ignorant, but those with the highest reputation for
wisdom – both knew the Jews and admired those whom they

(176) met. Clearchus, the disciple of Aristotle, second to none among
the Peripatetic philosophers, mentions in his first book *On
Sleep* that his master Aristotle tells this story about a certain
Jew. He ascribes the conversation to Aristotle himself, and it
runs as follows:

(177) ' "It would be a long business to tell the whole story, but
it may be no bad thing to mention the wonderful and
philosophical elements of it. Be warned, Hyperochides", he
said, "you will think that I am telling you dream-like
phantasies." Hyperochides tactfully answered: "That is why

(178) we are all anxious to hear it." "Very well, then", said
Aristotle, "let us follow the rules of rhetoric, and first study
his race, that we might not ignore the advice of those who
teach the narrative art." "Take it that way if you like", said

(179) Hyperochides. "By race" (replied Aristotle) "the man was a

Jew from Coele-Syria. These Jews are descendants of the philosophers in India. Among the Indians, they say, the philosophers are known as Kalanoi, but among the Syrians as Jews, the name being taken from the territory, for the land they inhabit is called Judaea. The name of their city is

(180)   extremely strange; they call it Hierousalēmē. Now this man, who was enjoying much hospitality as he travelled down from the hills to the coast, was Greek not only in speech but in spirit.

(181)   While we were staying in Asia he toured the same places as we did, and shared our company and that of certain other scholars, trying out their learning. And as he had enjoyed close contact with many well-educated prople, it was he who had something to offer us rather than vice versa."'

(182)   This was the account of Aristotle, as given by Clearchus; and Aristotle went on to describe at length the Jew's large and wonderful endowment of physical stamina and mental poise in his daily life.

Having demonstrated to his satisfaction that the Greeks were poor and recent historians compared with the Babylonians, Egyptians, Phoenicians, and Jews, Josephus goes on to explain why the Greek historians said so little about the Jews (because there was so little contact) and to quote Egyptian, Phoenician, and Babylonian evidence for the antiquity of the Jews. He then turns to Greek references to the Jews, quoting allusions from Pythagoras of Samos (*c.* 500 BC), Theophrastus (a fourth-century BC pupil of Aristotle, most famous for his *Characters*), the fifth-century BC Herodotus of Halicarnassus, 'the father of history', his contemporary the poet Choerilus of Samos, and, in this excerpt, from the philosopher Aristotle himself (384–322 BC), a pupil of Plato and the teacher of Alexander the Great. With this story Josephus apparently demonstrates that the wisest of the Greeks could accept the Jews as fellow philosophers, and even go so far as to describe one member of the race as being Greek 'not only in speech but in spirit' and to accept tuition from him.

(176) *Clearchus* of Soli in Cyprus lived from the mid fourth to the mid third century BC. An inscription found in Afghanistan containing sentences of wisdom from the Delphic oracle notes that they were brought to Bactria by Clearchus. If this is the same person, Clearchus is an example of those who travelled in the footsteps of Alexander.

Peripatetic philosophers were named after the cloistered walk that was built for Aristotle's philosophical school in Athens. Nothing else is known of Clearchus' work *On Sleep*, though other works on education, zoology, erotica, paradoxes, ways of life, and Plato are known.

(177) *Hyperochides* is an otherwise unknown character in the dialogue.

(179) *Coele-Syria* referred to Syria south of the River Eleutherus, the 'hollow' (Greek, *koilē*) part of Syria between Lebanon and the anti-Lebanon. (See Map 4.) *descendants of the philosophers in India*: to the Greeks the Jews were clearly a remote and inaccessible people with strange laws and customs. Various learned attempts were made to connect them with people or religious or philosophical groups from the east. A diplomat of Seleucus I, Megasthenes (*c.* 350–290 BC), wrote a four-volume history of India; a surviving fragment mentions the Indian Brahmans and Syrian Jews among the philosophers outside Greece. Diogenes Laertius (third century AD) says that according to some accounts the Jews were descendants of the Magi, whom Clearchus saw as the ancestors of the Indian gymnosophists (Diogenes Laertius, *Lives* 1.9). In the present passage, Clearchus links the Jews with the *Kalanoi*; according to Plutarch (*Alexander* 65) there was an Indian philosopher called Kalanos who told Alexander to strip and listen naked if he wished to hear Kalanos' doctrines, enacted a parable in front of Alexander to teach him how to rule his empire from the centre, and finally, suffering from an intestinal disease, immolated himself. *Jews...Judaea*: in Greek, *Ioudaioi, Ioudaia*, from which derives the Latin *Judaea*. The name *Hierousalēmē* is a unique Greek form for the more usual Hierosoluma. The Greeks turned the first two syllables of the Hebrew name Jerusalem into the Greek form *hiero-* from the adjective *hieros*, 'holy', or the noun *hieron*, 'temple'.

(181) *Asia*: after the death of Plato (348–347 BC) Aristotle went to stay at Assos in Mysia, and then at Mytilene on the island of Lesbos, until in 343–342 he was invited to become Alexander's tutor in Macedonia. (See Map 1.) There is little evidence for Jews in Asia at this period, but there were perhaps some at Sardis. Aristotle's chance acquaintance, however, seems to have been a traveller, not a permanent resident. Although Josephus says that there were Jews with citizen rights in Syria and Asia in the reign of Seleucus I Nicator soon after 300 BC (*Ant.* XII.3.1 (119–24)), and that Jews in Ionia were given citizenship by Antiochus II (261–247 BC; *Ant.* XII.3.2 (125–8)), there are reasons for thinking that Josephus is not entirely accurate here, and that the Jews received no particular rights before the time of Antiochus III

(223–187 BC), who according to Josephus (*Ant.* XII.3.4 (147–53)) transported 2000 Jewish families from Mesopotamia to act as 'loyal protectors of our interests' in Phrygia and Lydia. (See Map 1.)

(182) *physical stamina and mental poise*: Josephus apparently summarises the remainder of Clearchus' account. But this emphasis on Jewish physical stamina and mental poise begins to sound remarkably like an extra piece of Jewish apologia, perhaps replacing the original sequel to Clearchus' story.

This meeting and conversation between Aristotle and a Jew seems unlikely. A similar story was told of a meeting between Socrates and an Indian philosopher. The story reflects hellenistic Greek hearsay and curiosity about the wisdom of the East. Originally it portrayed from the Greek side Aristotle's willingness to learn from the fabled philosophers of the East; Josephus makes it serve his purpose of demonstrating the superiority of Jewish philosophy.

Josephus concludes *Apion* Book I by 'demonstrating the falsity of the accusations and insults that certain people have hurled against our nation' (1.24 (219)). He corrects the errors of Manetho (a third-century BC Egyptian priest who wrote a three-volume history of Egypt), Chaeremon (librarian of Alexandria and tutor of Nero), and Lysimachus (an Alexandrian writer of the second to first century BC). In Book II Josephus turns to his *bête noire*, Apion. Apion was by birth an Egyptian who had managed to acquire Alexandrian citizenship (a rare achievement for an Egyptian), and who taught in Rome and led the Alexandrian delegation against the Jews in AD 39 to the Emperor Gaius Caligula. The Roman writer Pliny (*Nat. Hist.* Preface 25) comments on Apion's vanity and quotes the nickname 'cymbal of the world' given to him by the Emperor Tiberius. Josephus criticises Apion's interpretation of Moses and the Exodus, before going on to attack Apion's accusations against the Jewish residents of Alexandria (*Apion* II.4ff (37ff)).

APION'S CHARGE OF SEDITION

Apion II.6 (68)   In addition, he lays charges of sedition against us. Even if this accusation of his against the Jews at Alexandria has any truth in it, why does he make that unity for which we are famous

(69)   a reason for blaming us all wherever we are settled? And further, as anyone who looks into the matter will find, the real authors of sedition are Alexandrian citizens like Apion. For while it was

the Greeks and Macedonians who held this citizenship, they directed no pogroms against us but allowed us to keep our own ancient religious usages. But when on account of the troubles of the age the number of Egyptians in the citizen body increased, there always came with them this extra performance. Our race,

(70) however, remained uncontaminated. These people, therefore, were the origin of the trouble, for they were neither self-possessed like the Macedonians nor cautious like the Greeks, and all of them inevitably practised the appalling Egyptian standards of behaviour and exercised their longstanding hostility towards us.

(71) In fact, the reproach they presume to throw at us should be reversed. For while most of them have no proper claim to citizenship of this state, they give the name of 'aliens' to our people, who are known to have acquired this privilege from

(72) their rulers. No past king, no present emperor seems to have granted the right of citizenship to the Egyptians. But we were given our initial status by Alexander himself, our position was improved by the Ptolemies, and our permanent tenure has been approved by the Romans.

(73) Apion therefore has tried to discredit us because we do not erect statues of the emperors – as if the emperors did not know that or needed Apion to act in their defence! He should rather have admired the magnanimity and restraint of the Romans in not compelling their subjects to transgress their ancestral laws, and accepting only such honours as are consistent with the religious laws of those who offer them. For the Romans give no thanks for honours conferred out of obligation and oppres-

(74) sion. The Greeks and certain others approve of setting up statues; it gives them great joy to paint the portraits of fathers and wives and children. Indeed, some people acquire the portraits of persons who have no connection with them, while others do this for much-loved household servants. Why then is it surprising if they are seen to offer this honour to emperors

(75) and rulers as well? Our lawgiver, however, prohibited the making of any animal images – and even more the making of

any images of God, who, as will be shown below, is not animate. He did this, not as one in prophetic style denying honour to the Roman power, but as one who despised a practice profitable
(76) neither to God nor man. He did not forbid the bestowal of honours, so long as they were not divine honours, upon good men; we dignify both emperors and Roman people alike with
(77) just such honours. We offer continual sacrifices on their behalf – and not only do we celebrate such sacrifices every day out of the common fund of all the Jews but we offer this special honour to the emperor alone. As a people, we offer no other such sacrificial victims, not even for the emperor's children. We
(78) pay such honour to no other human. I hope that this is a fully adequate answer to Apion and what has been said about Alexandria.

For a description of the background to the trouble at Alexandria between the Jewish inhabitants and the Greek population, and the resulting delegations to the Emperor Gaius Caligula, see A. R. C. Leaney, *The Jewish and Christian World 200 BC to AD 200*, pp. 137–40. Josephus himself outlines the story in *Ant.* XVIII.8.1 (257–60). The problem lay in the status of the large Jewish community at Alexandria; they were called 'Alexandrians', but in what sense? Were they full citizens (*politai*, *Ant.* XIV.10.1 (188)), with equal citizen rights, as Josephus says, granted by Alexander (*War* II.18.7 (487f)) and Ptolemy I Sōtēr (*Ant.* XII.1.1 (8)) and recognised by the Emperor Claudius (*Ant.* XIX.5.2 (280–5))? Or did the term 'Alexandrian' imply no more than the undeniable fact that the Jews resided in Alexandria? Or was the Jewish citizenship limited to their membership of a *politeuma*, a community of resident aliens with its own magistrates, assembly, and cult, and a certain amount of autonomy (cp. Josephus' description, taken from Strabo, in *Ant.* XIV.7.2 (110–18))?

The question has been virtually settled by the discovery of a copy of Claudius' reply to an Alexandrian address to him. He told the Alexandrians to be forbearing to the Jews who had lived for so long in the city and to allow them to observe their traditions; he told the Jews not to involve themselves in the city's gymnasia and to enjoy prosperity 'in a city not their own'.

In practice the Jews held a social position between the native Egyptian people of the country (*chōra*) and the full citizens of the Greek city of Alexandria. They were not *astoi* (Greek citizens) nor *autochthones* (natives) but *katoikoi* (resident aliens). They had certain privileges as members of a *politeuma*, but they were not allowed to participate in the gymnasium with its many related activities, which was the prerogative and mark of the full citizen. Hellenised Jews naturally coveted this privilege, which the Greek citizens were in no hurry to extend to people whose religion and customs were so alien to their own and whose support for and from the occupying Roman power was regarded with such suspicion. There were inevitably some Jews (and other foreigners) who had gained Alexandrian citizenship, and Claudius in his rescript confirmed the citizenship of all who had held that status before he became emperor 'except to those who may have intruded themselves among you and contrived, though low-born, to become *epheboi*' (see above, p. 103, for the *epheboi*; for the rescript, see H. I. Bell, *Jews and Christians in Egypt* (British Museum: London, 1924), pp. 28f). Apion himself may have belonged to this last category, for Josephus sharply castigates his false accusations as made by way of return to the Alexandrians for his citizenship. 'Knowing the Alexandrian hatred for the Jews who share their city as their home, he has set himself to abuse them, and he includes all the other Jews with them' (*Apion* II.3 (32)).

(68) *charges of sedition*: compare the report made about Jerusalem to the King of Persia in Ezra 4: 15: 'You will discover by searching through the annals that this has been a rebellious city, harmful to the monarchy and its provinces, and that sedition has long been rife within its walls.' In Alexandria, some such slander would have been an obvious way of destroying the Jews' standing with the Romans, and there were men in Alexandria at the time capable of it, 'Alexandrian citizens like Apion' (69). Philo mentions them: 'demagogues like Dionysius, record-porers like Lampo, faction leaders like Isidorus, busy-bodies, mischief-makers, and disturbers of cities' (*Flacc* IV.20). He calls Lampo a 'poison pen' (*Flacc* XVI.132) and Isidorus 'a genius at manufacturing commotions and disorders when they did not exist' (*Flacc* XVII.135). Both men served with Apion on the Alexandrian delegation to Gaius, and they would have found it easy to present as sedition such events as Agrippa's royal parade in Alexandria at the Jews' behest, or allege seditious plots as the reason for Flaccus' arrest of the Jewish council. In particular, the Jews' unwillingness to sacrifice to Caesar (as distinct from their willingness to sacrifice on Caesar's behalf) could be construed as seditious, though Gaius himself spoke of it as merely lunatic. *Greeks and Macedonians*: Alexandria was founded by Alexander as a Greek city,

and its citizenship was basically confined to them. The position of the Macedonians is a little obscure. According to *Apion* II.4 (35) (cp. *Ant.* XII.1.1 (8) and *War* II.18.7 (487f)), the Jews in Alexandria had the same privileges as the Macedonians (though Josephus appears to imply full citizenship). But the Macedonians may have been a separate ethnic group like the Jews, with limited privileges. According to P. M. Fraser (*Ptolemaic Alexandria* (Oxford, 1972), vol. I, p. 54), there is no reason to suppose that they had any special or privileged status; Josephus may simply have assumed that Alexander of Macedonia would have given Macedonians a special status, and drawn a further wrong conclusion from the fact that some Jews bore the false ethnic name 'Macedonian'. *But when...the number of Egyptians...increased*: Josephus blames the unrest on the increase of native-born Egyptians (of whom Apion was one) among the Alexandrian citizenry. In fact, native Egyptians were rarely given Alexandrian citizenship. Pliny the Younger got himself into difficulty when he asked the Emperor Trajan to give Roman citizenship to his doctor, Harpocras. This was granted, but Pliny then discovered that, as Harpocras was Egyptian, for Roman citizenship he needed the prior qualification of Alexandrian citizenship. Trajan noted that like his predecessors he was cautious in allowing this. The native Egyptians had a reputation for being 'sharp and politically-minded' (Polybius, *Histories* XXXIV.14); but Philo (*Leg Gaj* XXVI.166) calls them 'a worthless breed, whose souls were infested with the poison and bad temper alike of the crocodiles and asps of their country'.

(72) *Alexander*

'...who had been given enthusiastic help by the Jews against the Egyptians, rewarded their support by giving them permission to reside in the city on equal terms with the Greeks. This privilege was also continued by the *Diadochoi* [i.e., the Ptolemies], who in addition assigned them their own quarter, in order that by having less social contact with non-Jews they might more easily preserve the holiness of their own way of life; and they were allowed to be designated Macedonians.'

(*War* II.18.7 (487–8))

According to *Ant.* XII.1.1 (8), Ptolemy I, recognising the loyalty of the Jews, took many of them to serve in his garrisons, and at Alexandria 'granted them equal rights with the Macedonians'. *approved by the Romans*: in *Ant.* XIV.10.1 (188), Josephus says that Julius Caesar had a bronze tablet set up in Alexandria declaring that the Jews were citizens of Alexandria. In *Ant.* XIX.5.2 (280–5), Josephus quotes an edict of

Claudius to Alexandria and Syria that recognises 'that the Jews in Alexandria called Alexandrians were from the beginning co-settlers with the Alexandrians and won equal constitutional rights from the kings...and that after Alexandria was subjected to our empire by Augustus, their rights were protected by the governors sent at different times', and pronounces that 'none of the Jewish rights should lapse by reason of Gaius' insanity; their former privileges should be protected as long as they adhere to their national customs'. This edict of Claudius must be interpreted in the light of the genuine rescript quoted above (pp. 184f). The crux of the matter is the meaning of 'won equal constitutional rights' (*isēs politeias*), which should probably be taken to mean no more than that they received equal status with other Alexandrian residents belonging to autonomous *politeumata* (see above, p. 184).

(73) *do not erect statues of the emperors*: Apion and Josephus presumably have in mind Caligula's order of AD 39 that his statue should be erected in the Jerusalem Temple. When the Jews objected, the emperor sent Petronius to enforce the order. Petronius, discovering the strength and determination of the Jewish opposition, urged Gaius to reconsider. He replied by threatening Petronius with execution for delaying but, fortunately for Petronius, news of Gaius' own death arrived ahead of Gaius' letter to Petronius (*War* II.10.1–5 (184–203); *Ant.* XVIII.8.2–9 (261–309)).

(75) *Our lawgiver...prohibited the making of any animal images*: cp. Exod. 20: 4; Deut. 4: 16; 5: 8.

(77) *We offer continual sacrifices on their behalf*: there was nothing new in this. According to Ezra 6: 9ff, Darius of Persia decreed that animals for burnt-offerings should be provided for the Jerusalem Temple, 'that they may offer soothing sacrifices to the God of heaven and pray for the life of the king and his sons'. 1 Macc. 7: 33 refers to the sacrifices offered by the Jewish priests for the Syrian king in 161 BC. According to Philo, the Emperor Augustus 'gave orders for regular holocausts of sacrifices to be made daily in perpetuity at his own expense as an offering to the Most High God. These sacrifices continue to this day' (*Leg Gaj* XXIII.157; XL.317). According to Josephus (*War* II.10.4 (197)), the Jews pointed out to Petronius that they sacrificed twice daily (i.e., morning and evening) on behalf of the emperor and Rome. When the Jewish delegates from Alexandria made the point to the Emperor Gaius in person, however, the emperor's response was to say: 'But even if it was for me, it was to another god. What use is that? You have not sacrificed to me.' He went on to comment that the Jewish refusal to

acknowledge his divinity was foolish rather than criminal (*Leg Gaj* XLV.367). *not even for the emperor's children*: the word *emperor's* has been supplied from the context and is not in the Latin text. It is therefore also possible that the phrase should be translated 'not even for our own children', but in view of the established practice quoted above of praying 'for the life of the king and his sons', the former translation seems more likely.

DIPLOMACY IN ROME AND JERUSALEM

Life 3 (13)   At the age of twenty-six, I had the opportunity of going up to Rome. The reason was as follows. When Felix was governor of Judaea, he arrested several priests, colleagues of mine, good and honest men, on some minor and inconse-quential charge, and sent them in chains to Rome, to give
(14)   an account of themselves to Caesar. I wanted to find some way of saving these men, especially when I discovered that in spite of their troubles they had not forgotten their religious practices, and were nourishing themselves on figs and nuts.
(15)   I reached Rome after a hazardous journey by sea, for our ship sank in the middle of the Adriatic, and about six hundred of us spent the whole night swimming. About dawn, by divine providence, a Cyrenean ship appeared, and I and some others, about eighty of us altogether, swam ahead of the rest and were
(16)   taken on board. We were brought safely to Dikaiarcheia (the Italian name is Puteoli). I became friendly with the actor Aliturus, a particular favourite of Nero's and Jewish by birth. Through him I made the acquaintance of Caesar's wife Poppaea, and as soon as I could, I made plans to enlist her aid in the release of the priests. After receiving her help, together with substantial gifts, I returned home.

4 (17)   Here I found the beginnings of revolution already at work, and many people enthusiastic for revolt from Rome. I tried to discourage and dissuade the seditious; they should keep clearly in view that their intended opponents, the Romans, were superior to themselves both in military skill and in
(18)   fortune of war, and that they should not impetuously and foolishly bring the risk of utter disaster upon their fellow

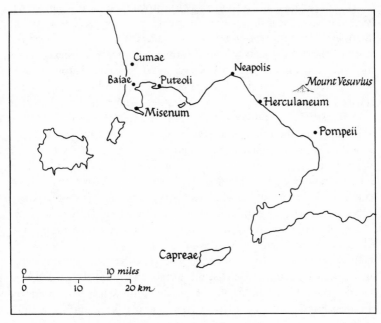

Map 7   The Bay of Naples

(19)   countrymen, their families, and upon themselves. With these
       words I persistently tried to dissuade them, because I foresaw
       that the result of the war would be ultimate disaster for us.
       I failed, however, for the insane determination of these
       desperate men was overpowering.

This passage from the *Life* shows Josephus undertaking his first public
commitment and making his first contact with Rome. Josephus is
careful in this passage to emphasise two things: first, that he had high
regard for Jewish religious practices and for the Jerusalem priesthood
and, secondly, that in Jewish politics he was a moderate and had
strongly attempted to dissuade the Jews from rebellion against Rome.
In this connection one should note also the contrast drawn between
Josephus' diplomatic success at Rome and his failure at Jerusalem, and
between the political good sense of the Romans and the self-destructive
instincts of the Jews. The story of the shipwreck, in some ways
reminiscent of Paul's shipwreck in Acts 27, adds drama to the
adventure; but it also serves to reveal one of Josephus' less appealing
traits, his readiness to sacrifice others in the interests of self-preservation.

(13) *At the age of twenty-six*: this visit probably took place in AD 64. *Felix* was procurator in Judaea from AD 52 to perhaps as late as AD 60. Josephus' mission therefore takes place several years after the original arrest of the priests. Felix and his brother Pallas were originally slaves and then freedmen of the Emperor Claudius' mother Antonia. Pallas became Claudius' financial secretary but was eventually killed by Nero; Felix married three times into royal families; Tacitus notes of him that 'he practised every kind of cruelty and lust, and exercised the power of a king with the mind of a slave' (*Histories* v.9). Paul was brought before Felix, who deferred judgement on him for two years in hope of a bribe (Acts 24: 26f). *give an account of themselves to Caesar*: Josephus does not tell us what the charge was. Possibly the event is that related in *War* II.13.7 (266–70) (cp. *Ant.* xx.8.7 (173–7), and 9 (182–4)), where fighting between Jews and Syrians at Caesarea forces Felix to send the leaders of both sides to Nero for arbitration. For a similar problem at Alexandria, see above pp. 182–8.

(14) *figs and nuts*: the priests were concerned to avoid incurring ritual uncleanness by eating meat that might have been killed in sacrifice to gentile gods; this was a problem that gave some Christians an uneasy conscience at Corinth (cp. 1 Cor. 8). The *nuts* may be walnuts, chestnuts or almonds.

(15) *the Adriatic*: cp. Acts 27: 27. *Cyrenean ship*: Cyrenaica was a North African district administered from the Roman province of Crete. It had a substantial Jewish colony (cp. Mark 15: 21; Acts 2: 10; 13: 1). According to Acts 6: 9 there was a synagogue of Cyrenians at Jerusalem. *by divine providence*: here as elsewhere (see p. 121), Josephus ascribes to this cause his deliverance from dangerous circumstances. He does not scruple to tell us that he was among the eighty to reach the boat first. Presumably the boat's capacity to take on board survivors was limited, and the rest were left to their fate.

(16) *Dikaiarcheia*: this Greek colony was first settled in 529 BC. Under the Romans, as Puteoli, it was an important port in the bay of Naples, especially for traffic from the eastern Mediterranean (cp. Acts 28: 13). In Josephus' time, the lower town had a large market-place, a breakwater built on masonry piles, a colonnaded quay and docks, and a temple of Augustus. The upper town had an amphitheatre, baths, and a circus. A few miles away across the Golfo di Pozzuoli was the important resort of Baiae, where Nero's mother, the Empress Agrippina, was murdered. Beyond Baiae lay the naval base of Misenum. This whole region was of great importance to the rulers of Rome. *Poppaea* was married twice before she became Nero's mistress and then his wife

(AD 62). She died in AD 65. According to Josephus, Poppaea was *theosebēs*, 'a worshipper of God', with Jewish sympathies, who used her influence on behalf of a Jewish delegation that came to Nero to protest against King Agrippa II's new palace built overlooking the Temple in Jerusalem (*Ant.* xx.7.11 (189–96)).

(17) *I tried to discourage and dissuade the seditious*: on Josephus' attitude to the War, and his aims in the *Life*, see above, pp. 89–92. His description of the course of events leading up to the War in *War* II.14.1–16.5 (271–404) culminates in the speech credited to King Agrippa (*War* II.16.4 (345–401)). Its theme is very similar to the view Josephus expresses here as his own.

A Note on Further Reading

This book of necessity contains only a limited selection of Jewish writings from the hellenistic world. The reader who wishes to explore the subject further might begin by finding the standard editions of the writers we have studied here.

The Letter of Aristeas may be found in R. H. Charles (ed.), *The Apocrypha and Pseudepigrapha of the Old Testament* (Clarendon Press: Oxford, 1913), vol. II, pp. 83–122, translated by H. T. Andrews, or in the translation by H. St J. Thackeray (Translations of early documents, 2nd series; S.P.C.K.: London, 1917). A very useful edition of the Greek text with English translation and notes is that of M. Hadas, *Aristeas to Philocrates* (*Letter of Aristeas*) (Jewish Apocryphal Literature; Harper and Brothers: New York, 1951). The Sibylline Oracles also appear in R. H. Charles, *A.P.O.T.*, vol. II, pp. 368–406, translated and annotated by H. C. O. Lanchester, and more recently in J. H. Charlesworth (ed.), *The Old Testament Pseudepigrapha* (Darton, Longman and Todd: London, 1983), vol. I, pp. 317–472, translated and introduced by J. J. Collins.

Eupolemus' fragments were preserved in the *Praeparatio evangelica* of Eusebius, Book IX, and the Greek text and English translation and notes may be found in E. H. Gifford, *Eusebii Pamphili Evangelicae Praeparationes, Libri XV* (4 vols., Clarendon Press: Oxford, 1903), and now in C. R. Holladay, *Fragments from Hellenistic Jewish authors* (Scholars Press: Chico, California, 1983), vol. I: 'Historians', pp. 93–156. This most useful volume includes also the remaining fragments from Demetrius, Pseudo-Eupolemus, Artapanus, Cleodemus Malchus, Aristeas, Pseudo-Hecataeus, Theophilus, Thallus, and Justus of Tiberias.

English translations of Josephus are not so common as might be expected; the best known is that of William Whiston, first published in 1737 and reprinted many times since. Penguin Classics published *Josephus: The Jewish War*, translated by G. A. Williamson, in 1959; a revised edition, by E. Mary Smallwood, appeared in 1981, complete with notes, appendices, a chronological table, maps, plans, a bibliography, and an introduction. At much greater expense, the Paternoster Press, Exeter, and the Zondervan Publishing House, Grand Rapids, Michigan, have published a profusely illustrated new 'simplified' translation and commentary, *Josephus: The Jewish War*, under the general editorship of Gaalya Cornfeld (1982); this presents vividly much recently-discovered archaeological detail. However, for the serious student the most convenient and useful edition of Josephus, containing a Greek text and English translation of all his writings, with much useful annotation, remains that of the Loeb Classical Library (Heinemann: London; and Harvard University Press: Cambridge, Massachusetts, 1926–55), under the editorship of H. St J. Thackeray (vols. I–IV), H. St J. Thackeray and R. Marcus (vol. V), R. Marcus (vols. VI–VII), R. Marcus and A. Wikgren (vol. VIII), and L. H. Feldman (vol. IX).

Recent years have shown a renewal of interest in these writings, and a vast amount of scholarly literature has appeared in books and journals. A full bibliography would cover many pages, but much of it will be found in the works by Charlesworth and Holladay cited above, and for Josephus the reader should turn to L. H. Feldman's *Scholarship on Philo and Josephus, 1937–61* (Studies in Judaica, 1; Yeshiva University: New York, 1963) and H. Schreckenberg, *Bibliographie zu Flavius Josephus* (Brill: Leiden, 1968). But a number of books stand out as important. The Letter of Aristeas is given careful treatment by S. Jellicoe, *The Septuagint and Modern Study* (Clarendon Press: Oxford, 1968). A major and enlightening study of the Sibylline Oracles is presented by J. J. Collins, *The Sibylline Oracles of Egyptian Judaism* (Society of Biblical Literature Dissertation Series 13: Missoula, Montana, 1972). A stimulating monograph entitled *Eupolemus: a study of Judaeo-Greek literature* by Ben Zion Wacholder was published in 1974 by the Hebrew Union College Press: Cincinnati. On Josephus there are many books. Earlier important works include H. St J. Thackeray, *Josephus, the man and the historian* (Jewish Institute of Religion Press: New York, 1929), and F. J. Foakes Jackson, *Josephus and the Jews* (S.P.C.K.: London, 1930). R. J. H. Shutt's useful *Studies in Josephus* (S.P.C.K.: London) appeared in 1961. A new, important, and very readable study of the *War* is Tessa Rajak's *Josephus: the historian and his society* (Duckworth: London, 1983). In recent years, however, scholars have been turning their attention more to Josephus' other works, and attempting to discover his theological interests and apologetic concerns. Illuminating and influential here is H. W. Attridge, *The interpretation of biblical history in the* Antiquitates Judaicae *of Flavius Josephus* (Harvard Dissertations in Religion 7; Scholars Press: Missoula, Montana, 1976). Equally stimulating is S. J. D. Cohen's *Josephus in Galilee and Rome: his* Vita *and development as a historian* (Brill: Leiden, 1979).

The place of the Jews in the hellenistic and Roman worlds has been much studied. The reader will derive great pleasure and insight from M. Hadas, *Hellenistic culture: fusion and diffusion* (Norton: New York, 1959); from A. Momigliano, *Alien wisdom: the limits of hellenization* (Cambridge University Press, 1975); and from V. Tcherikover, *Hellenistic civilisation and the Jews* (Jewish Publication Society of America: Philadelphia, 1966). Particularly valuable are M. Hengel's *Judaism and Hellenism* (2 vols., S.C.M. Press: London, 1974) and *Jews, Greeks and barbarians* (S.C.M. Press: London, 1980). For a wide-ranging study of Alexandria, P. M. Fraser's *Ptolemaic Alexandria* (3 vols., Clarendon Press: Oxford, 1972) must be consulted. For the historical background to the Jewish War of AD 66–74, the recent works of D. M. Rhoads, *Israel in revolution 6–74 CE* (Fortress Press: Philadelphia, 1976) and of

S. V. Freyne, *Galilee from Alexander the Great to Hadrian, 323 B.C.E. to 135 C.E.*
(Michael Glazier and Notre Dame University Press, 1980) are valuable.
Helpful surveys will be found in M. Grant's two books, *The ancient historians*
(Weidenfeld and Nicolson: London, 1970) and *The Jews in the Roman world*
(Weidenfeld and Nicolson: London, 1973). On this last subject, see particularly
E. Mary Smallwood, *The Jews under Roman rule* (Brill: Leiden, 1976). An
important work of reference is E. Schürer, *A history of the Jewish people in the
age of Jesus Christ (195 BC − AD 135)*, a new English version revised and edited
by G. Vermes, F. Millar, and M. Black (T. and T. Clark: Edinburgh), vol.
I (1973), vol. II (1979), vol. III (forthcoming).

Lastly, it is important to note that this book should be read in conjunction
with the other volumes of this series, and in particular with M. Whittaker,
Jews and Christians: Graeco-Roman views, and with A. R. C. Leaney, *The
Jewish and Christian World 200 BC to AD 200*.

Index